Infant Assessment

Developmental Psychology

Series Editor, Wendell E. Jeffrey, U.C.L.A.

Communication Development During Infancy, Lauren B. Adamson

How Divorce Affects Offspring,
Michael R. Stevenson and Kathryn N. Black

Reading and Writing Acquisition, Virginia Berninger

Human Auditory Development,
Lynne A. Werner and G. Cameron Marean

The Development of Peer Prejudice and Discrimination:
Evolutionary, Cultural, and Developmental Dynamics,
Harold D. Fishbein

Moral Psychology, Daniel K. Lapsley

A History of Developmental Psychology in Autobiography,
Dennis N. Thompson and John D. Hogan, editors

Parents and the Dynamics of Child Rearing, George W. Holden

Infant Assessment, M. Virginia Wyly

Infant Assessment

M. Virginia Wyly
STATE UNIVERSITY COLLEGE AT BUFFALO

WestviewPress

A Division of HarperCollins*Publishers*

Developmental Psychology

Copyright © 1997 by Westview Press, A Division of HarperCollins Publishers, Inc.

Published in 1997 in the United States of America by Westview Press, 5500 Central Avenue, Boulder, Colorado, 80301-2877, and in the United Kingdom by Westview Press, 12 Hid's Copse Road, Cumnor Hill, Oxford OX2 9JJ

A CIP catalog record for this book is available from the Library of Congress.
ISBN 0-8133-3087-4—ISBN 0-8133-3088-2 (pbk.)

Typeset by Letra Libre

The paper used in this publication meets the requirements of the American National Standard for Permanence of Paper for Printed Library Materials Z39.48-1984.

10   9   8   7   6   5   4   3   2   1

To Jack

Contents

Tables, Figures, and Boxes

Preface

Interest in the development, competencies, and needs of infants has burgeoned in recent years. Infancy is now acknowledged to be a period of rapid growth and change. The process of assessing infant development provides an understanding of an infant's abilities as well as the infant's caregiving environment.

Early efforts to assess infants evaluated developmental performance using traditional psychometric scales based on normative schedules of development. These assessment methods enabled clinicians to compare an infant's attainment of developmental milestones with that of a normed population sample. Such assessments also provided an understanding of how infants develop. Although the traditional standardized testing movement dominated the field of assessment for thirty years, there have been dramatic changes in infant assessment since 1990. This evolution has been guided by the implementation of Public Law 99-457 Part H, which includes directives for identifying and providing intervention for at-risk infants and their families. Assessments are now performed to identify risk, diagnose developmental problems, and plan programmatic early intervention. Assessment strategies include traditional assessments as well as a range of developmental measures within the scope of comprehensive assessment that involves parent participation and the use of multiple criteria tailored for individual infants.

Recent theory and research in infancy has also contributed to innovations in infant assessment. The recognition that infants are complex social beings whose behaviors and competencies combine and recombine to organize more sophisticated skills has challenged clinicians to develop new assessment measures. New procedures and assessment processes are being refined with the goal of reaching a deeper understanding of infant competencies and the optimal elements of the caregiving environment.

This book was written to introduce readers to the general principles and practices in the assessment of infants. Chapter 1 discusses the history of infant assessment and the historical influences on current assessment approaches. Neonatal assessment is the focus of Chapter 2. It contains an overview of the competencies of newborns and a description of the procedures used to measure them. Chapter 3 examines the purposes and methods of infant screening for developmental problems. Chapters 4 and 5 address assessment of infants' cognitive and information-processing skills. Their relationship to later intellectual outcomes is discussed. The importance of infant play and play assessment procedures is outlined in Chapter 6. Chapter 7 provides background information on parent-infant interaction assessment and discusses its rationale. The role of infant temperament and emotion in development is presented in Chapter 8. Finally, in Chapter 9, some of the challenges and new directions in assessment are covered.

M. Virginia Wyly

Acknowledgments

I am especially grateful to Mary Mueller, whose assistance was invaluable in the preparation of the text. Her good humor, support, and competence helped make possible the preparation of this book. I extend my gratitude to my colleague and friend Richard C. Towne, professor emeritus at Buffalo State College, for his skillful editing of this manuscript. I thank Robert Pollaro and Lori Atherton, who read drafts of the manuscript as it was being prepared and carefully reviewed the references. My special thanks go to the infants and their families at the Bornhava Early Intervention Program, who have shared their journey and taught me the wisdom of collaborative assessment.

M. V. W.

1

Infant Assessment: Overview

What is the little one thinking about?
Very wonderful things no doubt! . . .
Who can tell what a baby thinks.

—*J. G. Holland*

In this chapter, we will review the history of infant assessment and explore recent trends and issues concerned with measuring infant development, intelligence, and skills. We will start over one century ago, when infants were seldom assessed, and end with the 1990s, when it seems as though almost everybody is probing, observing, measuring, and assessing infants. We will spend most of our time on developments and issues that have taken place during the explosion of scientific interest in infancy that has occurred since the 1970s.

You should come away from this chapter feeling that the twenty-four-month period of infancy is an exciting time of development that has a dramatic effect on the entire life span. You should learn that infants engage in social interactions and process information about the world in which they live. You should have a good feel for how far our understanding of infancy has come and an equally good understanding of the many questions that remain.

In addition to helping you understand general outcomes, your study of this chapter should broaden your knowledge of a variety of specific developments and issues that have evolved in the study of infant assessment. You should be able to

- Outline the development of infant assessment, know what the major tests used and their purposes are, and understand the theoretical foundations and approach to assessment
- Describe the uses of infant assessment
- Describe the assessment process
- Discuss current trends in infant assessment

You can do a number of things that will help you get the most out of this chapter.

- Keep the above general and specific outcomes in mind when studying the chapter. They will help focus your thinking.
- Review the terms listed in Table 1.1 before reading the chapter. Look for the terms in the chapter. Be sure you understand their meaning and how they are being used.

Table 1.1 defines some of the basic terms used in this text.

Introduction

Infancy is a brief but important period of development. When a baby is born, parents and society are challenged to optimize the child's potential. As parents have asked questions about what they can do to provide a foundation for their baby's development, researchers have provided answers regarding the unique behaviors and capabilities of infants. Infant research has shown that the rapid developmental changes that occur in the first twenty-four months after birth have a dramatic effect on the entire life span. Infants are now recognized as competent beings who from birth learn and process information about the world around them.

Infants have not always been thought of as competent beings. In 1890, William James, the well-known American psychologist, said that infants experience the world as "blooming, buzzing confusion," whereas the behaviorist J. B. Watson (1924) described infants as passive creatures who needed experience to shape their minds. These views of infant incompetence persisted until the 1950s, when scientists began to identify a rich array of infant abilities.

Currently, infancy is conceptualized as a unique period of development. Infants have social skills and individual temperaments. For example, shortly after birth, newborns become both quiet and alert in response to their caregiver's voice or face. Later, they engage in turn-taking interactions, including playing games with their caregivers. Very early in life, they imitate facial gestures and differentiate between facial expressions of joy, sadness, and anger. They learn, remember, and problem solve. In fact, they process information in sophisticated ways. They communicate pleasure and displeasure at birth and in two short years learn a language—something we adults have a difficult time doing! All of their senses are present at birth, and they use them to organize incoming information from their environment.

Despite all that is known about infant competency, questions still remain. How do infants think? How can we measure infant cognition? What is the relationship between infant play and the development of intelligence? How do infants process information? What is the relationship between parent-infant interactions and infant development? Can infants' personalities be measured? These are just some of the questions that guide the development of infant assessments.

TABLE 1.1   Assessment Terms

Assessment: The process of collecting data to identify infants for developmental risk, to make a diagnosis, or to plan infant interventions. The assessment process can determine an infant's strengths and weaknesses and level of developmental functioning.

Screening: A procedure used to identify infants at risk for developmental delays. Screening is done to determine if an infant needs further in-depth assessment or early intervention services. Screening tests are usually relatively quick and easy to administer; they are often done on a large scale. One example of an infant screening test is the Denver Developmental Screening Test (Frankenburg, Dodds, and Fandel 1975).

Norm-Referenced Assessment: Assessment based on comparing infants' performance with the performance of a large reference group of age-equivalent infants. These assessments are usually standardized. Scores indicate whether the infant is average, below average, or above average compared to the age-equivalent standard. An example of a norm-referenced test is the Bayley Scales of Infant Development (Bayley 1969).

Criterion-Referenced Assessment: A test that measures an infant's performance on a particular developmental skill or on test tasks. The infant's performance is assessed using a performance criterion rather than established norms. Thus, an infant is not compared to age-equivalent infants. An example of a criterion-referenced test is the Carolina Curriculum for Handicapped Infants and Infants at Risk (Johnson et al. 1986).

Standardized Assessment: A test that has a uniform procedure used in administering test items and scoring.

Validity: Does a test measure what it is supposed to measure? Several methods are used to determine the validity of a test instrument. Content validity involves careful analysis of the test items. Construct validity is concerned with the underlying theoretical construct of the test. Predictive validity measures how well a test is able to predict future performance in a selected situation.

Reliability: Refers to the consistency and accuracy of the test items in measuring what they are supposed to measure.

At the same time that knowledge of infant development has increased, we have come to understand better the causes and outcomes of developmental disorders. Approximately 10 percent of the infant population has a disabling condition at birth or shortly after birth (Anastasiow 1993). In addition, there are numerous genetic, prenatal, and ecological factors such as prematurity, mother's age, socioeconomic status, maternal nutrition, disease, and environmental hazards that place a fetus or infant at risk for developmental problems. Professionals who work with infants use the terms *at risk, high risk,* or *developmental risk* to indicate that certain infants are in jeopardy of acquiring developmental problems.

The impetus for assessing infants at risk for developmental problems came about with the 1986 passage of Public Law 99-457, the Education of the Handicapped Act Amendments. The provisions of Public Law 99-457 require the availability of multidisciplinary assessment for infants and toddlers with disabilities. Part H of this law provides funding for states to implement and provide early intervention services for children from birth to age two who are developmentally delayed or disabled. The criteria for developmental delay and risk are established by each state. Accurate assessment of eligible infants is an integral part of this directive. Early intervention takes the form of programs and services directed toward helping disabled infants and toddlers develop as normally as possible (Meisels, Dichtelmiller, and Liaw 1993). These services include special education programming, developmental programming, services in physical therapy, occupational therapy, and speech therapy, as well as psychosocial intervention for families. Early intervention providers are concerned with accurately identifying infants at risk as well as with skillfully following their developmental progress (Widerstrom, Mowder, and Sandall 1991).

Uses of Infant Assessment

Why assess infants? The answer is that it depends on your purpose. The reasons for assessing infants have changed as the goals of the consumers of such information have changed.

Historically, the primary purposes of infant assessment were to document developmental maturation and make long-term predictions about development, hence the rise of norm-referenced instruments (Honzik 1983). These assessments allowed the comparison of an individual infant's performance with the performance of a normed sample. Typically, these instruments focused on the "average child" rather than on individual differences.

Initially, investigators also used infant assessment measures to learn more about the content and progression of sensorimotor development during infancy. Later, screening instruments were developed to detect which infants, because of risk factors present in the infant's environment or within the infant, were at risk for developmental delay. If these infants were assessed as being at risk, then they were thought to need in-depth assessments to determine whether they should be recommended for special education services. These service programs have come to be known as infant early intervention. Infant early intervention programs exist throughout the United States. The programs provide special education services, physical and occupational therapies, speech and language therapy, and psychosocial interventions, as well as specialized activities geared toward improving social and language skills. Figure 1.1 shows how the processes of screening and assessment are

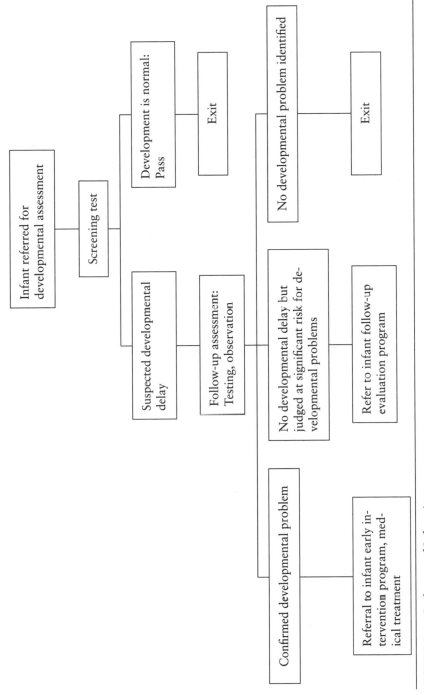

FIGURE 1.1 Pathways of Infant Assessment

used to determine which infants should be referred for infant early intervention services. An infant girl, for example, might be referred for assessment because she is low birth weight. Following hospitalization in a neonatal intensive care unit (NICU), she would be referred to a follow-up clinic for developmental screening. If no problems were detected she would continue to be developmentally screened every three months because of her at-risk status. However, if the screening test revealed a developmental problem, she would then be referred for an in-depth assessment to diagnose the extent of her delays. If developmental problems were confirmed, she would be eligible for early intervention services.

Developmental assessment is thus a process designed to enhance understanding of infants' skills, competence, or personality characteristics. According to Greenspan and Meisels (1993), the goals of developmental assessment are to

- Identify infants who may be at risk for developmental delay
- Diagnose the presence and extent of a developmental problem
- Identify an infant's specific abilities and skills
- Determine appropriate intervention strategies

The assessment process is usually undertaken within a broad clinical scope that involves several professionals representing different disciplines.

As intervention programs for infants with disabilities have increased, many additional uses for infant assessment have evolved. Infant assessment information is used for program planning for individual infants (Bricker and Littman 1982). Such programs involve specific educational activities or therapies designed to remediate specific problems. Another purpose is to evaluate the developmental progress of an infant in an intervention program (Sheehan 1982). Infant assessment data are also used to evaluate the effectiveness of infant intervention programs (Benner 1992).

A variety of assessment tools and techniques have been designed to detect developmental disabilities, in order to provide quick screens of specific aspects of infants' development. The Developmental Screening Inventory (Knobloch, Stevens, and Malone 1980) and the Denver Developmental Screening Test (DDST) (Frankenburg, Dodds, and Fandal 1975) are examples of tests that screen for developmental problems. The Callier-Azusa Scale (Stillman 1978) is a scale designed to assess infants and children with severe handicaps. In 1978, the Diagnostic Inventory of Early Development, a criterion-referenced assessment, was introduced for use in developing intervention strategies for at-risk infants (Brigance 1978).

Donald Bailey (1989) identified five major reasons for assessing an infant.

Screening: To identify infants who may be at risk for developmental problems and need further in-depth assessment
Diagnosis: To confirm or disconfirm a developmental problem

Placement: To assist in decisions as to what type of intervention, that is, educational or medical, the infant should receive

Program planning: To aid in planning goals and developmental activities for individual infants in an early intervention program

Evaluation: To measure the progress of infants who are in intervention programs or undergoing medical treatment

Assessments are now often used as vehicles for teaching parents about their infants. The Brazelton Neonatal Behavioral Assessment Scale (NBAS) (Brazelton 1984), for example, has been widely used by clinicians to teach parental involvement with neonates and to assist parents to more accurately read their infant's cues and responsiveness (Worobey 1985).

Let's look at some case examples of situations that call for screening or assessment. Clinicians and educators who work with infants must decide whether infants are at risk and whether there is a need for screening and assessment. Each of the following examples highlights an infant at risk for developmental delay. Read the examples, and for each, answer these questions:

Why is this infant at risk for developmental problems?
Should this infant be developmentally screened? If so, why?

Then compare your ideas with the answers provided after each example.

Cordell, age three months, is the only child of a fifteen-year-old single mother. He was full term, with no birth complications. His mother brought him to the well-baby clinic because he has difficulty holding his head steady. She describes him as a fussy baby who sleeps for only short periods of time.

Answer: Cordell is considered at risk because of the age of his mother. The research literature indicates that infants born to young adolescent mothers are at risk for delays. Cordell's inability to maintain head control and his sleep pattern indicate he may have developmental problems. He is a candidate for screening.

Dana, a five-month-old girl, is a graduate of the neonatal intensive care nursery where she spent two months. Dana was a low birth-weight infant and was eight weeks premature. During the two weeks after her birth, Dana was medically critical and had a questionable prognosis. She recovered slowly. Today, she is still small but appears alert and responsive. Her parents are hopeful that she will develop normally.

Answer: Dana's medical history and low birth weight place her in an at-risk category. Although Dana appears to be developing normally, low birth-weight infants are at greater risk for developmental and learning dysfunction in childhood. Periodic screening should be done to monitor her progress and detect developmental lag.

Benjamin is an eighteen-month-old healthy infant. His medical history is good except for his birth. For a few seconds, his umbilical cord was wrapped around his neck, cutting off his oxygen supply. However, that was quickly remedied. At birth, he was administered the newborn screening test, the Apgar, and his score of 7 was in the normal range. His parents have described him as a little slow in reaching such developmental milestones as babbling and crawling. They compare him to his older sister, who walked and talked by fourteen months of age. Only recently, they have become concerned because Ben says only a few single words and has shown little improvement in his walking skills since he took his first step at thirteen months.

Answer: Benjamin experienced a perinatal insult to his nervous system. His parent's observation initially indicates that he is attaining normal developmental milestones expected at his age. In this case, an in-depth assessment of Benjamin's abilities might yield more information than a screening test.

Carin is a healthy full-term six-month-old infant girl with Down syndrome. Her development to date has been on target, with only minor problems with head lag and some motor hypotonia.

Answer: Down syndrome is a genetic defect with an established risk of cognitive and motor problems. Carin is in an established risk category in which a developmental delay will occur; therefore, screening is not necessary. Instead, she is eligible for infant intervention services, where she will receive ongoing in-depth assessment.

At birth, Shawna weighed less than 1,500 grams (3.3 pounds). She spent three months in the neonatal care nursery. Her mother had no prenatal care and is a suspected drug user. Shawna has been discharged from the hospital for two months. She has been assigned a visiting home nurse.

Answer: Because Shawna was a low-birth-weight baby with possible prenatal drug exposure, she is both at biological and environmental risk for developmental delay. She is a candidate for developmental screening.

History of Infant Assessment

Infant assessment and infancy have been the subject of scientific scrutiny since 1970. Although the climate of intensive theorizing and heightened interest in infancy that began in the 1960s has contributed to infant assessment, the search for ways to measure infant intelligence originated in the late nineteenth century (Brooks-Gunn and Weinraub 1976). During this historical period, a number of disparate scientific interests and perspectives guided the study of intelligent behavior and its relationship to development. The assessment of intelligence grew out of the research interests of scientists, who first studied children and later, infants. With more systematic research on infant development, the quest for measuring infant intelligence took on a developmental perspective (Lewis and Sullivan 1985). Currently, the focus of infant testing is on cognition, language, perception, motor, and social development.

Origins of Infant Testing

The era of infant study began with the systematic documentation of infant development, observations that were then published as "baby diaries" by parents who took a formal interest in their infants' development. The first recorded baby biography, titled *Record of an Infant's Life*, was published in 1787 by Dietrich Tiedemann, a German philosopher (Tiedemann [1787] 1927). The following example from Tiedemann describes what today would probably be identified as the Moro reflex: "If he was held in arms and then suddenly lowered from a considerable height, he strove to hold himself with his hands, to save himself from falling, and he did not like to be lifted very high" (Tiedemann [1787] 1927:216).

An especially important baby biography was published in 1877 by Charles Darwin, who is best known for his theory of evolution. Because of Darwin's reputation, his detailed day-by-day account of his baby's development spawned interest in infant development and influenced numerous other parent observers to publish their own baby diaries (Preyer 1882; Shinn 1900). This segment of Darwin's diary (Darwin 1877:288) reveals both his careful observations and his interpretations.

> At the age of 32 days he perceived his mother's bosom when three or four inches from it, as was shown by the protrusion of his lips and his eyes becoming fixed; but I much doubt whether this had any connection with vision; he certainly had not touched the bosom. Whether he was guided through smell or the sensation of warmth or through association with the position in which he was held, I do not at all know.
>
> It was difficult to decide at how early an age anger was felt; on his eighth day he frowned and wrinkled the skin round his eyes before a crying fit, but this may have been due to pain or distress, and not to anger. When about ten weeks old, he was given some rather cold milk and he kept a slight frown on his forehead all the time that he was sucking, so that he looked like a grown-up person made cross from being compelled to do something which he did not like.
>
> When four and a half months old, he repeatedly smiled at my image and his own in a mirror, and no doubt mistook them for real objects; but he showed sense in being evidently surprised at my voice coming from behind him. Like all infants he much enjoyed thus looking at himself, and in less than two months perfectly understood that it was an image; for if I made quite silently an odd grimace, he would suddenly turn round to look at me.

One of the most famous baby biographies was written by Wilhelm Preyer (1822), who organized the description of his son's first year into intelligence, sensation, and motor development categories. Baby biographies such as these often suffered from *observer bias*, in which the observer's expectations about behaviors affected the observational data; nevertheless, they were the beginnings of systematic observations of infant behavior and provided a rich understanding of infant behavior. In addition, they alerted the scientific community to developmental trends and individual differences in infant development, two concepts now accepted as central to the field of infancy study.

Another early influence on infant assessment theory was the Child Study Movement founded at the beginning of the twentieth century by G. Stanley Hall, an American psychologist (Hall 1904). Hall helped to initiate the normative approach to child development, which involves assessing and describing the average age at which a behavior occurs within a specific population. This effort resulted in child development becoming a legitimate area of inquiry. In the 1920s, Arnold Gesell used the normative approach to establish normative curves for developmental milestones during infancy.

The scientific movement to assess intelligence was profoundly influenced by Sir Francis Galton's 1869 book *Hereditary Genius* (1974), which described the occurrence of genius within families. Galton's studies of the relationship of genetics to inherited traits influenced the emerging testing movement in Europe and the United States and generated scientific interest in the innate intellectual capacities of children.

Concern about individual differences in intellectual functioning was evident in the testing movement that emerged in Europe in the late 1800s. In 1904, Alfred Binet, a French psychologist, was commissioned by the Paris public instruction minister to develop a screening test that would identify children in the Paris school system who were mentally retarded and might need remedial education. The resultant thirty-item test focused on attention, comprehension, and memory, elements that Binet identified as the higher mental processes (Binet and Simon 1905). The test, which was organized from least to most difficult items, was designed to yield a mental-age score. Although the Binet test of intelligence was intended for school-age children, the scale included items appropriate for infants below the age of two. Consequently, some consider Binet's test to be the first infant intelligence test. Some examples of infant test items included visual tracking of a lighted match and imitating gestures. At a minimum, the test provided the impetus for intelligence testing and led to questions about the origins of infant intelligence.

In the United States, Lewis Terman (1916) revised and standardized the Binet-Simon Scale. In the process, he eliminated the infant test items, since they had been included in the original Binet-Simon Scale to identify school-age children who were mentally retarded. Still, the format of the resultant Stanford-Binet Intelligence Scale became a prototype for subsequent infant assessments that focused on infant intelligence.

1920–1930: Measuring Infant Intelligence

During the 1920s, the construct of intelligence was refined, and the first infant tests of intelligence were developed. Infant intelligence was considered a simpler version of adult intelligence. During this period, the unique competence of infants had not yet been discovered, and consequently, tests for infants tried to measure an infant intelligence quotient (IQ). Revisions of the Stanford-Binet Scale and the Linfert and Hierholzer Scale (1928) were early attempts to apply to infants the measurement techniques designed to measure the intelligence of older children (Kuhlmann 1922). One such test, for example, included measures of imitation, recognition, and language for two-, six-, twelve-, eighteen-, and twenty-four-month-old age groups (Kuhlmann 1922). There were obvious limitations in this approach to assessing infants, and neither test was widely used. Work with the intelligence scales, however, did set the stage for the publication of the Gesell Developmental Schedules and the Bayley Scales of Infant Development (BSID) in the 1930s.

Arnold Gesell (1925) and his associates at the Yale University Clinic of Child Development revolutionized infant assessment by using the normative approach previously identified by Hall to describe infant development. Based on a theory that emphasized biological maturation, these norms and their related test items were published as the Gesell Developmental Schedules (Gesell and Amatruda 1947). Using extensive observations of infants and young children, Gesell identified norms of infant behavior in four developmental domains: motor, adaptive (constructive exploration), social, and language. Sample test items from each of the developmental domains measured by the Gesell Developmental Schedules appear in Box 1.1. Maternal reports rather than direct observation are primarily used for test items in the language and personal-social areas. The combination of scores from the four areas of performance are calculated to obtain a developmental quotient (DQ). The DQ was originally conceptualized as analogous to the IQ, but in fact the DQ measures very different behaviors than the IQ.

The Gesell schedules were widely used as diagnostic tools and still continue to receive considerable use, particularly by pediatricians. In addition, many of the Gesell schedule items have been borrowed by authors of subsequent infant assessment scales, apparently because the items tap naturally occurring events in infant development.

While Gesell was working on the East Coast, Nancy Bayley was investigating the development and modification of patterns of infant behavior on the West Coast. Like Gesell, Bayley focused on normative behavior and in 1933 used the findings of the Longitudinal Berkeley Growth Study of Infant Development to publish the first version of the Bayley Scales of Infant Development (Bayley 1933). She subsequently revised her initial scale, and the BSID became the best known and most widely used test of infant development.

Bayley's research led to an expanded interest in the relationship of infant intelligence and later IQ measures. This was a predictive validity issue directly related to questions about the stability of intelligence and the impact of infants' environments on emerging mental capacities (Bayley 1949). Eva Abigail Fillmore (1936), for example, designed the Iowa Tests for Young Children to assess mental development and predict IQ, and the Cattell In-

BOX 1.1   Sample Test Items from the Gesell Developmental Schedules

	Motor Schedule
4 weeks	Rolls partway to side
12 weeks	Lifts foot while standing
36 weeks	Leans forward in sitting position and re-erects

	Language
16 weeks	Laughs aloud
36 weeks	Imitates sounds

	Personal-Social
8 weeks	Eyes follow moving person
20 weeks	Smiles at mirror image

	Adaptive
12 weeks	Follows dangling ring 180 degrees
44 weeks	Points out pellets through the glass bottle

SOURCE: Data from Gesell Developmental Schedules (New York: Psychological Corporation, 1940).

fant Intelligence Scale (Cattell 1940) was designed for infants from two to thirty months as a downward extension of the Stanford-Binet. Some sample test items from the Iowa test include the following:

- Reacting to image in mirror
- Picking up pellet
- Walking with help

Box 1.2 shows sample test items from the Cattell scale. Test items in the Cattell scale were chosen for ease of administration, as well as for the capacity to capture the child's interest. The test, however, met with little success in predicting subsequent Stanford-Binet scores (Honzik 1983).

1940–1960: Developments in Infant Testing

Infant tests were markedly improved between 1940 and 1960. Infant tests were standardized more carefully and included more items that assessed infants' sociability and linguistic skills. However, with few exceptions, infant tests were designed to assess behaviors that could be used to measure intelligence as well as to predict later IQ. These proved to be elusive goals, for although the assessments yielded information about the normative course of human development, infant test scores did not predict scores on childhood intelligence tests (Bayley 1949; Honzik, MacFarlane, and Allen 1948;

BOX 1.2 Cattell Infant Intelligence Test

• Lifts head from prone position (2nd month) • Regards cube while sitting (3rd month) • Lifts cup (6 months) • Says "DaDa" (8 months) • Imitates sounds (9 months) • Secures cube under cup (11 months) • Identifies objects by name (23–24 months)

SOURCE: P. Cattell, *The Measurement of Intelligence in Young Children* (New York: Psychological Corporation, 1940).

Honzik 1983). The issue of predictive validity remained unresolved, but infant assessments began to be used more widely as diagnostic tools of infant development (Lewis and Sullivan 1985).

The Griffiths Mental Development Scale (Griffiths 1954) provides a good example of a test concerned with diagnosis rather than prediction. Griffiths did not believe that her test should measure or predict IQ. The Griffiths scale resembled the Gesell schedules in that it contained locomotor, personal-social, hearing and speech, hand-eye, and performance subscales, based on Griffiths's view that social relationships were important to intellectual development, but Griffiths included more measures of social interactions in her test. See Box 1.3 for sample test items from the Griffiths test. Although this test was regarded as innovative because it included test items that measured social responsiveness, it was not widely used outside of England (Brooks-Gunn and Weinraub 1976).

The inability to predict later intelligence from infant measures led to a reexamination of the idea that intelligence is a stable attribute that is continuous and can be measured during infancy. This is known as the continuity-discontinuity hypothesis. Carl Dunst and Regina Rheingrover (1986) and others point out that research efforts that tried to predict adult intelligence from infant tests in fact measured the stability of individual infant assessment measures over time, while assuming that development is a continuous, cumulative process. These investigators argue that development is not additive; they believe that intelligence changes qualitatively over time. What is measured in intelligence tests in later childhood or adulthood is qualitatively different from what developmental assessments measure. Thus, it would not automatically follow that an infant who had a high score at eight months on an infant measure would have a high IQ at eight years.

Longitudinal studies of infant cognitive development found little stability in infant performance related to later intellectual performance. Investigators argued that this lack of stability was explained by the fact that the

BOX 1.3   Sample Test Items from the Griffiths Mental Development Scale

Locomotion

- Kicks vigorously
- Lifts head and chest when prone
- Rolls from side to back

Personal—Sound

- Vocalizes when talked to
- Frolics when played with
- Anticipatory movements when about to be lifted

Hearing and Speech

- Startled by sounds
- Laughs aloud
- Talks (babbles) to people

Eye and Hand

- Glances from one object to another
- Clutches at dangling ring
- Visually explores new environment

Performance

- Plays with own fingers
- Looks at toy on table
- Drops first cube for second

SOURCE: Data from R. Griffiths, *The Abilities of Babies: A Study in Mental Measurement* (New York: McGraw-Hill, 1954).

infant developmental period is qualitatively different from later periods of development. Early infant development is much more reliant on sensorimotor skills. For example, measures on the Bayley scales primarily assess sensorimotor abilities such as eye-hand coordination and orienting to objects, whereas measures on traditional childhood intelligence tests assess conceptual skills such as language, perceptual learning, and memory.

Some authorities have argued that early infant tests do not appropriately measure infant mental cognition. Marc H. Bornstein and Marian D. Sigman (1986), for example, contend that assessments of infants should measure information-processing skills such as decrement and recovery of attention to changing aspects of the environment known as *habituation* and *dishabituation*. Measures of both decrement and recovery of attention to visual and auditory stimuli in infants were found to be positively associated with cognitive performance later in childhood (McCall 1971; Olson and Sherman 1983).

Recent studies indicate that there is more stability in infant mental development than was previously thought. Measures of visual recognition of objects and pictures, object permanence, habituation, and attention do indicate significant relations between infant cognition and later intelligence (McCall and Carriger 1993; Rose and Feldman 1995).

1960–1980: A New Look at Infants

Between 1960 and 1980, remarkable advances in the study of infancy occurred. In fact, infant development became recognized as a legitimate field of its own (Fogel 1991). Psychological research led to a growing awareness of individual infant temperament, the infant's role in social dynamics, infants' capacities to make sense of the world, the transactional interplay between infants and their environments, and the importance of secure infant-parent bonds in promoting optimal infant development. The rich array of neonatal behaviors in human infants was acknowledged. Medical knowledge of infants also expanded. Advances in medical technology fostered high-risk infant survival, which resulted in the establishment of infant intervention programs throughout the United States. Clinicians more clearly recognized that assessment of infants is different from assessment of children or adults.

Assessment instruments were needed for developmental screening and educational planning for high-risk infants. Norm-referenced infant assessments such as the Gesell and Bayley scales designed for normal populations were found to have limited use in documenting progress of infants with disabilities. Assessments were needed to provide information about infants' strengths and progress as well as their weaknesses. There was a decided need for infant assessment to extend beyond its traditional approaches.

Infant assessment techniques developed during these two decades reflected new approaches to measuring infant capabilities. Two notable contributions in this period were the Uzgiris-Hunt Ordinal Scales of Psychological Development and the Brazelton Neonatal Behavioral Assessment Scale.

The Uzgiris-Hunt Ordinal Scales of Psychological Development (Uzgiris and Hunt 1975), based on Jean Piaget's theory of sensorimotor intelligence in the first two years of life, was a departure from traditional infant assessments. The theoretical focus of the scales was on measurement of infant cognition. These scales focused on the emergence of sensorimotor intelligence and measured such skills as problem solving, object permanence, play, and imitation. The ordinal scales were designed to assess the progression of conceptual understanding from simple to more complex levels. Rather than simply passing or failing a test item, which typified the approach of traditional standardized tests such as the Bayley scales, infants receive qualitative ratings on their task performance. The ordinal scales are widely used as research instruments as well as for infant assessment.

The Brazelton Neonatal Behavioral Assessment Scale (Brazelton 1973, 1984) resulted from the recognition of newborn competence. The scale not only measures newborn responses and reflexes but has also been used as an index of newborn individuality and interactive capabilities. Changes in infant state behaviors, for instance, sleep-wake patterns, are measured as indications of infants' central nervous system integrity.

During this period, other instruments were developed to tap into the behavioral capacities of infants. For example, attachment classifications between parent and infant were measured using the Ainsworth Strange Situation procedure (Ainsworth et al. 1978). Various measures of the styles and patterns of infant temperament were developed for clinical practice and research (Rothbart and Goldsmith 1985), and the recognition of the importance of parent-infant interactions prompted the development of a number of parent-infant interaction scales (Farran et al. 1987; Bromwich and Parmelee 1979). Strategies for assessing infant play behaviors began in the 1970s and continued to be refined in the next two decades (Rubenstein and Howes 1976). New directions in assessing infants with disabilities also began in the 1970s (DuBose 1979).

Current Trends in Infant Assessment

In the 1990s, assessment of infants is being closely scrutinized and studied. Traditional infant tests provide information on infants' skills but leave many questions about infants' abilities unanswered. For example, how does a baby solve a problem? What does a baby need in order to learn? What is a baby unable to do and why?

Public Law 99–457 mandates multiteam evaluation of infants at risk and their families. This has challenged infant interventionists to examine the purpose of assessment and identify effective methods for gathering information. The development of new assessment methods includes a more comprehensive approach to measuring infants as well as an emphasis on infant development within the familial and sociocultural environment.

A recent trend in infant assessment is the development of a multidimensional, interdisciplinary approach. This approach starts with the assumption that developmental domains are inextricably linked and that one domain affects all domains. Language, for example, is assumed to affect cognitive and social-emotional development parent-infant social interaction patterns. Such assessments may be done by a team of professionals, including physicians, psychologists, infant development specialists, speech therapists, occupational therapists, and physical therapists. Thus the "new look" in infant assessment requires assessment not only of infants' developmental status but also of their home environment (Bradley and Caldwell 1976), their interactions with family members, and family functioning (Fogel 1991).

Multidisciplinary team assessment is provided for by Part H Public Law 99–457 to implement the early intervention assessment process for at-risk infants and their families. The early intervention assessment process includes each of the following steps, each of which requires assessment:

- Finding infants and their families who are qualified to receive early intervention services
- Screening that uses a quick developmental screen to determine whether more assessment is needed
- Assessment that uses an in-depth assessment to determine diagnosis and referral
- Planning intervention strategies that use assessment to promote the infant's development
- Monitoring change that uses ongoing assessment to determine change and progress in the infant's developmental status

At each stage of the intervention process, the assessment team must decide which assessment methods will be most useful in obtaining the needed information. Ideally, the team works together in a positive collaborative relationship. The family of the at-risk infant is also included as a team member and is involved in decisionmaking at each stage of early intervention. Assessment in early intervention is an evolving process that is guided by family needs and priorities.

The impetus to reformulate traditional approaches to infant assessment has come from the recent upsurge of early intervention programs for infants who are disabled or at risk. Whereas early infant measures were designed to yield information about normal infant development, a need now exists to assess atypical developmental patterns and to make recommendations about intervention procedures. So too must assessments document the developmental progress of atypical infants within the family context (Sheehan 1982).

Standardized norm-referenced infant scales have not established their validity assessing atypical populations. Clinicians who work with infants who are disabled do not gain a clear picture of the infants' performance and progress from a norm-referenced assessment. These assessments provide a general assessment of developmental progress. The emphasis on infants' functional behavior, so necessary to implementing effective infant intervention, cannot be determined from traditional infant assessments such as the Bayley Scales of Infant Development (Bayley 1993). Consequently, criterion-referenced scales have been developed for use with infants with special needs. These assessments sample functional behaviors and developmental tasks used in most infant or preschool early intervention educational curricula. Infants are measured on the extent to which they meet a specific criterion for each developmental task. Some examples of criterion-based assessments include the Early Learning Accomplishment Profile (ELAP) (Griffin and Sanford 1975), the Brigance Diagnostic Inventory of Early Development (1978), and the Hawaii Early Learning Profile (HELP) (Furuno et al. 1987). Typically, these assessments contain many more items than traditional infant tests. The test items are used to structure the infant's individual intervention plan. Sample assessment activities from HELP are presented in Box 1.4.

BOX 1.4   Examples from Hawaii Early Learning Profile

Hawaii Early Learning Profile
1.35   Plays 2–3 minutes with single toy (6–9 months). Use squeeze toys for the child to hit, bang, touch, look at, taste different parts, and so on.
1.42   Imitates familiar, then new gesture (7–11 months). Pick new gestures similar to the ones the child knows, such as "patting the floor" if he knows "patting his stomach."
5.26   Cooperates in games (6–10 months). The child enjoys the give-and-take of simple games, such as pat-a-cake.
5.35   Engages in simple imitative play (9–12 months). Give the child an extra washcloth in the bath and encourage her to wash her tummy.

SOURCE: Data from S. Furuno, K. A. O'Reilly, C. M. Hosaka, T. T. Inatsuka, T. L. Allman, and B. Zeisloft, *Hawaii Early Learning Profile (HELP): Activity Guide* (Palo Alto, CA: VORT Corporation, 1987).

An example of a recent alternative to traditional infant tests is the use of information-processing measures. Information-processing techniques used include infant habituation, preference for a novel stimulus, and infant visual recognition. These measures are now thought to produce more accurate assessments of intelligence than previous test measures did. Research evidence offers support for the development of more accurate measures of infants' intellectual functioning using information-processing procedures (Zelazo and Kearsley 1989). Measures of memory and information processing are currently being developed as alternatives to conventional infant tests (Zelazo and Weiss 1990).

The habituation-recovery procedure was adapted to measure infant intelligence (Fagan and McGrath 1981). In this paradigm, infants are tested for their ability to habituate to a new stimulus and then dishabituate or recover when a second novel stimulus is presented. Habituation occurs when infants are repeatedly exposed to a visual or auditory stimulus such as a bell ring or flashing light. The first time the stimulus is presented, the infant startles or blinks. As the stimulus is repeated, the infant's response begins to lessen. The infant's gradual decline when looking at or responding to the stimuli over repeated trials is known as habituation, whereas the recovery of interest in a novel stimulus is called dishabituation. Similarly, recognition memory has been used with a visual preference procedure as a measure of infant intellectual ability (Fagan and Singer 1982). In this procedure, two pictures are simultaneously shown to the infant. One of the pictures has been previously viewed by the infant. Infants prefer to look at the visual stimulus they have seen before, indicating memory of a familiar picture. Other techniques assess short-term and long-term memory in infants as well as psychophysiological responses to novel stimuli.

Infant Assessment Process

The process of infant assessment yields information about infant development, temperament, personality, cognitive style, and parent-infant interaction. The assessment process can involve direct testing in which standardized tasks and stimulus items are presented to an infant in a controlled setting. Assessment may also include structured observations of the infant in natural settings such as the home, parent interviews, and observations of parents and infants in play situations.

The quality and amount of information gathered depends on what occurs during the assessment process, the skills of the examiner, and the infant's cooperation. For example, infants are often wary of strangers, so an experienced examiner would allow enough time for the infant to adapt to the new situation. A novice examiner might overlook an infant's behavioral cues such as looking away or fussing. Such cues say in effect "I'm tired" or "I'm not ready for this activity."

In 1993, the National Center for Clinical Infant Programs identified a Zero to Three Work Group on Developmental Assessment (Greenspan and Meisels 1993). This task force proposed a number of recommended practices for developmental assessment of infants and young children. Some suggested practices include the following: Instead of testing an infant using a single standardized procedure, examiners should attempt to gather a picture of the whole child, using multiple sources of information. Infants should be observed interacting with their caregivers. The assessment should measure an infant's functional capacities, which include organized behavior, attending to people and events in the environment, engaging others, taking part in reciprocal interactions with others, and constructing and using symbolic relationships. Multiple sources of information should provide a clear view of the infant's current competencies as well as the skills needed to attain further skills.

The Zero to Three Work Group also suggests that a developmental assessment should encompass the following steps. The examiner should do the following:

- Obtain a picture of the infant within the family experience. This involves establishing a working alliance with the family over time by discussing family members' views of the infant's strengths and weaknesses as well as their expectations of the assessment process.
- Obtain a developmental history of the child through ongoing observations.
- Observe the infant playing with parents or caregivers.
- Observe infant interaction with a clinician.
- Make specific assessments of the infant's individual functions.

• Integrate all data obtained from observations, parent reports, and other assessments, using a developmental model as a basic framework.

The process of infant assessment requires a skilled examiner who is patient, creative, and knowledgeable about infants and infant development. The examiner should have extensive experience with a broad range of infants and families and should also be knowledgeable about infant development. The examiner must be comfortable in handling and working with infants. It is crucial that the infant be alert and that the examiner be able to determine when to stop or proceed with an assessment based on the infant's behavioral cues. The assessment tasks and routine must match the infant's availability and readiness. Test materials should be organized and easily accessible. This may seem easy, but in fact it is difficult for inexperienced testers. Novice assessors can gain experience by engaging in practice testing with many infants of different ages. New testers should be supervised and observed and should receive feedback on their testing skills from experienced practitioners.

Current "best practices" in assessment point to the assessment process as the first step in a potential early intervention approach. Assessments that occur in just one meeting and that are conducted by a strange examiner in a new setting unnecessarily challenge infants. Assessments should provide an integrated understanding of an infant's development rather than a limited view of one developmental domain such as language or motor development. Assessments of infants should involve more than a structured test approach, characteristic of formal tests (Greenspan and Meisels 1993).

Infant assessment can take place in a variety of settings, including intensive care nurseries, hospital clinics, physicians' or psychologists' offices, social service agencies, or the infant's home. Assessments may include formal standardized procedures combined with informal or structured observation. Infants may be tested just one time or repeatedly throughout the infant period. In the case of an infant who is disabled or at risk for developmental problems, repeated testing is recommended. Often a single assessment may be able to elicit only a limited sample of the infant's behavior. Usually, infants have a broader array of behaviors than those exhibited during a testing session. Serial assessments allow for a more comprehensive picture of an infant's developmental pattern.

Parents are a valuable source of information about the infant. Usually prior to a formal assessment, the parents are interviewed by the examiner. In that interview, the examiner obtains information about the medical history of the infant and family, the infant's developmental history, family demographics, and concerns or questions the parents may have about their infant's development. This information is useful in planning and interpreting the assessment data.

Testing infants poses many challenges. Young infants sleep a lot. They get fussy. Infants cannot tell the tester what they are feeling or thinking.

Sometimes infants are uncooperative or uninterested in a particular test task. Infants are often distracted by an unfamiliar testing environment or even by the examiner. Establishing rapport with a wary infant takes time. The examiner may introduce a game such as peekaboo or simply allow the baby to play with an interesting toy until the infant becomes relaxed.

The following example illustrates the difficulty of successfully completing an assessment in one session.

Six-month-old Eric is brought to the psychologist's office for developmental assessment. He is alert and quiet. The psychologist spends forty minutes collecting his history and explaining the test to the parents. The test is then begun. Initially, Eric shows interest in the test items but then begins to fuss and arches his back. The parents try to soothe Eric, but to no avail.

Often an infant's parents are present during the assessment; in fact, Bayley (1969) recommends that parents accompany their infant in the exam. Parents should be informed of the exam's purpose and be made to feel comfortable in the examination process. Transmitting the assessment findings to the parents should be done in a nonthreatening, informative manner. The informing conference can be used to assist parents to identify and appreciate their infant's individual behaviors.

Communicating diagnostic findings to parents of infants with developmental delays requires sensitivity on the part of the professional. In such cases, parents often report feelings of alienation and dismay that the examiner focused only on the infant's limitations (Murphy 1990). Since the diagnostic conference is often difficult for parents of infants with disabilities, providing emotional support for parents is as important as conveying factual information about the infant. Most practitioners recommend more than one information session with parents to discuss test results and answer questions.

Summary

Infancy is an immensely important period for cognitive development. In the 1930s, the Gesell Developmental Schedules and the Bayley Scales of Infant Development were developed to measure infant development. The early tests of infant mental functions yielded information on developmental norms but did not predict IQ in later childhood.

Screening involves a quick developmental check on infant status. Assessment is a more in-depth analysis of infant behaviors and development. These processes are used to determine infants' eligibility for early intervention services.

The current state of infant assessment is undergoing close scrutiny by researchers. A major influence on the field of infancy was Public Law 99–457, which provided education and therapy services for at-risk infants and their families. Multidisciplinary team assessment is used to assess infants suspected of having developmental delays. Another recent trend in infant assessment is the use of information-processing techniques such as habituation and visual preference recognition to measure cognitive function. Because of the interdependence of developmental domains for infant development, it is now recognized that in order to fully understand infant development, infant assessments must be comprehensive and interdisciplinary. As the field of infant assessment continues to evolve, the likely result will be improved measures for diagnosis and prescription.

References

Ainsworth, M.D.S., M. C. Blehar, E. Waters, and S. Wall. 1978. *Patterns of Attachment: A Psychological Study of the Strange Situation*. Hillsdale, NJ: Lawrence Erlbaum Associates.

Anastasiow, N. J. 1993. The effects of early intervention. In *At-Risk Infants: Intervention, Families, and Research*, edited by N. J. Anastasiow and S. Harel. Baltimore: Paul H. Brookes.

Bailey, D. B. 1989. Assessment and its importance in early intervention. In *Assessing Infants and Preschoolers with Handicaps*, edited by D. B. Bailey and M. Wolery. Columbus, OH: Merrill.

Bayley, N. 1993. *Bayley Scales of Infant Development*. 2d ed. San Antonio, TX: Psychological Corporation.

_____. 1969. *Manual for the Bayley Scales of Infant Development*. New York: Psychological Corporation.

_____. 1949. Consistency and variability in the growth of intelligence from birth to 18 years. *Journal of Genetic Psychology* 75:165–196.

_____. 1933. *The California First Year Mental Scales*. Berkeley: University of California Press.

Benner, S. M. 1992. *Assessing Young Children with Special Needs*. New York: Longman.

Binet, A., and T. Simon. 1905. Méthodes nouvelles pour le diagnostic du niveau intellectual des anormaux. *L'année psychologique* 11:191–244.

Bornstein, M., and M. D. Sigman. 1986. Continuity in mental development from infancy. *Child Development* 57:251–274.

Bradley, R. H., and B. M. Caldwell. 1976. Early home environment and changes in mental test performance in children from 6 to 36 months. *Developmental Psychology* 2:93–97.

Brazelton, T. B. 1984. *Neonatal Behavioral Assessment Scale*. Philadelphia: J. B. Lippincott.

_____. 1973. *Neonatal Behavioral Assessment Scale*. Clinics in Developmental Medicine, no. 50. Philadelphia: J. B. Lippincott.

Bricker, D., and D. Littman. 1982. Intervention and evaluation: The inseparable mix. *Topics in Early Childhood Special Education* 2(4):23–34.

Brigance, A. 1978. *Brigance Diagnostic Inventory of Early Development*. Worcester, MA: Curriculum Associates.

Bromwich, R., and A. Parmelee. 1979. An intervention program for preterm infants. In *Infants Born at Risk*, edited by T. Field. New York: Spectrum Publications.

Brooks-Gunn, J., and M. Weinraub. 1976. A history of infant intelligence testing. In *Origins of Intelligence*, edited by M. Lewis. New York: Plenum.

Cattell, P. 1940. *The Measurement of Intelligence in Young Children*. New York: Psychological Corporation.

Darwin, C. 1877. *Biographical Sketch of an Infant*. *Mind* 2:286–294.

DuBose, R. 1979. Adaptations in measurement procedures: Should you make alterations for handicapped children? In *Perspectives on Measurement: A Collection of Readings for Educators of Young Handicapped Children*, edited by T. Black. Chapel Hill, NC: TADS.

Dunst, C. J., and R. M. Rheingrover. 1986. Concurrent validity of the Uzgiris and Hunt Scales: Relationship to Bayley scale mental age. *Social and Behavioral Sciences Documents* 16:65.

Fagan, J. F., and S. N. McGrath. 1981. Infant recognition memory and later intelligence. *Intelligence* 5:121–130.

Fagan, J. F., and L. T. Singer. 1982. Infant recognition memory as a measure of intelligence. In *Advances in Infancy Research*. Vol. 2. Edited by L. P. Lipsitt. Norwood, NJ: Ablex.

Farran, D. C., C. Kasari, P. Yoder, L. Harber, G. Huntington, and M. Comfort-Smith. 1987. Rating mother-infant interactions in handicapped and at-risk infants. In *Stimulation and Intervention in Infant Development*, edited by D. Tamir. London: Freund Publishing House.

Fillmore, E. A. 1936. Iowa tests for young children. *University of Iowa Studies on Child Welfare* 11(4).

Fogel, A. 1991. *Infancy*. 2d ed. St. Paul: West.

Frankenburg, W. K., J. Dodds, and A. Fandal. 1975. *Denver Developmental Screening Test*. Denver: LADOCA Project and Publishing.

Furuno, S., K. A. O'Reilly, C. M. Hosaka, T. T. Inatsuka, T. L. Allman, and B. Zeisloft. 1987. *Hawaii Early Learning Profile (HELP): Activity Guide*. Palo Alto, CA: VORT Corporation.

Galton, M. S. [1869] 1974. *Hereditary Genius*. New York: St. Martin's Press.

Gesell, A. 1940. *The First Five Years of Life: A Guide to the Study of Preschool Children*. New York: Harper.

_____. 1925. *The Mental Growth of the Preschool Child*. New York: Macmillan.

Gesell, A., and C. S. Amatruda. 1947. Developmental Diagnosis. New York: Hoeber.

Greenspan, S. I., and E. Meisels. 1993. Toward a new vision for developmental assessment. *Zero to Three* 14:1–8.

Griffin, P., and A. Sanford. 1975. *Learning Accomplishment Profile*. Winston-Salem, NC: Kaplan Press.

Griffiths, R. 1954. *The Abilities of Babies: A Study in Mental Measurement*. New York: McGraw-Hill.

Hall, G. S. 1904. *Adolescence*. Vols. 1–2. New York: Appleton-Century Crofts.

Honzik, M. P. 1983. Measuring mental abilities in infancy: The value and limitations. In *Origins of Intelligence in Infancy and Early Childhood*, edited by M. Lewis. New York: Plenum.

Honzik, M. P., J. W. MacFarlane, and L. Allen. 1948. Stability of mental test performance between 2 and 18 years. *Journal of Experimental Education* 17:309–324.

James, W. 1890. *The Principles of Psychology*. New York: Henry Holt.

Johnson, B., N. Martin, K. G. Jens, and S. M. Attermeir. 1986. *The Carolina Curriculum for Handicapped Infants and Infants at Risk*. Baltimore: Paul H. Brookes.

Knobloch, H., F. Stevens, and A. F. Malone. 1980. *The Revised Developmental Screening Inventory.* Houston, TX: Gesell Developmental Test Material.

Kuhlmann, F. 1922. *A Handbook of Mental Tests.* Baltimore: Warwick and York.

Lewis, M., and M. A. Sullivan. 1985. Infant intelligence and its assessment. In *Handbook of Intelligence: Theories, Measurements, and Applications,* edited by B. B. Wolman. New York: Wiley.

Linfert, H. E., and H. M. Hierholzer. 1928. *A Scale for Measuring the Mental Development of Infants During the First Years of Life.* Baltimore: Williams and Wilkins.

McCall, R. B. 1971. Attention in the infant: Avenue to the study of cognitive development. In *Early Childhood: The Development of Self-Regulatory Mechanisms,* edited by D. N. Walcher and D. L. Peters. New York: Academic Press.

McCall, R. B., and M. S. Carriger. 1993. A meta analysis of infant habituation and recognition memory performed as predictors of later IQ. *Child Development* 64:57–77.

Meisels, S. J., M. Dichtelmiller, and F. Liaw. 1993. A multidimensional analysis of early childhood intervention programs. In *Handbook of Infant Mental Health,* edited by C. H. Zeanah, Jr. New York: Guilford Press.

Murphy, A. 1990. Communicating assessment findings to parents. In *Interdisciplinary Assessment of Infants,* edited by E. Gibbs and D. M. Teti. Baltimore: Paul H. Brookes.

Olson, G. M., and T. Sherman. 1983. Attention, learning and memory in infants. In *Handbook of Child Psychology. Vol. 2: Infancy and Developmental Psychobiology.* Edited by M. M. Haith and J. J. Campos. New York: Wiley.

Preyer, W. 1882. *The Mind of the Child.* New York: D. Appleton.

Rose, S. A., and J. F. Feldman. 1995. Prediction of IQ and specific cognitive abilities at 11 years from infancy measures. *Developmental Psychology* 31:685–696.

Rothbart, M. K., and H. H. Goldsmith. 1985. Three approaches to the study of infant temperament. *Developmental Review* 5:237–260.

Rubenstein, J., and C. Howes. 1976. The effects of peers on toddler interactions with mothers and toys. *Child Development* 47:597–605.

Sheehan, R. 1982. Infant assessment: A review and identification of emergent trends. In *Intervention with At-Risk and Handicapped Infants: From Research to Application,* edited by D. Bricker. Baltimore: University Park Press.

Shinn, M. 1900. *The Biography of a Baby.* Boston: Houghton Mifflin.

Stillman, R., ed. 1978. *The Callier-Azusa Scale.* Dallas: University of Texas at Dallas.

Terman, L. M. 1916. *The Measurement of Intelligence.* Boston: Houghton-Mifflin.

Tiedemann, D. [1787] 1927. Tiedemann's observations on the development of the mental faculties of children. Trans. S. Langer. *Pedagogical Seminary and Journal of Genetic Psychology* 34:205–230.

Uzgiris, I. C., and J. McV. Hunt. 1975. Assessment in Infancy. Urbana: University of Illinois Press.

Watson, J. B. 1924. *Behaviorism.* New York: Norton.

Widerstrom, A. H., B. A. Mowder, and S. R. Sandall. 1991. *At-Risk and Handicapped Newborns and Infants.* Englewood, NJ: Prentice-Hall.

Worobey, J. 1985. A review of Brazelton-based interventions to enhance parent-infant interaction. *Journal of Reproductive and Infant Psychology* 3:64–73.

Zelazo, P. R., and R. B. Kearsley. 1989. Validation of an information processing approach to infant-toddler intellectual assessment.

Zelazo, P. R., and M. J. Weiss. 1990. Infant information processing. In *Interdisciplinary Assessment of Infants*, edited by E. D. Gibbs and D. M. Teti. Baltimore: Paul H. Brookes.

2

Neonatal Assessment

Small traveller from an unseen shore,
By mortal eye, ne'er seen before,
To you, good-morrow.

—*Cosmo Monkhouse*

Introduction

A new baby comes into the world, but what can the newborn do? What does a baby at birth know? Are neonates able to learn and remember? Can newborns communicate with others? How do newborns interpret environmental events? Scientific research is providing some answers to these questions, and as a result, we are learning that newborns are indeed remarkable. Documenting the rich repertoire of newborn skills and potential is the goal of neonatal assessment.

The assessment of the newborn infant is a relatively recent and rapidly growing area of clinical application. As compared to traditional assessments of older infants—assessments with origins in education and psychology—neonatal assessment derives from medicine. Newborn assessment is unique when viewed from other perspectives as well. For example, many neonatal assessments rely on structured observations of the infant in states of rest or alertness. State behaviors are organized patterns of arousal that encompass sleep and waking states. In typical full-term infants, there are distinct periods of rest and activity. The attention to state behaviors marks a major difference between tests of newborns and older infants because state of arousal is considered an indicator of newborn central nervous system integrity. Another difference is that assessment of the newborn relies on observations of subtle motor movements. Also, as part of the assessment, the examiner handles the neonate and thus must be skilled in handling newborns. Since newborns can become easily taxed by environmental input, accurately reading newborn signs of stress and using flexibility in assessment is a requisite in newborn testing.

In this chapter, you will be introduced to the uses and purposes of neonatal assessment. First, we will review the development of neonatal assessment. Then, neonatal capabilities are briefly reviewed, as are ways to assess premature infants. Next, practicalities involved in testing newborns are discussed. In the last section of this chapter, types and examples of neonatal tests are presented. To guide your reading, review the study questions, read the case examples, and answer the questions.

When you finish reading this chapter you should be able to

- Describe newborns' capacities and abilities
- Identify types of newborn assessments
- Describe the key elements of neurobehavioral assessments

Historical Background of Newborn Assessment

Historically, neonates were tested to learn more about the relevant dimensions of their behavioral repertoire, to screen and identify neonates at risk for developmental delay, and to make developmental predictions (McCall 1971). These goals remain today, and though promising experimental neonatal assessment methods exist, accurate prediction of later developmental outcomes from neonatal assessments has still not been achieved.

Neonatal assessment procedures have their beginnings in medicine, with later contributions deriving from psychology (St. Clair 1978). Early neonatal assessments focused on neurological functioning and neonatal adaptation to birth trauma (Polani 1959). These tests were primarily developed and carried out by physicians who were trying both to determine the neonate's medical status and to predict developmental potential. For the most part, such tests reflected a static view of the newborn infant that included the assumption that newborns are passive and capable only of a very limited range of behaviors. Typically, these tests focused on neurological responses, postural control, skin color, respiration, and reflex abilities (Prechtl and Beintema 1964; Andre-Thomas, Chesni, and Saint-Anne Dargassies 1964; Saint-Anne Dargassies 1977).

As clinicians began to understand the importance of neonatal behaviors and their relationship to neurological functioning, traditional neurological assessments gave way to more comprehensive approaches that evaluate newborn behavior as reflective of central nervous system integrity (Britt and Myers 1994; Berg and Berg 1979).

Contemporary approaches to newborn assessment are based on the view that the newborn is an active being who, within the context of the caregiving environment, organizes behaviors and interacts with others. Newborn behaviors reflect meaning for both the newborn's individuality and neurological integrity. Recognition of the significance of the neonatal period (the first fourteen days of life) is reflected in the proliferation of neonatal assessment instruments since the 1970s (Gorski, Lewkowicz, and Huntington 1987). These instruments measure reflexes, neonatal neurological status, arousal abilities, stress signals, individual differences, interaction with caregivers, the ability to organize behaviors, and a range of behavioral capacities.

The first of these neonatal behavioral exams was developed by F. K. Graham (1956) and revised by Judith Rosenblith in the 1960s; together, they published the Graham/Rosenblith Behavioral Test for Neonates (Rosenblith 1961, 1979a). Later, the Neonatal Behavioral Assessment Scale was developed by T. Berry Brazelton (1973). Brazelton's neurobehavioral test embodies a dynamic view of newborn-environmental interaction and measures the newborn's capacity to organize responsivity to environmental changes. Thus, contemporary neonatal testing goes beyond assessment of neurological markers such as reflexes to include measures of neonatal behavioral characteristics and social responsiveness.

Capacities of the Neonate

Until recently, newborns have been regarded as incompetent, helpless, and fragile. These beliefs about newborn incompetence prevailed largely until relatively recently, when a surge of scientific interest in newborn behavior resulted in knowledge and appreciation of the newborn's behavioral repertoire. Since 1970, there have been numerous studies on newborns' abilities and responses to their caregivers. In this section, we will examine some newborn behaviors.

Reflexes

Infants are born with a set of reflex behaviors. These are involuntary responses that occur automatically in response to particular stimuli. Once triggered, the reflex continues through its natural course. Many of these reflexes, such as sucking and grasping, begin to function during the prenatal period. Some of the reflexes of the newborn are described in Table 2.1. It is believed that many of these reflexes have evolved to promote the survival of helpless infants. Some reflexes, for instance, the walking reflex, are the rudimentary elements of later voluntary movements, in this case, walking. Reflexes such as rooting and sucking help infants locate and consume nutrients, whereas other reflexes appear to be evolutionary vestiges of early survival behaviors. Some reflexes such as the Moro reflex are defensive reactions—responses to changes in the environment.

During the first month of life, newborns begin to adapt their reflexes to match the demands of their environment. For example, the sucking reflex, which is vital to feeding, is highly adaptable to such features as the size of the object placed in the mouth, the object's position, the nourishment obtained, and the room temperature (Elder 1970; Kaye 1966). Some theorists (Piaget 1954) consider this ability to adapt reflexes as the beginning of cognition.

Reflexes are also used as neurological markers, in that assessors can note whether they are present at expected times. This is possible because not all reflexes are present at birth; they appear later, on a fairly precise schedule. Some reflexes such as the startle reflex persist through the life span. In addition, certain reflexes disappear on schedule. This happens because reflexes are controlled by the lower center of the brain and disappear or are replaced by vol-

TABLE 2.1   Newborn Reflexes

Reflex	Description	Usual Age of Appearance	Usual Age of Disappearance
Hand grasp	Place small object in newborn's hands. Infant grasps object tightly.	4–6-month fetus	3 months
Rooting	Stroke corner of infant's mouth. Infant turns head toward side of stimulation.	2–3-month fetus	Weakens by 2 months. Disappears by 5 months.
Sucking	Place nipple or finger in newborn's mouth. Newborn sucks.	2–3-month fetus	7 months
Babinski	Sole of infant's foot is stroked. Toes spread out.	4–6-month fetus	12–18 months
Moro	With infant on back, remove head support. Arms move in toward midline of body, then extend, then in again. Hands are held open.	7-month fetus	4 months
Foot withdrawal	Lightly prick sole of foot with pin. Foot withdraws with leg flexion.	4–6-month fetus	8–12 months
Walking reflex	Hold infant upright with soles of feet touching surface. Infant makes walking movements when moved forward.	8–9-month fetus	8 weeks

untary, self-directed responses when the higher cortical centers develop and take control. For example, when a reflex that should be present at birth is either absent or weak, there may be neurological dysfunction. Likewise, when a reflex persists beyond the time when it should diminish, a central nervous system defect may be denoted. Some researchers propose that the disappearance of certain reflexes also involves motor and physical factors that alter infants' ability to express reflexes (Thelen, Fisher, and Ridley-Johnson 1984).

Sensory Capacities

At birth, all of the newborn's sensory modalities are functional. Although the senses are not yet operative at an adult level, newborns are able to organize and integrate sensory information.

Vision.   Vision provides newborns with most of their information about the world. They can see at birth, and their visual acuity, the ability to see details, is estimated to be approximately 20/600, compared to the adult level of 20/20 (Banks and Salapatek 1983). Newborns are able to track or follow slow-moving objects with their eyes, although the tracking is jerky (Greenman 1963; Aslin 1981). They focus best on objects at distances of about eight inches (Haynes, White, and Held 1965).

Newborns have the ability to integrate sensory experiences. They will turn their heads to visually search for a sound that they hear (Turkewitz, Birch, and Cooper 1972). There is some evidence that by the age of one month, newborns usually perceive a looming object moving on a trajectory as an impending collision (Nanez 1988). Newborns prefer to look at complex rather than simple visual patterns and can detect contrast between light and dark edges (Fantz 1963). They look longer at stimuli that have sharp contrast such as black and white and prefer looking at circles rather than straight lines (Fantz, Fagan, and Miranda 1975). Newborns also look longer at patterns with high-contour density, that is, patterns with many edges or contours like a checkerboard (Karmel and Maisel 1975). Tiffany Field (1982) found that newborns were able to visually distinguish human emotional expressions. They even discriminated among happy, surprised, or sad faces. Newborns were also shown to have preferences for the less bright of two stimuli, regardless of color (Adams 1987). It is not certain whether they can perceive differences in color, but neonates have shown some sensitivity to color differences (Jones-Molfese 1977).

Hearing.   Full-term neonates have a well-myelinated auditory nerve; however, myelination of the auditory cortex is still underdeveloped at birth. Although the hearing of human newborns is not mature at birth, they can respond to auditory stimulation. They respond to the loudness or intensity of different sounds (Bridger 1961). Newborns can localize sounds (Muir and Field 1979), respond to sounds within the range of the human voice (Wolff

1963; Wolff 1966), and make identifiable reactions to sudden loud noises (Steinschneider 1968). Newborns also prefer their mother's voice over that of a stranger (Fifer 1987).

William S. Condon and Louis W. Sander (1974) reported that newborns move their bodies in rhythm to human speech. They called the movement *interactional synchrony* and suggested that the infant movement in response to linguistic sounds rather than nonlinguistic sounds such as tapping indicates that infants are born with the ability to perceive human speech sounds. Peter Eimas et al. (1971) reported that newborns have the capacity to distinguish speech, as opposed to nonspeech, sounds.

Smell, Touch, and Taste.   Newborns are able to react to different smells and different tastes. Newborn infants are able to discriminate among odors on the first day after birth (Engen, Lipsitt, and Kaye 1963). They turn their heads away from unpleasant odors such as vinegar or ammonia and can differentiate odor intensity (Rovee 1969). One study demonstrated that within a few days of their birth, infants recognized the smell of their mother over the smell of a stranger (MacFarlane 1977).

Newborns prefer some tastes over others; for example, they prefer sweetness over saltiness (Crook 1976). Research on taste sensitivity shows that infants will suck more of a sweeter solution than one that is less sweet (Rosenstein and Oster 1988). Newborns show negative facial expressions for salty, bitter, and sour solutions.

Neonates are highly responsive to touch because of the density of their skin receptors in relation to skin surface. When touched, neonates show heart rate changes. Tactile sensitivity is particularly higher around the mouth and the hands.

Learning Capacities of Newborns

Learning is defined as permanent changes in behavior resulting from experience. Newborns show several kinds of learning, ranging from the very simple response called *habituation* to a more complex form of learning known as *operant conditioning*.

Habituation.   Habituation is the lack of a response after continued exposure to a repeated stimulus. For example, when a bright light is shown repeatedly in newborns' eyes, they blink or stop moving at first, but then they decrease their response if the light continues to be flashed in their eyes. And if a bell is rung, newborns typically respond by widening their eyes and ceasing movement, but after about the eighth ring, they do not respond. It is inferred that they stop responding because they remember the earlier sounds. Habituation is thought to be a basic form of learning in that it is a primitive memory process mediated by the central nervous system. Habituation is an important protective skill that allows infants to shut out distracting noise or light.

Conditioning.   Both classical and operant conditioning have been attempted with newborns. Classical conditioning occurs when an unconditioned stimulus such as seeing or biting a crisp dill pickle induces an unconditioned response such as salivation. When an unconditioned stimulus is paired systematically and repeatedly with a conditioned stimulus, such as a loud tone or bell, the unconditioned response will be elicited by the conditioned stimulus. In this case, when the bell or tone sounds alone without the sight of the pickle, salivation occurs. This is called the conditioned response and indicates learning has taken place. Several researchers have reported success at classically conditioning newborn infants (Lipsitt and Kaye 1964). In one such study, newborn rooting and sucking reflexes were used as the unconditioned response (UCR) and the unconditioned stimulus (UCS). When the sweet fluid was presented, the neonate's head was stroked, which was the conditioned stimulus (CS). Following pairing of the CS and UCS, the infants showed rooting and sucking responses to the stroking alone. Other conditioning experiments could not elicit classical conditioning responses from newborns and have been criticized because of their lack of appropriate control groups (Sameroff 1972).

Operant conditioning procedures, however, have met with greater success with neonates (Clifton, Siqueland, and Lipsitt 1972). *Operants* were defined by B. F. Skinner (1938) as spontaneously emitted behaviors. Reinforcers are consequences that increase or decrease an operant's occurrence. Operant conditioning is the process by which the frequency of an operant is controlled by its consequences. In newborns, a conditional sucking procedure is frequently used to demonstrate operant conditioning. For example, newborns can be trained to suck vigorously to elicit the sound of their mother's voice. One study showed that newborns could be operantly conditioned to increase the efficiency of their sucking behavior in order to obtain a sugar solution, as compared to a nonsugar reinforcement (Bosack 1973). In this case, newborns learned to associate their response with the immediate consequence of tasting a sugar solution.

Newborn States

Infant states are characteristic sleep and arousal behaviors and physiological markers that occur with regularity over a twenty-four-hour period. They were first described by Peter Wolff in 1966 and quickly became an important consideration in neonatal testing since the degree of infant alertness to the environment is determined by the infant's state (Wolff 1966). Brazelton (1973) identified six states in the newborn, as shown in Table 2.2.

Infant state is an important consideration in neonatal testing because it determines the degree of infant alertness to the environment. The quality of a baby's response to environmental input will vary depending on the state of the infant at the time. Consequently, the state will affect a newborn's behavior during an assessment. A newborn who is in the quiet sleep state or

TABLE 2.2   Newborn Behavioral States

	State	*Description*
State 1	Quiet sleep	Characterized by no movement except startles Eyes closed. Regular breathing.
State 2	Active sleep	Bursts of movement. Rapid eye movement (REM). Respiration irregular.
State 3	Drowsy	Eyelids flutter. Increasing activity level. Irregular breathing.
State 4	Quiet alert	Few body movements. Regular breathing. Eyes open for more than 15 seconds.
State 5	Active alert	Eyes open. Spontaneous motor activity. Bursts of fussiness.
State 6	Crying	Cries for longer than 15 seconds. Skin color change to red. Body movements.

SOURCE: Data from T. B. Brazelton, *Neonatal Behavioral Assessment Scale,* National Spastics Society Monograph (Philadelphia: J. B. Lippincott, 1973).

drowsy state will not be as responsive as an infant in the quiet alert state. Through physical or environmental manipulations, it is possible to move a newborn from one state to another. For example, swaddling a crying baby will quiet the baby and assist transition into the quiet alert state, whereas undressing a sleeping baby will bring the baby to a drowsy or alert state. Infants' capacity to control their level of arousal directly affects their environmental experiences, including their interactions with caregivers. The Brazelton Neonatal Behavioral Assessment Scale measures infants' responses to the environment as they are assisted through state changes. State organization is assessed via measures of the distinctness and lability of infant states.

Fragile, high-risk newborns such as preterm infants typically spend more time in transitions across states. When they do show state behaviors, these are brief and lack clarity (High and Gorski 1985). Premature infants of less than twenty-five weeks gestational age spend most of their time in a drowsy sleep state. As the infant matures, brief alert states will emerge for very brief periods. By thirty-three to thirty-five weeks' gestation, premature infants will have quiet alert states.

Testing the Newborn: Practical Considerations

What are some of the practical considerations in neonatal assessment? Practice and familiarity with the particular assessment to be employed is essential to good testing. The examiner should be well versed in a wide range of infant behaviors, neonatal neurological responses, and movement patterns. The neonate's changing behavioral states must be closely monitored in order to elicit optimal responses during the assessment. Flexible procedures that allow observations rather than handling are essential when testing high-risk newborns. These neonates may show physiologic instability when moved or handled. Stressful procedures must be minimized during testing. `

Newborn infants are sensitive to changes in their environment. High levels of stimulation such as visual input can be stressful and change infant behavior. The fragile, preterm infant is particularly vulnerable to multimodal stimuli such as noise, handling, and bright lights (High and Gorski 1985). Even social stimuli such as a parent's smiling face too close to a medically fragile infant may result in infant distress and physiological decompensation. The following are examples of signs of infant stress:

- Looking away
- Body arching
- Grimacing
- Respiration change
- Color change
- Drooling
- Hiccuping
- Body goes limp
- Yawning

These stress signs are particularly apparent in premature infants.

During a neonatal assessment, the examiner must continuously monitor infant stress, look for signs of recovery, and use those support systems that assist infants to recover from stress. When infants show signs of stress, are unable to recover, and physiologically decompensate, examiners should assist them to self-regulate. This may be done by reducing environmental stimuli, providing brief physical containment of the infant, or providing a pacifier for the infant.

Contemporary approaches to neonatal assessment focus on neurological, behavioral, and individual temperament indices of the newborn. An important underlying assumption is that these measures provide information not only about the newborn but also about the transactions between the infant and the environment. Brazelton (1978) described the newborn as working on gaining control via state behavior and interactions with the caregiver.

Neonatal testing thus requires close attention to the neonate's individual arousal levels, organization, and responses to environmental stressors.

Generally, a neonatal test takes place in a hospital clinic, neonatal intensive care unit, or physician's office. As much as possible, these settings should be quiet and free of distractions since test results can be quite different in a noisy nursery compared to a dimly lit quiet room.

Parents are often present during the assessment. Brazelton recommends using the NBAS with the infant's parents present so as to address parents' concerns and questions. This allows parents the opportunity to learn about their baby's uniqueness. The test can be used to enhance parental responsiveness to their infant.

The decision to test a newborn is often based on the neonate's medical and risk status. Premature infants and other neonates at risk for developmental disabilities are more likely to be assessed. The examples that follow represent situations in which neonatal testing is a likely possibility.

Baby Keith was a thirty-week preterm infant. He was hospitalized in the neonatal intensive care nursery for six weeks. Since discharge, he has been physiologically stable and has no major medical problems. His parents have questions about his responsiveness and eating difficulties.

Baby Alex was born three weeks prematurely. He weighed 5 pounds and was hospitalized for thirteen weeks in the neonatal intensive care unit. His mother had no prenatal care and had a long, difficult delivery.

Baby Anne is the full-term newborn daughter of a sixteen-year-old single mother. Her Apgar score at birth was 7, and there is no indication of health difficulty. The baby and her mother are about to be discharged from the hospital; however, the hospital staff is expressing concern about the mother's ability to care for her infant.

In each of the examples, the infant is at potential risk for developmental delay because of birth status or the social risk factors in the environment.

Premature Infants

Preterm Infant Behaviors

Technological advances have dramatically improved the life chances of preterm infants. Consequently, there is a significant increase in the number of high-risk infants who survive the neonatal period. Forrest C. Bennett (1987) reported that between 1960 and 1980, the number of low birthweight infants doubled. Many of these infants are at risk for biological and developmental disabilities. Because of their risk status for developmental problems, premature infants are often the recipients of neonatal assessment.

Premature infants are neurologically immature, and as a result, they often have difficulty adapting to the intensive environment of the NICU, which is often noisy and brightly lit. Premature infants face qualitatively different experiences in the hospital than do full-term infants. Further, their systems development is different from that of full-term infants (Wyly, Allen and Wilson 1995).

Heidelise Als (1986) has described the premature infant as an organism ideally suited to intrauterine life who must make dramatic adaptations to the NICU environment to survive. Survival depends on the infant's ability to stabilize and grow in the extrauterine environment. Als's synactive theory identifies five distinct subsystems within the infant:

1. Physiological or autonomic system
2. Motor system
3. State attentional system
4. Attentional-interactional system
5. Self-regulatory system

In full-term infants, these subsystems interact dynamically and support each other, reflecting a well-organized, mature nervous system. Full-term infants have little or no difficulty negotiating the environment because a stable autonomic and motor system allows the infant to control state behaviors, self-regulate stress response to the environment, and remain available for interaction with caregivers. Premature infants, depending on their gestational age and neurological maturation, have varying degrees of emergence of these subsystems.

Physiologic or autonomic stability is an absolute prerequisite for the emergence of the other subsystems. In fact, it is the first subsystem to emerge. For very premature infants—those of twenty-four to thirty weeks—behavioral cues are primarily physiological. Heart rate, breathing, skin color, and autonomic mediated movements are all indicators of how well the premature infant is responding to the environment. The motor system gradually emerges as infants grow and mature. Very early premature infants have few purposeful movements of arms and legs. Poor energy and diminished muscle tone make movements that do occur very weak.

Unlike their full-term counterparts, premature infants have a limited repertoire of conscious states. In addition, very young premature infants move quickly between states, sleep restlessly, and have only fleeting moments of alertness. As they mature, premature infants remain in each behavioral state for a longer period of time and make state transitions more predictably.

The attentional-interactive subsystem refers to the quality of infants' alert state, or the ability to attend to and interact with others. Compared to full-term infants, premature infants have few, if any, periods of alertness. Similarly, premature infants' ability to self-regulate to maintain stability in the presence of stressors is poorly developed compared to healthy term infants.

Assessment of Premature Infants

Premature infants are assessed while they are hospitalized in the NICU and following discharge. Assessment in the hospital is done by neonatal nurses, physicians, educators, and therapists to determine infant status and to plan individualized developmental care. Neurobehavioral assessments provide information about the infant's behavioral organization and stability. Assessments also measure these infants' progress during hospitalization (Merenstein 1994).

The assessment of premature infants differs from the assessment of healthy term infants. Before undertaking an assessment of premature infants, assessors must consider several things. How intrusive is the assessment process? Because of premature infants' limited tolerance of handling or sensory input, the examiner must determine whether the assessment process itself will tax the infant. Why is the assessment being done? The examiner should be clear about the purpose of the assessment. What will be learned or changed as a result of the information gathered? Finally, examiners must consider their role as they plan assessments. During these assessments, the examiner interacts with the infant and becomes a part of the infant's social milieu.

Preterm Infant Assessments

Several assessments have been developed for assessment of preterm behavior. Some assessments require certification, a process that involves training and observation of the trainee's skills.

Assessment of Preterm Infant Behavior (APIB). The APIB was designed by Als for premature infants. This assessment used Brazelton's Neonatal Behavioral Assessment Scale as the template. A major construct of the NBAS is the importance of state and arousal in the infant's ability to regulate environmental stimuli.

The APIB assesses the five subsystems identified in Als's synactive theory (physiologic, motoric, state, attentional-interactional, self-regulation) before, during, and following environmental maneuvers (Als and Duffy 1989). The examiner determines how well the infant adapts to these manipulations and also determines the toleration level of the infant for stimulation. Within each subsystem, signs of stability and instability are assessed. The signs are shown in Table 2.3.

Naturalistic Observations of Newborn Behavior (NONB). The NONB is an observational assessment of preterm infants who are unable to tolerate handling or touch (Als 1984). The observation structure is couched in synactive theory. Through systematic observations, the examiner assesses the infant's levels of stability, instability, and self-regulation. Based on the assessment results, specific care recommendations are made, including modifications of the infant's environment.

Neurobehavioral Assessment of the Preterm Infant (NAP). The NAP is designed to measure preterm infants' level of functioning (Korner and Thom 1990). Premature infants from thirty-two weeks' gestational age to full term

TABLE 2.3   Signs of Stability and Instability in Assessment of Preterm
Infant Behavior

	Stability Signs	*Instability Signs*
Motoric	smooth coordinated movements good tone able to use motor strategies, e.g., hand-to-mouth maneuvers clasping	diffuse motoric activity hypertonicity hypotonic/flaccid jerky motion
Physiologic	regular respirations stable color stable digestion	irregular respiration color changes digestive problems, e.g., gagging, spitting up, hiccuping
State	clear states robust state behaviors self-calming behaviors maintains periods of quiet alert states	diffuse states transition states predominate state behaviors diffuse and change rapidly
Attentional/interactional	visually attends to stimuli quiets body movements to stimuli attends to auditory stimuli	gaze aversion fussiness shows physiologic instability to auditory/visual input

SOURCE: M. V. Wyly, *Premature Infants and Their Families* (San Diego: Singular Press, 1995), p. 69; data adapted from H. Als, "Toward a Synactive Theory of Development: Promise for the Assessment and Support of Infant Individuality," *Infant Mental Health Journal* 3 (4), pp. 229–243.

are assessed in this test. The test items measure motor development, orientation to animate and inanimate visual and auditory stimuli, behavioral states, and range of passage movements. Some test items have been adapted from Brazelton's NBAS. As in the NBAS, the examiner attempts to get the best performance from the infant through repeated observations. Much of the test consists of observing infant behaviors rather than handling the infant.

Types of Neonatal Assessments

Medical Risk Scales

Although many neonatal tests look at postnatal neurological functioning of the neonate, others are designed to assess the relationship of the effects of pregnancy, labor, and delivery on later development (Francis, Self, and Horowitz 1987). Collectively, these scales are known as medical risk scales, since they attempt to identify prenatal and perinatal factors such as age of the mother, maternal illnesses during pregnancy, or difficulties during delivery that might have an impact on the neurological functioning of the newborn (Gorski 1984). The identification of prenatal, perinatal, and postnatal risk factors, although useful, is not always clear-cut. The risk factors may vary quantitatively in terms of duration and severity. Risk factors vary in the degree to which they theoretically constitute a threat to the developing nervous system.

Medical risk scales assist clinicians in identifying what should be assessed and why the assessment should be done (Prechtl 1990). Well-known medical risk scales include those discussed in the following sections.

Obstetric Complications Scale (Parmelee 1974a). This method scores broad categories of optimal and nonoptimal events related to the prenatal and birth periods. A scoring system is used to measure maternal characteristics such as the mother's age and health as well as hazardous birth events that might jeopardize the well-being of newborn infants. In clinical practice, knowledge of obstetrical complications can assist with identification of the etiology of certain problems of the newborn infant.

Postnatal Complications Scales (Littman and Parmelee 1978). These scales examine the abnormal events that occur during pregnancy and the first month of life that might compromise the neonate.

Optimality Score of Prechtl (1980). The optimality approach evaluates the degree to which the optimal course of pregnancy and delivery have been met. Heinz Prechtl's Optimality Score assessment describes forty-two optimal prenatal and perinatal conditions. Each optimal condition is defined in terms of the best condition that carries the least risk of mortality and morbidity. Included are maternal age, maternal blood pressure, fetal heart rate, birth weight, gestational age, and onset of breathing following birth.

Pediatric Complications Scale (Littman and Parmelee 1978). This scale assesses the contributions of postnatal events on developmental outcomes. Specifically, it measures infants' physical development, neurological and behavioral responses, and health from one to four months and from four to nine months postnatally.

In general, medical risk scales alert practitioners to prenatal, perinatal, and postnatal risk events but have not shown strong predictive validity. However, the Pediatric Complications Scales have been more successful than most in predicting developmental outcome. Peter Gorski (1984) has suggested that these results support the view that postnatal events have a powerful effect on the developing infant. He therefore reasons that assessments should pay more attention to postnatal events than to medical crises at labor or birth.

Neonatal Screening Tests

The Apgar Screening Test (Apgar 1953) is the most well-known neonatal measure of neonatal risk. The ease and simplicity of its scoring system accounts for its wide use.

Apgar scores are taken at one, five, and sometimes ten minutes after birth. A score of 0, 1, or 2 points is given to the infant in five categories: heart rate, respiration, reflex response, muscle tone, and color. A 2-point rating is given for the best possible sign in a category, with a score of 0 indicating the absence of the sign. For example, 0 indicates no respiration, 1 indicates irregular breathing, and 2, regular breathing. See Table 2.4 for a description of the five test categories.

The highest Apgar score that can be obtained by a neonate is 10. A score of 0 or 1 indicates that the baby is in very serious trouble or already dead. A composite score of 7 or better means that the infant should be able to successfully adapt to the postnatal experience. Although newborns rarely score a 10 at the one-minute evaluation, most do manage to score 7. Improved scores are likely on the five-minute evaluation.

The Apgar is used as a screening test to quickly identify infants in need of attention and further scrutiny. As such, it has become part of routine hospital practice throughout the world. But it has not been particularly useful in identifying long-term neurological problems (Nelson and Ellenberg 1981). Research on the Apgar generally indicates some predictive correlation between low Apgar scores and infant mortality (Atkinson 1983), and to some degree, infants with low Apgars have low scores on the Bayley Scales of Infant Development (Serunian and Broman 1975). Despite its predictive limitations, the Apgar scale has proven clinically useful in documenting the immediate physical well-being of neonates.

Neurological Testing

Neurological examination of neonates has the advantage of directly assessing responses that reflect central nervous system processing. One of the best-known neurological tests is the Prechtl Neonatal Neurological Exam (Prechtl and Beintema 1964; Prechtl 1977). This test and its abbreviated screening version make use of infant states to assess full-term infants' reflexes, posture, and motoric activity. For example, a motor behavior is assessed while the infant is in an alert state and then when in the crying state. The neonate's ability to habituate to a repeated stimulus is one measure in the Prechtl exam that is thought to reflect higher brain regulation of behavior patterns. Prechtl identified three newborn patterns that include future neurological risk: (1) apathy, found in premature infants and infants with perinatal distress, (2) hy-

TABLE 2.4　Apgar Scale

Function	0	1	2
Heart rate	no heartbeat	below 100	100–140 beats per minute
Muscle tone	limp	moderate muscle tone	flexed extremities, good muscle tone
Respiratory	no breathing	irregular, weak cry	regular breathing, strong cry
Reflex response to stimulation	no response	slow response	facial grimace, cough or sneeze
Color	blue or gray	pink body but blue extremities	body completely pink

SOURCE:　V. Apgar, "A Proposal for a New Method of Evaluation of the Newborn Infant," *Anesthesia and Analgesia: Current Research* 32, pp. 260–267.

perexcitability, and (3) lack of symmetry in the right and left cerebral hemisphere due to perinatal insult such as the use of forceps.

The Prechtl test is considered by many clinicians to be a comprehensive neurological exam; however, it has come under some criticism since it does not measure an infant's ability to respond to nonsocial and social stimulation, which is now considered to be a key link to infant cognition. Furthermore, studies have demonstrated low relationships between neonatal neurologic function scores on the Prechtl and persistent long-term neurological abnormalities (Bierman-Van Eedenberg, Jurgen-VanDerZee, and Olinga 1981; Prechtl 1990).

S. Saint-Anne Dargassies (1977) designed a popular neurological test that assesses the unfolding of neuromaturational markers between the twenty-eighth and forty-first weeks of gestation. Since the test is repeated every few weeks, it is possible to observe the maturation of an infant's neurological functions. As a consequence, the test has been particularly useful in determining the deleterious effects of degrees of prematurity. The greater the prematurity, the more likely there will be negative long-term cognitive outcomes (Saint-Anne Dargassies 1965, 1954).

The Gestational Age Assessment, also known as the Dubowitz method (Dubowitz, Dubowitz, and Goldberg 1970), is used primarily to designate gestational age. Knowing an infant's gestational age is important in determining follow-up medical care. For the clinician, an accurate determination of gestational age can be useful in determining whether the presence or absence of a response or the inability of the infant to remain for a few moments in an alert state is related to immaturity or to neurological dysfunction.

The Dubowitz assessment is usually done by trained medical personnel with experience in handling newborns. Validity studies have shown scores to be highly correlated with known gestational age (Dubowitz et al. 1970).

Lilly and Howard Dubowitz (1981) recently added an exam to administer a neurological component in the Gestational Age Assessment that makes it more useful as a clinical and research tool. The two-part exam includes (1) an assessment of external criteria such as lanugo (body hair), plantar skin creases, skin color, skin texture, and edema, and (2) a neurological assessment of posture, arm and leg recoil, head lag, and ventral suspension. On both subscales, numerical ratings ranging from more mature to less mature are assigned. State behavior is indicated when administering the Dubowitz; however, the examiner does not maneuver the infant through states.

Although neurological assessments have generally not been useful in predicting developmental outcomes, there is general agreement among test developers regarding common neurological warning signs that can be identified in the neonatal period. Some conditions of concern include postural asymmetry, floppiness, hyperextension of limbs or trunk, feeding difficulties, uneven respiration, jittery movements, abnormalities in cries, persistent fussiness, and unusual head circumference. These signs indicate developmental risk.

Neurobehavioral Assessment

The neurobehavioral approach to newborn assessment reflects a changing conceptualization of infants. Behaviorally oriented newborn assessments build on existing neurological tests to assess various dimensions of neonatal behavior. These tests assume that newborn behavior organization is related to central nervous system integrity. Thus, an important component of a neurobehavioral assessment procedure is direct observation of newborn behaviors within different contexts. Two behavioral assessments, the Graham/Rosenblith Behavioral Test for Neonates and the NBAS, will be described in this section.

Graham/Rosenblith Behavioral Test. The first behavioral exam was developed by Graham (1956), a psychologist who was trying to differentiate normal newborns from those who had suffered brain injury resulting from birth trauma. In 1961, Rosenblith revised Graham's initial scale to provide the Graham-Rosenblith assessment, a test that could identify newborns at medical and developmental risk.

Many of the Graham/Rosenblith test items were borrowed from previously developed infant tests such as the Gesell and Bayley scales. The maturational scale includes items from the Gesell.

Administration of the General Maturation Scale yields a general maturation score that consists of (1) motor score, (2) tactile-adaptive score, and (3) visual and auditory response score. Ratings of auditory responses to bell and rattle, visual fixation, traction, and eye movement yield a visual and auditory responsiveness score, and a motor score is derived from ratings of muscle strength and coordination. The tactile-adaptive score is a measure of adaptive responses to stimuli applied to the mouth and nose.

Extensive research was conducted by Rosenblith and her colleagues on the relationships between neonatal test scores on the Graham/Rosenblith test and follow-up developmental measures (Rosenblith and Anderson-Huntington 1972; Rosenblith 1979b). Some significant correlations were found between specific neonatal scores and intelligence measures taken at ages four and seven. Analyses revealed that motor status scores were somewhat predictive of later IQ measures. Newborn irritability was found to be related to attention at four years of age (Rosenblith 1961).

The Graham/Rosenblith test was developed as a behavioral measure of newborn status. The test, however, has not been widely used by researchers and clinicians, in part because the behavioral repertoire measured by the test is somewhat limited. Nevertheless, this assessment paved the way for a newborn test that incorporated contemporary themes of newborn competence—the NBAS (Brazelton 1973).

Brazelton Neonatal Behavioral Assessment Scale. The NBAS measures the interactions and behavioral organization of full-term newborns (Brazelton 1973, 1984). The scales incorporate an approach that reflects current knowledge of the rich behavioral repertoire of newborn infants. A major construct underlying this assessment is the importance of state and arousal in the infant's ability to regulate environmental stimuli. The behavioral state of the infant is manipulated while observing the infant's capacity to attend to stimuli or process environmental events.

A basic tenet of the NBAS is that neonates are active rather than passive beings who interact with the environment and are affected by the environment. The behavioral range of the test items assesses the neonate's ability to respond to social and nonsocial stimuli, to habituate, to self-organize, and to control motor activity and states. The examiner maneuvers the newborn from the sleep to the awake state and notes the state robustness and state changes and how specific environmental responses occur within states. These are considered valid indicators of overall neurological functioning.

Since the NBAS considers state organization to be a critical developmental task of the newborn, the following are specifically evaluated through the course of the exam:

- The predominant state of the newborn
- The number of state changes
- The baby's ability to regulate states in response to external and internal stimuli

The assessment of state "control" involves observing the infant's capacity to shut out aversive stimuli such as a heel prick or bright light, the ability to engage in self-calming behaviors, and the level of stimulation required to produce irritability.

A unique feature of the NBAS is that the examiner attempts to elicit the infant's optimal or best performance rather than an average performance score. Obtaining the infant's best performance requires skill and considerable practice in administering the test. Not only must examiners know how to handle newborns but they must also have obtained an acceptable reliability level in conducting and scoring the test.

The examination is administered over a twenty- to thirty-minute period. It is given to full-term infants at least three days old. The NBAS includes observations of twenty reflex behaviors and twenty-six behavioral maneuvers that include response to human stimuli such as a voice or face, cuddliness, response to inanimate stimuli such as tracking the sound of a rattle, and habituation to visual and auditory stimuli.

Scoring the exam takes place in a ten-minute period following the assessment. As shown in Table 2.5, reflexes are assigned a score of 0 to 3 (not elicited, low, medium, or high). Behaviors are ranked on a nine-point scale.

NBAS data are often organized in clusters to facilitate clinical use. A cluster organization of the NBAS that includes state regulation, state range, motor status, habituation, stimulus orientation, and autonomic stability has been suggested by researchers (Lester, Als, and Brazelton 1982).

Because of its more comprehensive view of newborn behavior, the NBAS has become widely used as a clinical and research assessment tool (Myers 1982). It has been used extensively to help parents understand their newborn's capabilities and to increase parent responsiveness to their infant (Nugent 1985). Gena C. Britt and Barbara J. Myers (1994) reviewed the research on using the NBAS as an intervention tool to promote parent-infant interaction. Although the research results were inconsistent, the authors suggested that the effectiveness of the NBAS as an intervention may depend on the risk status of the population, the receptivity of the parents, and the intensity of the intervention. The NBAS has been used to describe the effects of maternal medication on newborns (Aleksandrowicz and Aleksandrowicz 1974), to correlate differences in newborn behaviors due to maternal drug abuse (Chasnoff, Burns, and Schnoll 1985), and to identify infants at risk for developmental problems (Tronick and Brazelton 1975).

Summary

In this chapter, we have reviewed various methods used to assess newborns' status and behaviors. Neonatal assessments have been developed for several purposes. Neonatal tests are used to learn how well the newborn is functioning in the extrauterine environment. Some evaluations assess the behaviors of newborns or document individual differences in newborns. Identifying risk factors that limit the newborn's optimal development is a primary function of many neonatal tests. Finally, neonatal assessment is

TABLE 2.5   Neonatal Behavior Assessment Scale

Behavior	*1*	*2*	*3*	*4*	*5*	*6*	*7*	*8*	*9*
Startle									
Alert responsiveness									
Response decrement to bell									

SOURCE: Brazelton 1984, chapter 2.

more and more frequently used as a research tool to assist practitioners in gaining more understanding of the dynamics of neonatal behaviors.

Historically, neonatal testing focused on reflexes and other neurological indicators of central nervous system functioning. More recently, clinicians have paid more attention to newborn behaviors and the availability of the newborn to interact with the environment. Contemporary neonatal assessment procedures now include behavioral measures as well as neurological items. Infant-environment transactions are considered legitimate aspects of newborn assessment. Newborn assessments have also been expanded to measure preterm infant behavior.

Assessments of premature infants have been developed to determine preterm infant status and stability. Preterm infant assessments typically focus on behavior and response to environment. These assessments are used by clinicians to plan individualized developmental care plans.

Studies have focused on the relationship of the newborns' performance on neonatal measures to later developmental outcomes. This research is still being pursued, with added emphasis being given to examining the impact of very early infant-parent interactions on subsequent developmental outcomes. Recognition of the quality and diversity of newborn competence will continue to influence the neonatal assessment movement.

References

Adams, R. J. 1987. An evaluation of color preference in early infancy. *Infant Behavior and Development* 10:143–150.

Aleksandrowicz, M. K., and D. R. Aleksandrowicz. 1974. Obstetrical pain-relieving drugs as predictors of infant behavior variability. *Child Development* 45:935–45.

Als, H. 1986. Synactive model of neonatal behavioral organization: Framework for the assessment and support of the neurobehavioral development of the premature infant and his parents in the environment of the neonatal intensive care unit. In *The High-Risk Neonates: Developmental Therapy Perspectives*, edited by J. K. Sweeney. New York: Haworth Press.

_____. 1984. *Manual for the Naturalistic Observation of Newborn Behavior in Preterm and Full-Term Infants*. Boston: Children's Hospital.

Als, H., and F. Duffy. 1989. Neurobehavioral assessment in the newborn period: Opportunity for early detection of later learning disabilities and for early intervention. *Birth Defects* 25:127–152.

Andre-Thomas, Y. Chesni, and S. Saint-Anne Dargassies. 1964. *The Neurological Examination of the Infant*. London: William Heinemann.

Apgar, V. 1953. A proposal for a new method of evaluation of the newborn infant. *Anesthesia and Analgesia: Current Research* 32:260–267.

Aslin, R. N. 1981. Development of smooth pursuit in human infants. In *Eye Movements: Cognitive and Visual Perception*, edited by D. F. Fisher, R. A. Monty, and J. W. Sanders. Hillsdale, NJ: Lawrence Erlbaum Associates.

Atkinson, D. 1983. An evaluation of Apgar scores as predictors of infant mortality. *North Carolina Medical Journal* 44:45–54.

Banks, M., and P. Salapatek. 1983. Infant visual perception. In *Handbook of Child Psychology. Vol. 2: Infancy and Developmental Psychobiology*. Edited by P. Mussen. 4th ed. New York: John Wiley.

Bennett, F. C. 1987. The effectiveness of early intervention for infants at increased biological risk. In *The Effectiveness of Early Intervention for At-Risk and Handicapped Children*, edited by M. J. Guralnick and F. C. Bennett. Orlando, FL: Academic Press.

Berg, W. K., and K. M. Berg. 1979. Psychophysiological development in infancy state, sensory function and attention. In *Handbook of Infant Development*, edited by J. D. Osofsky. New York: John Wiley.

Bierman-Van Eedenberg, M., A. D. Jurgen-VanDerZee, and A. Olinga. 1981. Predictive value of neonatal neurological examination: A follow-up study at 18 months. *Developmental Medicine and Child Neurology* 23:296–305.

Bosack, T. N. 1973. Effects of fluid delivery on the sucking response of the human newborn. *Journal of Experimental Child Psychology* 15:77–85.

Brazelton, T. B. 1984. *Neonatal Behavioral Assessment Scale*. 2d ed. Clinics in Developmental Medicine, no. 88. Philadelphia: J. B. Lippincott.

――――. 1978. Introduction. In *Organization and Stability of Newborn Behavior: A Commentary on the Brazelton Neonatal Behavioral Assessment Scale*, edited by A. J. Sameroff. Monographs of the Society for Research in Child Development, 43 (5–6, Serial no. 177) (Chicago: University of Chicago Press for the Society for Research in Child Development).

――――. 1973. *Neonatal Behavioral Assessment Scale*. National Spastics Society Monograph. Philadelphia: J. B. Lippincott.

Bridger, W. H. 1961. Sensory habituation and discrimination in the human neonate. *American Journal of Psychiatry* 117:991–997.

Britt, G. C., and B. J. Myers. 1994. The effects of Brazelton intervention: A review. *Infant Mental Health* 15:278–292.

Clifton, R., E. R. Siqueland, and L. P. Lipsitt. 1972. Conditioned headturning in human newborns as a function of conditioned response requirements and states of wakefulness. *Journal of Experimental Child Psychology* 13:43–57.

Condon, W., and L. Sander. 1974. Neonate movement is synchronized with adult speech: Interactional participation and language acquisition. *Science* 183:99–101.

Crook, C. K. 1976. Neonatal nutritive sucking: Effects of taste stimulation upon sucking rhythm and heart rate. *Child Development* 47:518–22.

Dubowitz, L.M.S., and V. Dubowitz. 1981. *The neurological assessment of the preterm and full-term newborn infant*. Clinics in Developmental Medicine, no. 79. Philadelphia: SIMP/J. B. Lippincott Co.

Dubowitz, L.M.S., V. Dubowitz, and C. Goldberg. 1970. Clinical assessment of gestational age in the newborn infant. *Journal of Pediatrics* 77:1–10.

Eimas, P. D., E. R. Siqueland, P. Jusczk, and J. Vigorito. 1971. Speech perception in infants. *Science* 171:303–306.

Elder, M. S. 1970. The effects of temperature and position on the sucking pressure of newborn infants. *Child Development* 41:95–102.

Engen, R., L. P. Lipsitt, and H. Kaye. 1963. Olfactory response and adaptation in the human neonate. *Journal of Comparative and Physiological Psychology* 56:73–77.

Fantz, R. L. 1963. Pattern vision in newborn infants. *Science* 140:296–297.

Fantz, R. L., J. F. Fagan III, and S. B. Miranda. 1975. Early visual selectivity as a function of pattern variables, previous exposure, age from birth and conception and expected cognitive deficit. In *Infant Perception from Sensation to Cognition. Vol. 1: Basic Visual Processes*. Edited by L. B. Cohen and P. Salapatek. New York: Academic Press.

Field, T. 1982. Social perception and responsivity in early infancy. In *Review of Human Development*, edited by T. Field, A. Huston, H. Quay, L. Troll, and G. Finley. New York: John Wiley.

Fifer, W. P. 1987. Neonatal preference for mother's voice. In *Perinatal Development: A Psychobiological Perspective*, edited by N. S. Krasnegor, E. M. Blass, M. A. Hofer, and W. P. Smotherman. New York: Academic Press.

Francis, P. L., P. A. Self, and F. D. Horowitz. 1987. The behavioral assessment of the neonate: An overview. In *Handbook of Infant Development*, edited by J. D. Osofsky. New York: John Wiley and Sons.

Gorski, P. 1984. Infants at risk. In *Atypical Infant Development*, edited by M. Hanson. Baltimore: University Park Press.

Gorski, P., D. J. Lewkowicz, and L. Huntington. 1987. Advances in neonatal and infant behavioral assessment: Towards a comprehensive evaluation of early patterns of development. *Developmental and Behavioral Pediatrics* 8:39–50.

Graham, F. K. 1956. Behavioral differences between normal and traumatized newborns: I. Test procedures. *Psychological Monographs* 70:20 (whole no. 427).

Greenman, G. W. 1963. Visual behavior of newborn infants. In *Modern Perspectives in Child Development*, edited by A. J. Solnit and S. A. Provence. New York: Hallmark.

Haynes, H., B. White, and R. Held. 1965. Visual accommodation in human infants. *Science* 148:528–530.

High, D. C., and P. Gorski. 1985. Rewarding environmental influences on infant development in the intensive care nursery. In *Infant Stress Under Intensive Care*, edited by A. W. Gottfried and J. L. Gaiter. Baltimore: University Park Press.

Jones-Molfese, V. 1977. Responses of neonates to colored stimuli. *Child Development* 48:1092–1095.

Karmel, B. Z., and E. B. Maisel. 1975. A neuronal activity model for infant visual attention. In *Infant Perception from Sensation to Cognition. Vol. 1: Basic Visual Processes*. Edited by L. B. Cohen and P. Salapatek. New York: Academic Press.

Kaye, H. 1966. The effects of feeding and tonal stimulation on non-nutritive sucking in the human newborn. *Journal of Experimental Child Psychology* 3:131–145.

Korner, A. F., and V. A. Thom. 1990. *Neurobehavioral Assessment of the Preterm Infant.* New York: Psychological Corporation.

Lester, B. M., H. Als, and T. B. Brazelton. 1982. Regional obstetric anesthesia and newborn behavior: A reanalysis toward synergistic effects. *Child Development* 53:687–692.

Lipsitt, L. P., and H. Kaye. 1964. Conditioned sucking in the human newborn. *Psychonomic Science* 1:29–30.

Littman, G., and A. H. Parmelee. 1978. Medical correlates of infant development. *Pediatrics* 61:470–474.

MacFarlane, A. 1977. *The Psychology of Childbirth.* Cambridge: Harvard University Press.

McCall, R. B. 1971. Behavioral and other measurements in the neonate. *Proceedings of the Royal Society of Medicine* 64:465.

Merenstein, G. B. 1994. Individualized developmental care: An emerging new standard for neonatal intensive care units? *Journal of the American Medical Association* 272:890-891.

Myers, B. J. 1982. Early intervention using Brazelton training with middle-class mothers and fathers of newborns. *Child Development* 53:462–471.

Muir, D., and T. Field. 1979. Newborn infants orient to sounds. *Child Development* 50:431–436.

Nanez, J. E. 1988. Perception of impending collision in 3- to 6-week-old human infants. *Infant Behavior and Development* 11:447–463.

Nelson, K. B., and J. H. Ellenberg. 1981. Apgar scores as predictors of chronic neurologic disability. *Pediatrics* 68:36–44.

Nugent, J. K. 1985. *Using the NBAS with Infants and Their Families.* White Plains, NY: March of Dimes Birth Defects Foundation.

Parmelee, A. H. 1974a. The obstetric complications scales and the postnatal complications scale.

_____. 1974b. Newborn neurological examination.

Piaget, J. 1954. *The Construction of Reality in the Child.* New York: BasicBooks.

Polani, P. 1959. Neurological examination of the newborn according to the work of Prof. Andre-Thomas. *Cerebral Palsy Bulletin* 5:19–22.

Prechtl, H. 1980. The optimality concept. *Early Human Development* 4:201–206.

_____. 1977. *The neurological examination of the full-term newborn infant.* Clinics in Developmental Medicine, no. 63. Philadelphia: J. B. Lippincott.

Prechtl, H.F.R. 1990. Qualitative changes of spontaneous movements in fetus and preterm infants are a marker of neurological dysfunction. *Early Human Development* 23:151–158.

Prechtl, H., and D. Beintema. 1964. *The Neurological Examinations of the Full-Term Newborn Infant.* Philadelphia: J. B. Lippincott.

Rosenblith, J. F. 1979a. The Graham/Rosenblith behavioral examination for newborns: Prognostic value and procedural issues. In *Handbook of Infant Development,* edited by J. Osofsky. New York: Wiley.

_____. 1979b. Relations between Graham/Rosenblith neonatal measures and seven-year assessments. Paper presented at the meeting of the Eastern Psychological Association, Philadelphia.

_____. 1961. The modified Graham behavior test for neonates: Test-retest reliability, normative data, and hypotheses for future work. *Biologia Neonatorum* 3:174–192.

Rosenblith, J. F., and R. B. Anderson-Huntington. 1972. *Relations between newborn and 4 year behavior.* Abstract Guide of the Twentieth International Congress of Psychology, Tokyo.

Rosenstein, D., and H. Oster. 1988. Differential facial responses to four basic tastes in newborns. *Child Development* 89:1555–1568.

Rovee, C. K. 1969. Psychophysical scaling of olfactory response to the gliphatic alcohols in human neonates. *Journal of Experimental Child Psychology* 7:245–254.

Saint-Anne Dargassies, S. 1977. *Neurological development in the full term and premature neonate.* Amsterdam: Elsevier.

_____. 1965. Neurological examination of the neonate. *Proceedings of the Royal Society of Medicine,* 58:5.

_____. 1954. Méthode d'examen neurologique du nouveau-né. *Etudes néo-natales* 3:101–123.

Sameroff, A. J. 1972. Learning and adaptation in infancy: A comparison of models. In *Advances in Child Development and Behavior.* Vol. 7. Edited by H. W. Reese. New York: Academic Press.

Serunian, S. A., and S. H. Broman. 1975. The relationship of Apgar scores and Bayley mental and motor scales. *Child Development* 46:696–700.

Skinner, B. F. 1938. *The Behavior of Organisms.* Englewood Cliffs, NJ: Prentice Hall.

St. Clair, K. L. 1978. Neonatal assessment procedures: A historical review. *Child Development* 49:280–292.

Steinschneider, A. 1968. Social intensity and respiratory responses in the neonate. *Psychosomatic Medicine* 30:534–541.

Thelen, E., D. M. Fisher, and R. Ridley-Johnson. 1984. The relationship between physical growth and a newborn reflex. *Infant Behavior and Development* 7:479–493.

Tronick, E., and T. B. Brazelton. 1975. Clinical uses of the Brazelton Neonatal Behavioral Assessment. In *Exceptional Infant.* Vol. 3. Edited by B. J. Freedlander, G. M. Sterritt, and G. E. Kirk. New York: Bruner/Mazel.

Turkewitz, G., H. G. Birch, and K. K. Cooper. 1972. Patterns of response to different auditory stimuli in the human newborn. *Developmental Medical and Child Neurology* 14:487–491.

Wolff, P. H. 1966. The causes, controls and organization of behavior in the neonate. *Psychological Issues* 5:1–58.

_____. 1963. Observations on the early development of smiling. In *Determinants of Infant Behavior.* Vol. 2. Edited by B. M. Foss. London: Methuen.

Wyly, M. V., J. Allen, and J. Wilson. 1995. *Premature Infants and Their Families: Developmental Interventions.* San Diego: Singular Press.

3

Infant Screening

"Begin at the beginning," the King said, gravely, "and go on till you come to the end: then stop."

—*Lewis Carroll,* Alice in Wonderland

Introduction

Screening refers to any activity used to identify infants in need of further evaluation or assessment. Screening often involves examining large numbers of infants to target those infants who might have a possible medical or developmental problem and should be referred for follow-up diagnostic evaluation. Screening can also be performed on an individual basis. Thus, screening is the initial measurement that may, if warranted, be followed by a more comprehensive assessment to determine if abnormalities or developmental delays are present. Infants and young children who are at risk for potential developmental delay are the population targeted for screening.

In 1986, the Amendment to the Education of the Handicapped Act (PL 99-457) Part H was enacted by Congress to provide education for high-risk and disabled infants and toddlers (Meisels 1991). Not only did this legislation mandate a comprehensive system of education for infants, toddlers at risk, and their families, but the law promulgated changes in assessment practices with young children. Developmental and health screening are considered essential in identifying infants at developmental risk. Typically, infants and young children are considered to be at risk if (1) there is a family history associated with risk factors such as poverty or drug abuse, (2) there are significant medical problems in the prenatal or perinatal period, and (3) there are identified conditions at birth associated with problematic developmental outcomes, for example, cerebral palsy.

In this chapter, we will examine what is meant by developmental screening. Types of screening tests will be discussed, along with such screening issues as the focus of screening, timing of screening, and elements of useful screening programs. Descriptions of several widely used screening tests will be presented. To gain a fuller understanding of developmental screening, you might practice administering a screening test such as the Denver Developmental Screening Test to several infants of different ages. Doing this should illustrate how to use a screening test and the relative ease with which it can be administered.

When you finish studying this chapter you should be able to do the following:

- Describe the purpose and focus of infant screening
- Outline several commonly used infant screening tests
- Describe effective program components for screening infants at risk for developmental disabilities

Screening Issues

Screening Focus

Screening tests are used to identify those infants who manifest a particular condition or are likely to do so in the future (Bailey and Rosenthal 1987). Screening alerts practitioners to the need for further diagnostic assessment.

Consider the following examples. The described infant in each example would be a candidate for developmental screening because each of these babies is at risk for abnormal development due to signs of developmental problems, birth trauma, or a prenatal experience such as drug exposures. Even if no developmental problems were detected in the initial screening, it is likely another screening would be done a month or two later, or perhaps on a regular basis, to monitor the infant's status.

A fifteen-year-old mother gave birth to a five-and-one-half-pound baby girl two months prematurely. The mother is from a low-income background and received no prenatal care. She had a long and difficult labor. At birth, her newborn had normal vital signs and no indication of birth defects or problems.

After an uncomplicated pregnancy, a thirty-year-old mother had a premature delivery. Her baby was born at twenty-eight weeks' gestational age and weighed a little over three pounds. The infant spent his first six weeks of life in a neonatal intensive care unit.

A single, twenty-two-year-old woman delivered a six-pound girl. During her first trimester of pregnancy, this young woman took cocaine daily. Her newborn had respiratory problems, showed tremors and signs of hyper-alertness, and was subsequently hospitalized for two weeks.

A healthy, alert, full-term baby was born to a middle-income couple. The mother had ongoing prenatal care and no birth complications. When the baby was six months of age, the mother reported to her physician that she noticed her child was unable to lift her head when placed in a prone position and that her head control looked "wobbly."

Screening may involve testing one developmental domain, for instance, language or cognition, or may entail comprehensive screening. Ideally, a comprehensive screening program looks at more than the infant's simply reaching a developmental milestone such as walking or crawling. In addition to gathering data on multiple developmental domains, auditory, visual, and medical screening tests are used to look at a single domain. Important data points are derived from other information, such as family medical history and the infant's and mother's prenatal care and birth experiences.

Newborns in a hospital nursery are routinely given a blood screening test to detect excess amounts of the amino acid phenylalanine. Excessive amounts of phenylalanine indicate an amino acid disorder called phenylketonuria (PKU). This disorder is associated with seizures, psychomotor disabilities, and mental retardation. Newborns who have high amounts of phenylalanine in their blood are put on a diet low in phenylalanine. Throughout infancy, these infants are periodically tested for blood phenylalanine levels.

Professionals or paraprofessionals trained to administer the assessment conduct infant screening. Proper administration of the screening measure is considered to be essential to effective screening, as is the examiner's ability to relate to infant needs (Thorpe and Werner 1974). For example, infants brought to a well-baby clinic might be screened by a nurse or psychologist. In some clinics, parents or volunteers are trained in screening procedures. Interpretation of the test is usually done by physicians, nurses, psychologists, or developmental specialists.

Infant screening can take place in different types of settings. The screening tests or strategies used may depend on the screening goals. One goal of screening is to identify infants or toddlers who may need early intervention or medical treatment services. Another goal is to locate those infants who, because of risk factors, will need ongoing screening to determine whether there are indications of developmental delay that would then require a full diagnostic assessment. Some examples of screening to meet various screening goals are illustrated in the case examples that follow:

A rehabilitation center in a large children's hospital located in an eastern city operates an infant screening program. Infants with a birth weight of 1,500 grams (3.3 pounds) or less or infants who were hospitalized in the neonatal intensive care unit at birth are referred for periodic screening. Screening at the center is described as comprehensive and includes developmental screening, speech and hearing tests, and a neurological examination. A nurse and social worker collect medical and family data. Diagnostic tests, if needed, are done at the hospital. Based on that evaluation, referrals are then made to infant intervention programs and to therapy and medical services.

In a large city, an inner-city storefront has been converted to an auditory screening clinic for infants and toddlers. Paraprofessionals and parents have been trained to use the auditory screening tool. If the screening raises questions about an infant's hearing ability, then a full diagnostic assessment is done at a nearby speech and hearing clinic.

A privately operated infant early intervention program located in a rural community conducts a developmental screening program one day a week. Infants are recruited for screening through radio, television, and newspaper announcements directed at parents concerned about their infant's development. Screening is done by special educators trained to use the Denver Developmental Screening Test. If an infant's test performance is classified as "questionable" or "abnormal," the infant is referred for more extensive developmental evaluation.

Target Population

How are infants selected for screening? Screening efforts typically target infants who are judged to be at risk for developmental disabilities. The task of identifying infants and young children with developmental problems is complex and difficult (Gordon and Jens 1988). In large part, this is because there are many different factors that can affect development. Infants may be exposed to one or more factors during the prenatal, perinatal, or postnatal periods in varying frequencies or duration, which in turn affects their development. Sorting out the cumulative effects of prenatal or postnatal insults is challenging because infants may enter a nurturing family environment that ameliorates the negative effects. For example, a low birth-weight baby who was hospitalized in an NICU for one month may go home to a family that has a strong support system and home environment that promotes positive physical and psychological outcomes. Long-term versus short-term outcomes for infants at risk are less easily predicted and identified because of the interplay with environmental influences (Ensher and Clark 1994).

Researchers have attempted to classify the characteristics that place infants at developmental risk. Theodore Tjossem (1976) identified three risk-factor categories: environmental, biological, and established. Table 3.1 shows examples of risk factors in each of the three categories. These factors interact to define the infant's degree of risk. The interaction of risk factors is a dynamic process that can potentially modify the infant's developmental status at any time during infancy.

Established risks are identifiable impairments or congenital syndromes whose outcomes are fairly well documented. For example, Down syndrome, a chromosomal disorder, would fall into this category. A visual impairment diagnosed at birth would also be classified as an established risk.

The environment of many infants puts them at risk for developmental problems. Environmental risk factors include poverty, inadequate parenting practices, neglect and abuse, social isolation, and emotionally disturbed parents (Bijou 1981). A baby with an adolescent mother or one whose parents were referred for infant neglect would be categorized as at environmental risk.

TABLE 3.1   Developmental Risk Factors

Established Risk	Biological Risk	Environmental Risk
Inborn errors of metabolism	Preterm birth	Parental substance abuse
	Low birth weight	Maternal age below 15
Down syndrome	Intraventricular	Parent with a psychiatric
Orthopedic disorders	hemorrhage	disorder
Cystic fibrosis	Respiratory distress	Mentally retarded parents
Cerebral palsy	syndrome	Poverty
Blindness	Fetal alcohol syndrome	
Deafness	Prenatal cocaine exposure	
Spina bifida	Anoxia	

SOURCE: T. D. Tjossem, *Intervention Strategies for High Risk Infants and Young Children* (Baltimore: University Park Press, 1976).

The third major source of risk is biological risk. Included in this group are premature or low birth-weight infants, infants who have suffered perinatal anoxia or trauma, and infants exposed to drugs or other pathogens during the prenatal or perinatal periods.

Infants categorized as at environmental or biological risk usually make up the bulk of the target screening population. In addition, infants whose parents suspect their babies might be developmentally delayed are also given high priority for screening activities. Infants with obvious handicaps such as spina bifida, Down syndrome, or severe motor impairments usually are not screening candidates since their handicapping condition is obvious. Rather, they are referred directly to infant intervention services, where diagnostic assessments are made to determine the level of intervention services.

Table 3.2 outlines risk factors that can be present in the prenatal, perinatal, and postnatal periods. Note that there are factors in the table from each of Tjossem's three risk categories and that the categories are not mutually exclusive. For example, a infant may be low birth weight and also environmentally vulnerable because of abuse or an impoverished environment. These factors may act alone or in combination to affect development. Infants exposed to multiple factors have an increased risk of developmental disabilities. The number of risk factors has been found to be more predictive of developmental problems than a single risk factor. Further, early risk factors measured in the first year are less predictive of developmental delay than are those found during years three and four (King, Logsdon, and Schroeder 1992). It has been proposed that rather than viewing infants as continuously experiencing risk factors, it is more appropriate to think of risk factors fluctuating throughout the lives of infants (Gordon and Jens 1988).

TABLE 3.2   Prenatal, Perinatal, and Postnatal Risk Factors

Prenatal Risk Factors	Perinatal Risk Factors	Postnatal Risk Factors
Maternal age (under 15 or over 40)	Prematurity	Drugs/toxin exposure
Parents of low socio-economic status	Neurologic problems	Postnatal infections
In utero infections	Low birth weight of less than 1,750 grams	Inadequate support systems
Maternal history of difficult pregnancies	Anoxia	Impoverished home environments
Chromosomal abnormalities	Birth injury	Poor parenting practices
Gene disorders	Severe respiratory distress	Undernutrition
Maternal nutrition	Congenital infections	Accidents
Maternal Rh blood sensitization		Extended separation of parents and infants
Exposure to drugs/toxins		

Screening Criteria

To be effective, screening procedures must meet several criteria. The screening tests should be easy to administer. They should also be relatively inexpensive to administer. Finally, the screening test used should appropriately identify the area of the suspected delay.

The scope of screening and the target population are usually determined by the availability of resources needed to carry out screening. Kenneth Thurman and Anne Widerstrom (1990) identify six guidelines for effective screening:

1. Screening should be carried out only if intervention services are available to the infant.
2. Screening should be the initial step in a process that includes further diagnostic assessment and treatment.
3. Infant outcomes should be improved by the treatment that follows screening, assessment, and diagnosis.
4. Screening should target relatively prevalent developmental problems, or if the problem is rare, there should be severe consequences for not screening and treating that problem.
5. The screening tests should be cost-effective, efficient, easy to administer, and acceptable to the target population being screened.
6. Compared to later intervention for the developmental disorder, the early intervention used for treatment should be superior.

Screening Decisions and Problems

Many decisions must be weighed in good screening programs. The case examples that follow illustrate several screening decisions. In screening programs, it must be decided whether to use single or multiple screening measures, which screening tests to use, and how many screening visits should be scheduled for infants. It must also be decided when to refer infants for an extensive evaluation.

Five-month-old Bryan is brought to a developmental screening clinic. The results of a developmental screen show Bryan as having questionable delayed development. When he is reassessed at eight months, the test indicates no developmental delay.

Should Bryan continue to be screened periodically? In this case, it is likely that Bryan will receive a screening follow-up test at least once to confirm that development is progressing within normal limits.

Tiffany was born six weeks prematurely. Because of her prematurity and the fact that her mother was seventeen years old when she was born, Tiffany received developmental follow-up screening. Her screening tests at one month and three months showed no indication of developmental problems. At the six-month screening, noticeable lags were apparent. Prior to this screening, Tiffany's mother had been referred to a social services agency for child neglect.

What is the next step for Tiffany in the screening process? Since noticeable developmental delays were identified at six months, Tiffany should be referred for in-depth assessment to determine the extent of the lags. It is highly probable that this infant will be recommended for early intervention services.

Screening measures must be selected that are appropriate and reliable. Screening programs must consider whether direct observations of infants or parent reports will be their primary data source. The choice of screening criteria used to refer infants for in-depth assessment or intervention is an important issue in any screening program. Criteria for referral are usually indicated in standardized screening tests, whereas other tests do not always specify referral criteria. Thus, service providers need to establish their own referral criteria.

Problems and Issues in Infant Screening

Identifying infants at risk is not without problems. For one thing, the course of normal development does not proceed evenly. And it is not always easy to define those behaviors that characterize normal infant development. Further, infants show individual differences in development within the normal range that can be misinterpreted as delays. For example, a twelve-month-old infant may not be speaking single words but may still be within the developmental norm for language skill.

Identifying infants who are at risk for delays in development is the goal of comprehensive screening programs. Yet this is sometimes a difficult goal to accomplish because of the dynamic nature of development. What appears to be atypical motor function at five months of age may disappear by the time the infant reaches one year. Conditions of risk during the early months of infancy can be ameliorated by a supportive environment, and that, in turn, affects development (Keogh and Kopp 1978). Likewise, an infant born with few problems may later show developmental delay as a result of inappropriate parenting or dysfunctional parent-infant interactions.

Another screening problem is that of *false positives*. This occurs when the screening test indicates that the infant is abnormal, yet an in-depth assessment shows no developmental problems. This can cause anxiety for an infant's caregivers, who have been alerted to possible problems when in fact there are none. The error of under-referral, or *false negatives,* occurs when infants have developmental delays that are not detected by screening procedures. In this case, infants will not receive additional assessment or needed remedial services.

Another screening issue facing clinicians is how long to follow up screening of at-risk infants to determine outcomes. Infants who are born at risk—that is, premature or medically fragile—may show immediate problems. But some infants may not demonstrate developmental problems for several years. Typically, follow-up clinics evaluate at-risk infants at six months and twelve months, then once during the second and third year.

Certain essential characteristics have been identified for good screening tests (Meisels, Wiske, and Tirnan 1984). The test must have *reliability*. This refers to the consistency of test performance. If, for example, the same test were administered several times, would the infant's test performance be stable or variable? *Validity* is another dimension of screening tests. Validity refers to the extent to which the test measures what it is supposed to measure. The *predictive validity* of a test means that the test predicts related characteristics that will appear in the future. The Apgar scale, a newborn screening test, was designed to assess newborn behaviors at birth. Although it is a useful screening tool for assessing immediate problems, it has not been shown to predict long-term developmental problems. *Concurrent validity* is important to screening measures. Concurrent validity is determined by the extent to which the screening test results correlate with more thorough developmental assessments such as the Bayley Scales of Infant Development.

Screening Tests

There are many types of screening measures. Pregnant women are screened for possible risk factors that could jeopardize the development of the fetus. At birth, neonates are screened for medical and developmental risk.

Throughout infancy, a variety of screening instruments is used to detect visual, hearing, or developmental problems that have not been identified or may arise during the course of development. Infants and toddlers may be screened for overall developmental delay, cognitive delay, communication problems, specific medical problems, sensory-motor abnormalities, or difficulties in social-emotional development. Environmental screening measures are also used to assess the effects of an infant's home environment on developmental progress.

Screening measures must be specific and sensitive in order to accurately select those infants who need to be referred for diagnostic evaluation. Test administration should be easy and straightforward. The test should be standardized by using an adequate sample of infants and toddlers representing an equal distribution of racial, ethnic, and socioeconomic groups.

Screening tests employ different means of data collection. Typically, three are used: infant observations, parent reports, and direct testing. Screening measures may use combinations of these. The Denver Developmental Screening Test, for example, includes questions directed at parents about their infant's behavior as well as employing direct testing procedures.

In the section that follows, several commonly used screening tests are described. These tests are representative of different types of screening measures used with different infant populations.

Prenatal Screening Tests

Prenatal screening tests are designed to assess the relative risk encountered during the fetal period. These screens alert clinicians to possible problems that may affect the developing fetus.

Prechtl Obstetric Optimality Scale.   The Prechtl scale (Prechtl 1982) is an example of a widely used prenatal screening test. Scale items are clustered into categories that focus on possible difficulties during the prenatal and perinatal periods that could result in reduced optimal development for the infant. The sixty-two optimality items include maternal age, family history of diabetes, parity, and fetal position. Some sample items from the scale are shown in the chart that follows:

Items	*Criteria for Optimality*
Previous baby with congenital anomalies	No
Illness first trimester	No
Vaginal bleeding	No
Frequency of prenatal care	9–15 visits
Complications during labor	None
Start of labor	Spontaneous

As can be seen, there is an optimality criterion for each item. If the item meets the criterion, it is given a score of 1, but if the item is absent, it receives a score of 0. Infants are categorized as low-risk, middle-risk, and high-risk, based on their total optimality scores.

Obstetric Complications Scale. The Obstetric Complications Scale (OCS), designed by Arthur Parmelee (1974), scores nonoptimal events during the prenatal period and immediately after birth. These scales have been used extensively by clinicians and researchers. Some examples of nonoptimal events measured by the OCS are illustrated in the following list.

Items

- Time since last pregnancy
- Maternal age
- Drug abuse
- Gestational age
- Blood group incompatibility

Neonatal Screening Tests

At birth and during the neonatal period, newborns are screened for defects of the ear, nose, and throat and for metabolic disorders, visual problems, motor impairments, attentional deficits, and other developmental problems. The most widely used newborn screening measure is the Apgar Screening Test (Apgar 1953). The Apgar, already described in Chapter 2, is an easy-to-administer five-item test given immediately following birth. It is used to alert medical practitioners to possible physiological problems at birth.

Vision Screening

Vision is important to all areas of development. Through vision, infants learn about the world and interact with others. At birth, the visual capacities of neonates are functional but not fully mature. Infants who are low birth weight, premature, or had fetal infections or a family history of visual disorders are at risk for visual impairments. Screening high-risk infants for visual problems is fundamental to comprehensive infant screening. Vision screening of high-risk groups entails testing for both visual acuity and functional vision. An example of each type of test follows.

The Teller Visual Acuity Cards (Vistech Consultants 1986) are used to screen the visual acuity of infants. This test consists of showing infants sixteen cards, each with vertical black stripes of differing widths. Preferential looking at the cards is the acuity measure. Infants who prefer to look at the cards with thinner stripes are judged to have more mature visual acuity.

Functional vision is defined as infants' use of vision in ongoing daily activities. The Functional Vision Screening Test (Langley 1980) is a frequently used infant screening measure. In this test, infants are scored for the presence or absence of visual tracking of a moving object, visual fixation, visual reflexes, and gaze shifts.

Auditory Screening

When infants cannot hear, their development is dramatically altered. Language and speech are delayed. Social interactions between infants and their caregivers are modified. A deaf infant will, for example, be unable to hear soothing sounds and words from his or her parents. The rich elaboration of the social dyad that normally occurs between infants and parents will be absent. For some infants, this leads to emotional difficulties.

Risk factors, such as low birth weight, defects of the ear, nose, or throat, or viral infections such as rubella increase the probability of hearing impairment. Screening infants for hearing loss is now considered essential to a comprehensive screening program. In fact, periodic three-month auditory screening starting at six months has been recommended by the Committee on Standards of Child Health Care of the American Academy of Pediatrics (1977).

Newborns are often screened for hearing impairments before they leave the hospital. Their response to sounds is observed by medical staff, but more accurate measures are made with the "Crib-o-gram," which measures newborn movements in the crib in response to loud sounds (Garrity and Mengle 1983).

The Behavioral Observation Audiometry (BOA) test is used for testing hearing in infants under twelve months in age (Garrity and Mengle 1983). In this test, infants' reactions to sound presentations are recorded. Behaviors are noted that indicate auditory functioning, including eye blink, looking for a sound source, eye widening, and changes in sucking patterns.

Developmental Screening Tests

As interest in infant developmental problems has increased in recent years, efforts have also increased to develop effective screening tools. Developmental screening instruments measure the attainment of developmental skills, for example, motor, social-emotional, language, and cognition skills. Although many developmental screening guides are now available, only a few have been standardized. In many medical clinics, infant screening is now a part of each health visit. The following are some representative examples of widely used developmental screening instruments for infants and young children.

Denver Developmental Screening Test.   The DDST (Frankenburg, Dodds, and Fandal 1975) was designed as a simple screening tool for children from birth to six years in age. Because it is easy to use, it is one of the most widely used screening assessments and is routinely employed in public health clinics to detect infants with possible developmental delays. The revised Denver Developmental Screening Test, the Denver-II (DDST-II), was published in 1991 (Frankenburg et al. 1991). The test was revised because the original DDST tended to underdetect those children needing in-depth assessment. The DDST-II includes more language items and identifies young children with mild developmental delays.

The DDST-II can be administered in fifteen to twenty minutes and involves both direct testing of the child and parent interview questions. The 105-item test measures gross motor, fine motor-adaptive, personal-social, and language functioning. Some of the test items include the following:

Fine Motor-Adaptive

- Stacking blocks
- Object manipulation

Gross Motor

- Crawling
- Jumping

Language

- Says words
- Understands directions

Personal-Social

- Imitation of gestures
- Interaction with strangers

Test items are presented according to instructions specified in the test protocol. Infant performance of each of the administered tasks is assigned a rating of one of the following: pass (P), failure (F), refused (R), or no opportunity for performance (NO). These are written on a one-page test protocol organized by age and developmental domains. The child is scored as normal, questionable, abnormal, or untestable. Further diagnostic testing is recommended when the child is judged to be in the abnormal category.

Validation studies of the DDST have shown correlations ranging from .86 to .97 with the Bayley Scales of Infant Development and the Stanford-Binet Intelligence Scale (Frankenburg, Goldstein, and Camp 1971). The validity studies of the DDST-II are limited (Kochanek 1993). In a study of infants who were rated as normal on the DDST, 13 percent received abnormal scores on the Bayley scales (Frankenburg, Camp, and Van-Natta 1971). The accuracy of the DDST-II was examined and was found to be more sensitive than the DDST in the language domain; however, the DDST-II produced more incorrect than correct identification of risk (Frankenburg, Camp, and Van-Natta 1971). One explanation offered for these discrepant results is that the Bayley test does not rely on parent report of an occurring behavior; rather, the infant must display the behavior during the examination. The DDST, however, allows passing scores on many test items based only on parent report. Another reason may be the relatively small sampling of test items within the infant period on the DDST compared to the Bayley scales. Still another explanation of discrepancies in assessing developmental risk is that a large validity study has not been conducted on the DDST-II, which means that test items that should have been discarded are still being used.

Battelle Developmental Inventory Screening Test (BDIST).   The BDIST (Newborg et al. 1984) is a screening test made up of a subset of test items from the Battelle Developmental Inventory (BDI). The test items are grouped into seven categories: gross motor, fine motor, personal-social, adaptive, receptive language, expressive language, and cognition. The test was standardized using a representative sample of eight hundred children. Multiple methods of collecting data are used: direct observation of behaviors, parent report, and elicitation of behavior. Because the test is lengthy and difficult to administer, the BDIST is not widely used as a screening tool.

Developmental Profile II.   The Developmental Profile II (Alpern, Boll, and Shearer 1980) is a skill checklist designed to provide a screening inventory of five developmental areas that include physical development, social skills, expressive and receptive language, self-help skills, and intellectual abilities. An individual profile of a child's level of developmental functioning is obtained in this inventory.

The five scales of the Developmental Profile II consist of 217 items grouped in age levels from birth to twelve years. Rather than directly testing the child, the tester interviews the parent regarding the presence of a particular ability. Because of its interview format, the test procedures can be self-taught by professionals who will administer the test.

Developmental Indicators for the Assessment of Learning–Revised (DIAL-R).
The DIAL-R is a revision of a normed preschool screening instrument designed to screen young children between the ages of two and six years for learning disabilities (Mardell-Czudnowski and Goldenberg 1983). The test

has been standardized using a population stratified across geographic location, age, sex, and ethnic groups. Direct testing is used to screen concepts, language, and motor domains. For each of these areas, separate scores are obtained. A total score is based on the scores of the three assessed areas. Based on the scores, the child is classified as OK, potential problem, or potential advanced. The test takes twenty to thirty minutes to administer.

Minnesota Child Development Inventory (MCDI). The MCDI is a norm-referenced screening test for children from ages one to six that relies on parents' responses to statements about their child's current development (Ireton and Thwing 1974). The 320 test items measure the following developmental categories: fine motor, gross motor, expressive language, general development, comprehensive conceptual situations, personal-social, and self-help.

Since the test relies on parent report, it is considered easier to administer than the DDST. However, the reliability of parental reports about their children's behavior has been questioned (Meisels and Waskik 1990). Not only is parent objectivity and knowledge in answering questions a concern in this assessment, but the population on which the test is normed was limited to middle-class parents.

Developmental Activities Screening Inventory–II (DASI-II). The DASI-II is a screening instrument spanning the age range of 0–60 months (Fewell and Langley 1984). The test is designed to assess a variety of developmental skills of infants and young children who have already been screened and determined to have sensory impairments. Typically, there is a time lapse between the time a child is identified as delayed until a comprehensive test battery is given. The DASI-II is intended to aid infant and preschool teachers in identifying the developmental functioning of a child in order to plan appropriate activities during this period.

The DASI-II has several unique features. The sixty-seven item scale can be administered by classroom teachers who have some familiarity with child development and a minimum of testing experience. It is a nonverbal test and includes procedures for administering items to children with visual and auditory impairments. For example, with children with hearing impairments, instructions can be communicated manually, by using sign language. Test items assess a range of behaviors that indicate sensory association, sensorimotor organization, imitation, spatial relationships, memory, reasoning, size discrimination, and object functions.

Scoring the test is relatively simple; one raw score point is given for each item passed. A basal and ceiling level is provided to establish the age-level reference point. Items passed are added to the basal score. The estimated developmental level is then used as a reference point for instructional programming until an in-depth assessment is done. Specific instructional activities are provided for each skill tested. These guidelines assist teachers in targeting individual programming so that emerging skills may be refined or developed.

Bayley Infant Neurodevelopmental Screen (BINS).   The BINS (Aylward 1995) is an infant screen used to determine risk of developmental delay or neurological impairment. The age range of the BINS is 3–24 months. Item sets are arranged by age groups: 3–4 months, 5–6 months, 7–10 months, 11–15 months, 16–20 months, and 21–24 months. Four areas of abilities are assessed: neurological functions/intactness (N), receptive function (R), expressive function (E), and cognitive process (C). Depending on their test performance, infants are judged to be at high, moderate, or low risk. Table 3.3 shows examples of BINS test items and the area of ability assessed.

Environmental Screening

Infants spend most of their time in their home. Because the home environment is considered central to developmental functioning of infants, researchers have turned their attention to assessing home environments (Wachs 1988). Many screening programs include some type of environmental screening measure as part of their test battery. Often, such screens take the form of parent interviews that address questions concerning the safety of the physical environment, parent-infant interactions, family routines, toys available to the child, and number of people in the household.

Home Observation and Measurement of the Environment (HOME) (Caldwell and Bradley 1972) is the most well-known environmental screening measure. The HOME scale was designed to identify high-risk environments of infants (0–3 years) and children (3–6 years). A home visitor rates the home environment through direct observation and parent interviews. Six categories of the environment are included in the scale: (1) mother's verbal and emotional responsiveness, (2) appropriate play materials, (3) avoidance of punishment, (4) organization of physical and temporal environment, (5) mother's involvement with infant, and (6) opportunities for variety in stimulating activities.

The HOME scale has been found to reliably measure environments that place infants at cognitive and developmental risk (Bradley and Caldwell 1977). Further, this scale can be used as a vehicle for promoting and reinforcing positive parent-infant interactions (Powell 1981).

Tracking Systems

A tracking system sequentially and periodically monitors infants and children who are at risk for developmental disabilities. Through a tracking system, infants with developmental disabilities or delays can be identified and

TABLE 3.3   Sample Items from the Bayley Infant Neurodevelopment Screen Abilities Test

Age	Test Item	Ability
3–4 months	vocalizes two different sounds	expressive function
5–6 months	sits with slight support	expressive function
7–10 months	rings bell purposely	cognitive function
11–15 months	demonstrates optimal muscle tone in lower extremities	neurological function
16–20 months	points to doll's body parts	receptive function
21–24 months	identifies four pictures	receptive function

SOURCE: G. P. Aylward, *Bayley Infant Neurodevelopmental Screener* (San Antonio, TX: Psychological Corporation, 1995).

provided with diagnostic evaluation and early intervention services. James Blackman (1986) suggested two sets of entry criteria for a tracking system. The first set of criteria is applicable to newborns or infants before discharge from the hospital. The second set applies after hospital discharge. The major categories for each are as follows:

Prior to Hospital Discharge

Prenatal and Psychosocial Factors
- Maternal drug use
- Maternal phenylketonuria
- Parental mental retardation
- Parental mental illness
- Parental impairment in psychosocial functioning
- No permanent housing
- Maternal age less than fifteen years old
- Parental sensory impairment

Newborn Factors
- Low birth weight
- Newborn seizures
- Intercranial hemorrhage
- Asphyxia
- Suspected visual and hearing impairment
- Central nervous system infection or abnormality
- Major congenital anomalies

After Hospital Discharge
- Health maintenance problems

- Newly diagnosed familial disorder
- Nutritional problems
- Evidence of growth deficiency
- Severe chronic illness
- Delayed or abnormal development (Blackman 1986)

Approaches to developing tracking systems are currently being implemented through various state initiatives. Public Law 99–457 specifies that the tracking systems should include a public awareness program, a comprehensive child-find system, and a system for compiling data. Although some states have made substantial progress in this arena, there is still no national tracking system (Meisels and Provence 1989). In 1989, the National Center for Clinical Infant Programs published *Keeping Track*, which outlines the efforts and strategies of fifteen states to implement tracking systems (National Center for Clinical Infant Programs 1989).

A national comprehensive tracking plan for at-risk infants is an important goal for the United States. The National Center for Clinical Infant Programs (1989) has identified the necessary elements for a comprehensive tracking program:

- Tracking that begins before birth
- Screening at multiple time points
- Sensitivity to family involvement and families' right to privacy
- Information linkage across agencies
- Appropriate follow-up and referral to services
- Availability of transition between agencies

Screening and Early Intervention

Use of Screening to Identify Infants for Intervention Services
Identifying suspected developmental problems as early in infancy as possible is the primary goal of screening. Since infants with developmental delays are not enrolled in a public school system, screening is considered necessary in order to find them and begin early treatment efforts. The passage of two federal laws, Public Law 94-142 and Public Law 99-457, has focused public attention on the need for infant screening (Meisels and Waskik 1990).

Public Law 94-142, the Education for the Handicapped Act, which was passed in 1972, required that free and appropriate educational services be provided for all children with handicaps between the ages of three and twenty-one in those states that were already providing educational services. The passage of Public Law 99-457 (Part H of IDEA [Individuals with Disabilities Education Act]) in 1986 extended the provisions of Public Law 94-142 from birth to age two by allocating incentive monies to those states

that wished to provide these services. Public Law 99-457, or Part H, distin-
guished between evaluation and assessment (Campbell 1991). Evaluation
includes the procedures used to determine an infant's eligibility for early intervention services. Assessment is the ongoing process used to determine a
child's strengths and needs, the family's strengths and needs, and the degree
of early intervention needed.

This legislation also requires states to make multidisciplinary evaluation
available for infants and toddlers with disabilities as well as to implement a
comprehensive child-find system. The child-find system requires screening
large numbers of infants and young children to assist states in deciding who
should be eligible for early intervention services.

As states begin to implement Public Law 99-457, many questions are
being raised. These include the following: How should the terms *at-risk* or
developmental delay be defined? How should states go about screening
large numbers of infants? How can a comprehensive screening be accom-
plished? What are valid screening tests? How often should infants and
young children be screened?

A fundamental screening issue concerns which infants and children
should receive early intervention services. Evidence regarding the incidence
and prevalence of developmental problems in infants and toddlers is incon-
clusive. *Incidence* refers to the frequency with which a disabling condition
occurs within a population, usually for a specified time. For example, actual incidence of a particular handicap would be defined as the number of
infants born with the disability during a given year. Incidence figures may
change depending on prevention efforts such as vaccinations, toxic dump
removals, or provision of intervention services.

Prevalence is the term used to refer to the actual number of individuals
with a specific disability at any particular point in time. Although several
prevalence studies have been done on disabilities in children, there are no
national data available for disabilities from birth to age three (Meisels
1988). A 1987 U.S. Department of Education survey of twenty-six states
showed a prevalence rate ranging from less than 1 percent to over 5 percent
in three- to five-year-old children. Prevalence data from several recent state
surveys reveal low rates of identification for children under three years of
age and a disparity between the prevalence rates reported on disabled children under and over the age of six.

There are several reasons for the differences in early and late prevalence.
One of the more compelling is the difficulty of clearly identifying an infant
or young child as disabled. Categories such as "learning disabled," "train-
able mentally retarded," and "speech disordered" are more clearly defined
than "developmentally delayed." Samuel Meisels and Barbara Waskik
(1990) have pointed out that prevalence rates are in flux in the first three
years of life because risk factors may dissipate or developmental problems
may be remediated with improvements in the infant's environment.

Early and late prevalence rates may also be affected by the availability of valid assessments that accurately identify and diagnose disabilities. As compared to assessments available for school-age children, there is a paucity of valid instruments available for infants and toddlers.

Rationale for Early Intervention

Screening is the first step in identifying infants in need of early intervention programming. After diagnostic assessment determines that an infant is developmentally delayed, then early intervention services are recommended.

Early systematic intervention is based on the rationale that early treatment can ameliorate infants' problems and promote optimal future development (Hayden and McGinness 1977). For over three decades, experts have emphasized the importance of the infancy period for later development (Hunt 1961). This period of life is characterized by a heightened response to the environment and by the many sensory experiences that promote intellectual growth.

The idea that there are certain critical or sensitive periods during which the infant is most susceptible to environmental stimuli was first supported by research on various mammalian species (Denenberg 1975; Lipton 1976). The concept was subsequently applied to human infants, lending strength to the argument that there are times when the infant is most likely to be responsive to learning experiences. The period from birth to four years is considered critical to infants' learning and development (Peterson 1987). Burton White's (1975) longitudinal research with children between ages one and three indicated that foundations for language, social development, curiosity, and cognitive development are established during this time. Moreover, infants' skills in these areas were found to be modified as a result of manipulating their environmental experiences.

Studies of the outcomes of specific early experiences during infancy on later development were the subject of many animal and human studies in the 1960s and 1970s (Melzack 1962; Provence and Lipton 1962). Harry Harlow (1965) presented convincing evidence that monkeys that had been separated from their mothers at birth and that lacked tactile stimulation became socially maladaptive. Reduced social competency was also typical of dogs reared in social isolation (Thompson, Melzack, and Scott 1956). Similarly, studies of human infants raised in orphanages or in other unstimulating environments showed them to have psychological and physical developmental lags (Spitz 1945; Goldfarb 1955).

A number of studies have examined the benefits of early stimulation for infants and young children (Dennis 1960; Egeland and Sroufe 1981). In a classic study, thirteen young children in an orphanage were placed under the partial care of retarded women who provided them with extra nurturance and stimulation. The children had a mean increase in IQ points of 27.5, in contrast to an average decrease of 26.2 IQ points in children without the extra stimulation (Skeels and Dye 1939).

Subsequent research with different populations of high-risk infants examined the effectiveness of single-sensory modalities or multimodal stimulation, including tactile and kinesthetic or visual and auditory input. Interventions with preterm infants, such as holding or rocking, talking to the baby, or placing the baby on a waterbed or sheepskin, have been used as interventions in the neonatal intensive nursery. Outcome measures found weight gain, increased head circumference, improved orienting response, overall enhanced sensory motor skills, or documented medical progress in preterm infants (Barnard and Bee 1983; Mouradian and Als 1994; Kraemer and Pierpoint 1976). Other studies have documented the beneficial effects of early stimulation on young disadvantaged infants and infants with handicaps (Bronfenbrenner 1974; Garber and Heber 1977; Yarrow 1965).

Early Intervention for At-Risk and Disabled Infants

Research evidence supporting the importance of early stimulating experiences for infant learning spurred the development of early intervention programs (Peterson 1987). The idea that infants' development can be modified by changing their environment is a primary tenet of early intervention. Furthermore, the concern, supported by research, that handicapping conditions in the infant period can limit infants' development and learning prompted the establishment of early intervention programs in the 1970s (Bricker, Bailey, and Bruder 1984). Since the 1970s, early childhood professionals have continued to refine programs for infants and young children with disabilities. The focuses of intervention vary depending on the infant population, intervention approach, and program model.

As infant intervention services have been made available for disabled infants, a key question has emerged: Is early intervention effective? At first, the answer to that question was clouded by unsystematic evaluations as well as by the difficulties inherent in evaluating the array of intervention approaches (Guralnick 1988). As research questions about the efficacy of intervention became more focused, studies began to suggest that these programs do indeed improve the lives of infants and their families (Guralnick and Bricker 1987; Oelwein, Fewell, and Preuss 1985).

Research on programs for Down syndrome infants has demonstrated that the progressive intellectual decline of these children is reduced with early intervention (Hayden and Haring 1977). Documentation of positive outcomes with other disability groups varies depending on the type of disability (Bricker and Sheehan 1981; Ramey and Bryant 1982). In general, however, early intervention has been found to have a positive impact on infants with disabilities and their families.

Summary

Screening is the method used to determine which infants are likely to have developmental disabilities and need further diagnostic assessment and early intervention. The large population of infants who are at risk for developmental problems is the screening target. Screening can take place at multiple times during infancy.

The concept of risk is complex. Three major types of risk have been classified: established risk, environmental risk, and biological risk. These risk factors often overlap and may be additive.

Screening tests should be accurate and easy to administer. Screening tests use direct observations of infants, parent reports, and direct infant testing. Screening tests range from prenatal scales and auditory and visual screening to standardized developmental scales based on norm-referenced assessments. One well-known developmental scale that relies on direct testing and parent reports is the Denver Developmental Screening Test-II.

Effective screening programs for detection of infants with disabilities should meet several criteria. The screening should begin prenatally and continue until school age. The programs should be cost-effective. The screening instruments used should have adequate psychometric properties, be simple to administer, and be appropriate to the screening goals. Family input should be an integral part of the program.

Screening is the first step in directing infants to early intervention services. The concept that early intervention is valuable is based on research demonstrating that experiences in early life affect later developmental outcomes. Recent studies on the efficacy of intervention have to some degree validated the ameliorating effects of intervention for infants with disabilities.

References

Alpern, G. D., T. J. Boll, and M. Shearer. 1980. *Developmental Profile II*. Aspen, CO: Psychological Development Publications.

Apgar, V. 1953. A proposal for a new method of evaluation of the newborn infant. *Anesthesia and Analgesia: Current Research* 32:260–267.

Aylward, G. P. 1995. *Bayley Infant Neurodevelopmental Screener*. San Antonio, TX: Psychological Corporation.

Bailey, D. B., and S. L. Rosenthal. 1987. Assessment in early childhood special education. In *Assessment in Special Education*, eds. W. H. Berdine, and S. A. Meyer. Boston: Little Brown.

Barnard, K. E., and H. L. Bee. 1983. The impact of temporally patterned stimulation on the development of preterm infants. *Child Development* 54:1156–1157.

Bijou, S. W. 1981. The prevention of retarded development in disadvantaged children. In *Psychosocial Influences in Retarded Performance. Vol. 1: Issues and Theories in Development*. Edited by M. J. Begab, H. C. Haywood, and H. C. Garber. Baltimore: University Park Press.

Blackman, J. 1986. *Warning Signals: Basic Criteria for Tracking At-Risk Infants and Toddlers*. Washington, DC: National Center for Clinical Infant Programs.

Bradley, R. H., and B. M. Caldwell. 1977. Home observation for measurement of the environment: A validation study of screening efficiency. *American Journal of Mental Deficiency* 81:417–420.

Bricker, D., E. Bailey, and M. B. Bruder. 1984. The efficacy of early intervention and the handicapped infant: A wise or wasted resource. In *Advances in Developmental and Behavioral Pediatrics*. Vol. 5. Edited by M. Wolraich, and D. K. Routh. Greenwich, CT: JAI Press.

Bricker, D., and R. Sheehan. 1981. Effectiveness of an early intervention program as indexed by measures of child change. *Journal of the Division for Early Childhood* 4:11–27.

Bronfenbrenner, U. 1974. *A Report on Longitudinal Evaluations of Preschool Programs. Vol. 2: Is Early Intervention Effective?* (DHEW Publication no. OHD 7630025). Washington, DC: U.S. Government Printing Office.

Caldwell, B. M., and R. H. Bradley. 1972. *Home Observation and Measurement of the Environment Inventory*. Center for Child Development and Education: University of Arkansas at Little Rock.

Campbell, P. H. 1991. Evaluation and assessment in early intervention for infants and toddlers. *Journal of Early Intervention* 15:36–45.

Committee on Standards of Child Health Care of the American Academy of Pediatrics. 1977. *Standards of Child Health Care*. 3d ed. Evanston, IL: American Academy of Pediatrics.

Denenberg, V. H. 1975. Effects of exposure to stressors in early life upon later behavioral and biological processes. In *Society, Stress, and Disease: Childhood and Adolescence*, edited by L. Levi. New York: Oxford University Press.

Dennis, W. 1960. Causes of retardation among institutionalized children: Iran. *Journal of Genetic Psychology* 96:47–59.

Egeland, B., and L. A. Sroufe. 1981. Attachment and early maltreatment. *Child Development* 52:44–52.

Ensher, G. L., and D. A. Clark. 1994. *Newborns at Risk*. 2d ed. Gaithersburg, MD: Aspen.

Fewell, R. R., and M. B. Langley. 1984. *Developmental Activities Screening Inventory (DASI-II)*. Austin, TX: Pro-ed Corporation.

Frankenburg, W. K., A. D. Goldstein, and B. W. Camp. 1971. The revised Denver Developmental Screening Test: Its accuracy as a screening instrument. *Journal of Pediatrics* 79(6):988–995.

Frankenburg, W. K., B. W. Camp, and P. A. Van-Natta. 1971. Validity of the Denver Developmental Screening Test. *Child Development* 42:475–485.

Frankenburg, W. K., J. Dodds, and A. Fandal. 1975. *Denver Developmental Screening Test*. Denver: LADOCA Project and Publishing Foundation.

Frankenburg, W. K., J. Dodds, P. Archer, B. Bresnick, P. Maschka, N. Edelman, and H. Shapiro. 1991. *Denver II*. Denver: Denver Developmental Materials.

Garber, H., and R. F. Heber. 1977. The Milwaukee project: Indication of the effectiveness of early intervention in preventing mental retardation. In *Research to Practice in Mental Retardation: Care and Intervention*. Vol. 1. Edited by P. Mittler. Baltimore: University Park Press.

Garrity, J., and H. Mengle. 1983. Early identification of hearing loss: Practices and procedures. *American Annals of the Deaf* 128:99–106.

Glascoe, F. P., and K. Byrne. 1993. The accuracy of three developmental screening tests. *Journal of Early Intervention* 17:368–379.

Goldfarb, W. 1955. Emotional and intellectual consequences of psychologic deprivation in infancy: A re-evaluation. In *Psychopathology of Childhood*, edited by P. H. Hock and J. Zubin. New York: Grune and Stratton.

Gordon, B. N., and K. G. Jens. 1988. A conceptual model for tracking high-risk infants and making early service decisions. *Developmental and Behavioral Pediatrics* 9:279–286.

Guralnick, M. J. 1988. Efficacy research in early childhood intervention programs. In *Early Intervention for Infants with Handicaps*, edited by S. L. Odom and M. B. Karnes. Baltimore: Paul H. Brookes.

Guralnick, M. J., and D. Bricker. 1987. The effectiveness of early intervention for children with cognitive and general developmental delays. In *The Effectiveness of Early Intervention for At-Risk and Handicapped Children*, edited by M. J. Guralnick and F. C. Bennett. New York: Academic Press.

Harlow, H. F. 1965. Total social isolation: Effects on macaque monkey behavior. *Science* 148:666.

Hayden, A. H., and G. D. McGinness. 1977. Basis for early intervention. In *Educational Programming for the Severely and Profoundly Handicapped*, edited by E. Sontag. Reston, VA: Division on Mental Retardation, Council for Exceptional Children.

Hayden, A. H., and N. G. Haring. 1977. The acceleration and maintenance of developmental gains in Down's syndrome school-age children. In *Research to Practice in Mental Retardation: Care and Intervention*. Vol. 1. Edited by P. Mittler. Baltimore: University Park Press.

Hunt, J. McV. 1961. *Intelligence and Experience*. New York: Ronald Press.

Ireton, H., and E. Thwing. 1974. *The Minnesota Child Development Inventory*. Minneapolis: Behavioral Science Systems.

Keogh, B. K., and C. B. Kopp. 1978. From assessment to intervention: An elusive bridge. In *Communication and Cognitive Abilities in Early Behavioral Assessment*, eds. F. D. Minifie and L. C. Lloyd. Baltimore: University Park Press.

King, E., D. A. Logsdon, and S. R. Schroeder. 1992. Risk factors for developmental delay among infants and toddlers. *Children's Health Care* 21:39–52.

Kochanek, T. T. 1993. Enhanced screening procedures for infants and toddlers. In *Implementing Early Intervention: From Research to Effective Practice*, eds. D. M. Bryant and M. A. Graham. New York: Guilford Press.

Kraemer, L. I., and M. B. Pierpoint. 1976. Rocking waterbeds and auditory stimuli to enhance growth of preterm infants. *Journal of Pediatrics* 88:297–299.

Langley, B. 1980. *Functional Vision Inventory for the Multiple and Severely Handicapped*. Chicago: Stoelting Co.

Lipton, M. A. 1976. Early experience and plasticity in the central nervous system. In *Intervention Strategies for High Risk Infants and Young Children*, edited by T. D. Tjossem. Baltimore: University Park Press.

Mardell-Czudnowski, C. D., and D. Goldenberg. 1983. *DIAL-R (Developmental Indicators for the Assessment of Learning–Revised)*. Edison, NJ: Childcraft Education Corp.

Meisels, S. J. 1991. Dimensions of early identifications. *Journal of Early Intervention* 15:26–35.

_____. 1988. Developmental screening in early childhood: The interreaction of research and social policy. In *Annual Review of Public Health*, eds. L. Breslow, J. E. Fielding, and L. B. Lave, 9:527–550. Palo Alto, CA: Annual Reviews.

Meisels, S. J., and B. A. Waskik. 1990. Who should be served? Identifying children in need of early intervention. In *Handbook of Early Childhood Interventions*, eds. S. J. Meisels and J. P. Shonkoff. New York: Cambridge University Press.

Meisels, S. J., M. S. Wiske, and T. Tirnan. 1984. Predicting school performance with the Early Screening Inventory. *Psychology in the Schools* 21:25–33.

Meisels, S. J., and S. Provence. 1989. *Screening and Assessment: Guidelines for Identifying Young Developmentally Vulnerable Children and Their Families.* Washington, DC: National Center for Clinical Infant Programs.

Melzack, R. 1962. Effects of early perceptual restriction on simple visual discrimination. *Science* 137:978–979.

Mouradian, L., and H. Als. 1994. The influence of neonatal care unit caregiving practices on motor functioning of preterm infants. *American Journal of Occupational Therapy* 48(5):527–533.

National Center for Clinical Infant Programs. 1989. *Keeping Track: Tracking Systems for High-Risk Infants and Young Children.* 2d ed. Washington, DC: National Center for Clinical Infant Programs.

Newborg, J., J. R. Stock, L. Wnek, J. Guidabaldi, and J. Suinicki. 1984. *Battelle Developmental Inventory Screening Test.* Allen, TX: DCM-Teaching Resources.

Oelwein, P. L., R. R. Fewell, and J. B. Preuss. 1985. The efficacy of intervention at outreach sites of the program for children with Down's syndrome and other developmental delays. *Topics in Early Childhood Special Education* 5(2):78–87.

Parmelee, A. H. 1974. The obstetric complications scales and the postnatal complications scale.

Peterson, N. L. 1987. *Early Intervention for Handicapped Children and At-Risk Children.* Denver: Love Publications.

Powell, M. L. 1981. *Assessment and Management of Developmental Changes and Problems in Children.* St. Louis: Mosby.

Prechtl, H.F.R. 1982. Assessment methods for the newborn infant: A critical evaluation. In *Psychobiology of the Human Newborn*, edited by P. Stratton. New York: Wiley.

Provence, S., and R. C. Lipton. 1962. *Infants in Institutions.* New York: International University Press.

Ramey, C. T., and D. M. Bryant. 1982. Evidence for prevention of developmental retardation during infancy. *Journal of the Division for Early Childhood* 5:73–78.

Skeels, H. M., and H. B. Dye. 1939. A study of the effects of differential stimulation on mentally retarded children. *Proceedings and Addresses of the American Association on Mental Deficiency* 44:114–136.

Spitz, R. 1945. Hospitalism: An inquiry into the genesis of psychiatric conditions in early childhood. *Psychoanalytic Study of the Child* 2:313–342.

Thompson, W. R., R. Melzack, and T. H. Scott. 1956. Whirling behavior in dogs as related to early experience. *Science* 123:939.

Thorpe, H., and E. Werner. 1974. Developmental screening of preschool children: A critical review of inventories used in health and educational programs. *Pediatrics* 53(3):362–370.

Thurman, S. K., and A. W. Widerstrom. 1990. *Infants and Young Children with Special Needs.* Baltimore: Paul H. Brookes.

Tjossem, T. D. 1976. *Intervention Strategies for High Risk Infants and Young Children*. Baltimore: University Park Press.

Vistech Consultants. 1986. *Teller Acuity Card Handbook*. Dayton, OH: Author.

Wachs, T. D. 1988. Environmental assessment of developmentally disabled infants and preschoolers. In *Assessment of Young Developmentally Disabled Children*, edited by T. D. Wachs and R. Sheehan. New York: Plenum Press.

White, B. L. 1975. *The First Three Years of Life*. Englewood Cliffs, NJ: Prentice-Hall.

Yarrow, L. J. 1965. Conceptual perspectives on the early environment. *Journal of American Academy of Child Psychiatry* 4(2).

4

Assessment of Infant Cognition

Making terms with reality, with things as they are, is a full-time business for the child.

—Milton R. Sapirstein

Introduction

Initially, newborn babies experience the world through reflex actions and by touching, looking, and hearing. Yet in a brief two years, they become purposeful problem solvers able to organize their behaviors in a meaningful way. They can, for example, manipulate their environment using the concepts of time, space, cause and effect, and permanence of objects. Obviously, remarkable changes occur during this period. Understanding these changes by assessing the development of infant cognition has been the goal of traditional infant tests.

Assessment of infant cognition has challenged researchers, since cognition cannot be directly observed. Instead, cognitive behaviors are inferred from behavioral changes within specific contexts. To assess infants' cognitive functioning, several abilities are considered, among them object permanence, imitation, and goal-oriented actions. It is generally agreed that the assessment of infants' cognitive functioning entails taking a global approach to infants. Thus, a cognitive assessment would include consideration of cognitive abilities as well as communication, motor, and social-emotional skills.

In this chapter, we will review the milestones in infant cognitive development, with particular attention given to the developmental cognitive stages described by Jean Piaget. Methods and tests currently used to evaluate the cognitive functioning of infants will also be outlined, and a critique of their usefulness with different infant populations will be offered.

Your study of this chapter should enable you to

- Outline the major components of infant cognition included in Piaget's six sensorimotor stages
- Describe several tests of infants' cognitive functioning
- Describe the strengths and limitations of traditional and ordinal infant tests for research and for assessing different infant populations, including infants at risk for developmental disabilities

Cognitive Development

From the beginning of baby studies, researchers have been interested in what babies know and how babies think. They have asked questions such as these: How do babies experience time? Do they understand the consequences of actions? In what ways do babies organize new information to make sense of their world? What early experiences help to shape infants' thought? For decades, the question of the relationship of infant cognition to maternal intelligence has been raised by clinicians (McCall and Mash 1995). Researchers organize all such questions under the term *cognition,* which they use to designate behaviors related to thinking and knowing. Cognition has been used to refer to symbolic and representational thought (Rossetti 1990). Cognition includes memory, perception, thought, and information processing. Thought will be the focus of this chapter. In Chapter 5, we will consider infant information processing.

Sensorimotor Development

Jean Piaget's theory of cognitive development laid the groundwork for much of our present-day understanding of infant cognition. Piaget, a Swiss psychologist, formulated his theory of how intelligence is structured from childhood to adulthood through careful and extensive observations of his own children (Piaget 1952). Piaget proposed that cognition is integrated into the overall functioning of humans. As they develop, the cognitive system also changes and develops in an organized way. The conceptual system changes in response to environmental stimuli. In the material that follows, we will first review two important assumptions Piaget made to build his theory and then examine Piaget's sensorimotor stage, which takes place from birth to two years. This is the first of Piaget's four major stages of cognitive development, and he believed that it is during the sensorimotor stage that infants use adaptive responses to the environment to develop the ability to engage in increasingly complex mental operations. It is in the first two years of life that an infant's cognitive structures are formed and begin systematic organization. This organization is known as *sensorimotor intelligence.*

Assumptions. Two assumptions are central to Piaget's theory. One is that knowledge is acquired through an infant's motor actions. According to Piaget, infants first act on their environment motorically and in the process begin to learn something about space, objects, and time relationships. For example, when a three-month-old baby girl accidentally kicks a mobile hanging over her crib, the mobile will move and momentarily catch her attention. Initially, she will not connect her kicking with the movement of the mobile. But over time, the kick sequence will be repeated through random motor movements, and by the time she is five months old, she will be able to aim her foot purposefully, kick, and thus make the mobile move. Through this repeated action sequence, she gains an understanding of the mobile, its properties, and its relationship to her movements. In effect, she has constructed a reality about her environment through action sequences. Piaget (1954) believed such a construction of thoughts is essential to building intelligence.

A second assumption underlying Piaget's theory is that the process of adaptation is fundamental to intellectual development (Piaget 1952). According to this precept, infants adjust their actions to meet the demands of the environment. For instance, in the previous example, when the baby girl is at different distances from the mobile and tries to kick it, she must modify her movements in order to make it move. When she is close, she can make the mobile move with little effort, but when the mobile is farther away, she must straighten her leg and perhaps even stretch. Piaget termed this adaptation to changes in the environment *equilibrium.*

Equilibrium between the infant and the environment involves two processes, *assimilation* and *accommodation.* With *assimilation,* infants incorporate new experiences that are consistent with their existing cognitive repertoire. For example, a baby of five months will suck on a crayon instead of attempting to use it as a writing tool. This occurs because sucking is part of the baby's existing cognitive state, whereas coloring is not. Consequently, the baby sucks the crayon but does not use it to color.

Through *accommodation,* infants modify their existing concepts or actions to meet new environmental demands. For example, an infant might alter the way he or she grasps an object when given a toy that is larger than previously encountered. Assimilation and accommodation are constantly operative, and through these mechanisms, infants build their understanding of the world. Thus, cognitive development is a dynamic process in which infants modify old actions while learning new ones. As infants develop, changes in their cognitive processes result from their actions on the environment.

Sensorimotor Substages.   Piaget called the first of the four major cognitive stages in his cognitive development theory the *sensorimotor* stage. This stage focuses on infant cognitive development during the first twenty-four months of life and consists of six substages, each of which is characterized by significant cognitive events that lay the groundwork for adult thinking. The salient characteristics of each stage appear sequentially in infant development, as described in the following sections on substages.

Substage 1 (0–1 Month).   Infants in this stage are predominately reflexive. They look at objects and people and hear sounds but do not relate the sounds to a particular person or thing. Most of their responses to the external world are protective; for example, they withdraw their foot from a pin-prick or close their eyes to bright lights. They suck and grasp objects and spend time practicing nonnutritive sucking. Although infants at this stage have not learned to separate means from ends and do not understand that objects exist apart from them, external stimulation helps their sensory and motor systems organize and get ready for learning.

With babies at this stage, you might try placing a finger or small object in the palm of the infant's hand to observe the grasp response or try presenting your face to the infant; then watch the responses to these movements. Infants' responses will become more directed and refined toward the end of their first four weeks, though these changes are subtle and may be difficult to detect.

Substage 2 (1–4 months).   Babies in this substage begin to coordinate sensory input with their motor actions. Piaget calls such sequences *primary circular reactions*. For example, babies turn their heads toward sounds, and they repeatedly kick or grasp and release objects. The reactions are called "primary" because they are limited to the infant's own body. They are called "circular" because they are usually repeated. Usually by chance, these repetitive actions result in an interesting consequence for infants such as making an object move or producing a sound.

What distinguishes Substage 2 from the first substage is that infants in Substage 2 gradually gain more voluntary control over their responses to the world around them. By four months, they become more skilled at adapting their actions to a variety of events and objects. Yet, infants in this substage are still unable to distinguish themselves from objects. This means, for example, that when a toy is removed from their view, infants in Substage 2 will not search for it. Try it. Show a toy to a baby at this stage, then slowly remove it from view. Babies will not move their eyes or head to find the missing toy. However, they are likely to look surprised for just a moment.

Substage 3 (4–8 Months).   Intentionality is the distinctive feature of Substage 3. Infants in this stage learn that they can affect their environment and make things happen. They intentionally repeat actions that produce pleasurable results. For instance, a six-month-old infant may bang first one object and then another against a table leg to produce different sounds. And infants will often examine each object after they have banged it, picking up one, then another. These repetitive activities are termed *secondary circular reactions*. "Primary" becomes "secondary" because infants not only use their own bodies but also use objects around them to produce desired effects. The result of the action rather than the action itself has become important. Toward the end of Substage 3, intentionality characterizes most of a baby's actions.

During Substage 3, infants visually and tactually explore objects. A typical five-month-old baby will pick up a toy, look at it, feel it, turn it over, and then place it in his or her mouth. Games with adults also become increasingly complex as babies pass through this period. Infants learn to anticipate interactive game sequences, then to respond, and finally to initiate games. A seven-month-old infant boy, for example, will tense his muscles and widen his eyes when his father begins a game of peekaboo. As the father covers his eyes, the baby will smile or show pleasure and then laugh when his father shows his face and says, "Peekaboo." Often the baby will use body and facial expressions that indicate he wants the game repeated. An eight-month-old infant might pull a cloth from the caregiver's face and laugh, thus imitating game playing.

Imitating adult actions is an important feature of this substage. Initial efforts to search for disappearing objects also appears during this period. An object dropped out of an infant's sight results in the infant looking at the place it was dropped. This activity indicates the beginning of the concept of objects existing separately in time and space.

You can see all of these things in babies at Substage 3. Watch them repeat pleasurable activities. Play peekaboo or another interactive game with them. Look for signs of anticipation in the baby's face and body. Give them a chance to imitate you and repeat Substage 2's disappearing toy sequence. Then observe their reactions. You should see increased sophistication in responses with older infants in this stage.

Substage 4 (8–12 Months).   During Substage 4, infants learn to be goal directed. It is even more impressive that they learn to put several behaviors together to accomplish a desired goal. For example, an infant will push aside a pillow to grab a toy or will hold the arms out, gesturing to be picked up. Piaget describes this major cognitive milestone as separating means and ends.

During Substage 4, infants' problem-solving abilities also become more refined. However, although intentionality characterizes the problem-solving efforts of Substage 4 infants, these infants do not generate new behaviors to accomplish goals. Rather, babies at this stage "try out" existing behavior schemes in order to solve a problem. Efforts at true experimentation are not seen until the next substage.

In Substage 4, infants come to recognize that objects have permanence and continue to exist in time and space even when the objects are not visible. Consequently, when a cloth is placed over an object, they will remove the cloth and retrieve the object. An interesting feature of this situation is that infants in Substage 4 will not systematically search for a hidden object under several displacements. Instead, they will persist in looking for the object where it was last found. This is known as the AB error.

Try this yourself. Hide an object again under a cloth at location A and allow an infant to watch you, then successfully find it. Do this several times. Then, after again hiding the object in place A, move the same object, in full view of the infant, to place B and hide it under another cloth. The infant will probably continue to look for it in place A, even after seeing you move the object to location B.

Substage 5 (12–18 Months).   This stage is marked by active experimentation. In Substage 5, infants learn new behaviors through trial and error, a process called *tertiary circular reactions.* "Circular" remains in the definition because the activities are repeated, but "secondary" becomes "tertiary" because infants deliberately vary their actions to produce new and interesting results. This can be seen when an infant in a high chair, for example, a twelve-month-old boy, accidentally tips his glass of milk and watches it spill. He may then turn his glass over to see what happens when the remainder of the milk pours out. To the dismay of his parents, he may continue experimenting with how things look and sound by dropping spoonfuls of applesauce or spaghetti or whatever is within his reach. Thus, chance discoveries become the basis for exploring how things work.

Substage 5 infants also display making systematic searches for hidden objects. They no longer make the AB error, but they will not search for a toy that has not been made visible while being hidden. However, it is evident in Substage 5 that infants now have a wide range of complex behaviors available to them. Their play becomes more complex and symbolic toward the end of the stage. Further, Substage 5 infants are able to organize their behaviors in a purposeful way not evident in previous stages.

Try giving an infant in this stage toys or objects that move or make sounds when touched, and watch the infant experiment with them. See what happens if you hide a toy under two successive displacements while the infant is watching. If you have real courage, watch closely while an infant experiments with his mashed potatoes and peas.

Substage 6 (18–24 Months).   Using symbolic representations is the characteristic feature of Substage 6 infants. An important cognitive leap for infants in this stage is language acquisition. Now infants can imagine where an object is hidden rather than having to watch it being placed. Substage 6 infants show *deferred imitation*; that is, they imitate an action that has occurred previously. A twenty-month-old infant girl, for example, might talk on her play phone using words and the tone of voice her mother used the day before. Or she may imitate her father's shaving routine, even though the father shaved hours before.

Equally important, Substage 6 infants are no longer limited to immediate sensory-motor actions to solve problems and experience the world around them. They can think of different ways to reach goals. This means that infants at this substage are not confined to the here and now. Their play involves pretending and symbolism. As a result, a pencil can become a spaceship or a projectile, and a block of wood may become a boat.

To observe this symbolic play, arrange some blocks or plastic cups and plates. Ask a child to play with you. Suggest that you cook dinner or build a tall building. Listen for the child's interesting descriptions while playing. Use your imagination; your subject will, too.

Substage 6 is the end of infancy. In twenty-four months, a remarkable series of transformations has changed reflexive newborns into insightful problem solvers capable of remembering, planning, and thinking.

New Views of Cognitive Development in Infancy

Recent research has challenged Piaget's theory of cognitive development during infancy (Mandler 1990). As described in the previous section, Piaget viewed the process of cognitive development as occurring over a two-year period. He believed that at the end of the sensorimotor period, infants are able to think using symbolic representation.

New research investigations indicate that sensorimotor foundations begin much earlier than predicted by Piaget. It has been found that infants as young as three months old use perceptual feedback from the motion of objects to determine the object's boundaries (Kellman and Spelke 1983). Evidence of early conceptual representation was demonstrated in another study; nine-month-old infants were found to imitate actions they had observed twenty-four hours before (Meltzoff 1988). Recent work suggests that very young infants are capable of sensory coordination and can conceptualize their perceptual world (Leslie 1988). There is no question that this evidence and the research now taking place will change our view of cognitive development during infancy. Further, it will require a closer look at Piaget's sensorimotor stage.

Current views of infants' developing cognitive capacities have moved toward considering cognitive behaviors as part of a complex internal organization (McCune et al. 1990). Infants' cognitive behaviors derive from an interaction of developmental domains, for example, language, motor, and social domains, combined with their experience with the environment. Specific cognitive behaviors such as memory or object permanence can be measured, and these behaviors result from a dynamic and complex interaction with the world.

Cognitive Assessment Instruments

Historically, researchers attempted to use traditional measures of infant development to predict a child's ability at school age, and even to predict later childhood IQ (Kopp and McCall 1982). The measures of infant development were poor at predicting later school performance (Shonkoff 1983). However, the standardized infant tests encompass more than cognitive skills measures. They include measures of social skills, gross and fine motor behaviors, language, and certain perceptual skills. More recently, studies of specific cognitive abilities such as habituation and visual recognition memory have been found to be more predictive of later IQ than traditional infant assessments (McCall and Carriger 1993; McCall 1994). Procedures for assessing infant information-processing and specific infant cognitive abilities will be discussed in Chapter 5.

In recent years, considerable effort has been devoted to designing measures that assess the cognitive skills of infants with sensory, motor, or intellectual deficits (Garwood and Fewell 1983). In this section, we will review the Piagetian assessment procedures known as ordinal scales, as well as the more traditional scales of infant development. In addition, we will examine some of the more recent approaches to infant assessment.

Before beginning, you should know that there are a number of fundamental differences between traditional infant assessments and more recent approaches involving ordinal scales (see Table 4.1). Traditional infant assessments typically sample a range of behaviors judged to be typical for given chronological age groups. The behaviors measure responses involving social interaction, receptive and expressive language, object play, problem solving, and responses to auditory and visual stimuli. For an infant of eight months, for example, the Bayley Scales of Infant Development (Bayley 1969) measure such items as these: pulls to standing position, combines spoons at midline, uncovers toy, says "da-da." Seemingly, these behaviors interact in various ways to affect cognition.

Ordinal scales, on the other hand, select cognitive items based on their hierarchical relationship to one another. For instance, such items are designated as follows: looks at object, follows moving object with eyes, uncovers hidden object. That is, items within a cognitive domain are selected and sequentially ordered based on their level of difficulty. Ordinal scales can provide more descriptive information about an infant's specific cognitive capabilities. Traditional assessments gather data for an overall developmental profile, whereas ordinal scales gather data on an infant's performance within a particular cognitive domain. With ordinal scales, it is possible to identify the highest cognitive landmark obtained by an infant.

Finally, traditional assessments use standardized administration procedures, whereas ordinal assessments vary scale administration procedures based on the child. Because of the flexibility allowed in administering these tests, ordinal scales are thought to more adequately measure the cognitive abilities of handicapped infants and young children (Langley 1989; Heffernam and Black 1984). We will examine these and other differences between traditional and ordinal scales as particular scales are highlighted in the next section.

TABLE 4.1   Comparison of Ordinal and Traditional Assessments

Ordinal	*Traditional*
Assesses specific areas of cognitive development such as problem solving, imitation, object use, and object permanence.	Assesses many developmental domains including cognition. Domains tested include language, cognition, gross motor, fine motor, and social-emotional.
Provides picture of infant's cognitive capabilities.	Provides picture of overall development.
Contains cognitive task items arranged in hierarchical order.	Contains norm-referenced items. Tasks chosen are typical of a certain chronological age.
Test administration is flexible, with the primary goal of eliciting infant response.	Test administration is standardized, allowing comparison of results with same chronological-age infants.

Traditional Cognitive Assessments

Traditional infant assessment scales are used to measure infants' cognitive abilities. Most traditional infant scales are norm-referenced. This means that a normative sample of children is established that is made up of representative ethnic, gender, and income levels and geographic areas. The average performance of this group is the standard against which the performance of individual children is compared (Bailey and Brochin 1989). Such tests differ from ordinal scales in that their test items are based on behaviors characteristic of statistically derived norm groups, whereas test items for ordinal scales are designed to specifically test cognitive development within Piaget's sensorimotor stages. In addition, compared to ordinal scales, traditional tests provide a view of cognitive development in the context of infants' overall developmental level. In the next section, we will examine several well-known traditional cognitive assessments.

Gesell Developmental Schedules

The Gesell Developmental Schedules (Gesell and Amatruda 1947) were developed by Arnold Gesell and Catherine Amatruda at the Yale University Clinic of Child Development to clinically assess infant development. The Gesell schedules, first published in 1925, were based on longitudinal observations and studies of 107 infants from birth through sixty months in age.

With the publication of the schedules, the first extensive normative data on infant development became available to clinicians and researchers. However, the test was faulted for lacking an extensive normative base. Subsequent refinements of the scales provided standardized procedures to assess the developmental progress of infants and expanded the normative group (Knobloch and Pasamanick 1974). The Gesell schedules were to become the basis for all subsequent infant tests. In fact, items from the original test have been borrowed by other infant test developers.

The Gesell Developmental Schedules were revised in 1974 (Knobloch and Pasamanick 1974) and again in 1980 (Knobloch, Stevens, and Malone 1980). The current Gesell schedules assess development between the ages of four weeks to seventy-two months. Infant performance is measured within five domains of development. They are

1. *Fine Motor:* Measures fine sensorimotor skills such as an infant's ability to grasp and pick up a small cube.
2. *Gross Motor:* Measures postural movements and balance in sitting and holding the head erect. Coordinated motor movements are also included as test items.
3. *Adaptive:* Measures problem-solving abilities.
4. *Language:* Measures infant's communication, whether vocal or facial.
5. *Personal-Social:* Measures infant's responses and behaviors related to the broader social culture. Included are such things as bladder control, feeding skills, and cooperation during play.

Within each domain, infants are observed in a number of situations. Table 4.2 illustrates some sample test situations at the three-, eight-, and fifteen-month levels. The examiner scores the infant's responses in each situation with a + or – symbol, rating the skill as fully acquired or absent. A ++ symbol is used to indicate that the response is advanced for the infant's age, and a + symbol indicates that the skill is emerging. To make such judgments, the examiner needs considerable expertise in evaluating infant behavior.

Following the direct observation, which takes about thirty to forty-five minutes, a questionnaire is completed by parents, who report behaviors that may not have been seen in the observation. A maturity level is estimated for each of the five developmental domains. Finally, a developmental quotient (DQ) is derived by dividing the maturity level by the infant's chronological age.

The Gesell schedules were designed for clinical use, primarily as diagnostic tools (Lewis and Sullivan 1985). As such, the schedules have been utilized extensively in clinical settings to assess infants' developmental status. Although the scale has been criticized for inadequate standardization validity and inadequate reliability tests, it nevertheless is a useful tool for assessing development since it incorporates naturally occurring infant activities into the assessment. Despite the psychometric limitations of the Gesell schedules,

TABLE 4.2   Example of the Gesell Developmental Schedules for Infants at Three, Eight, and Fifteen Months of Age

Age	Motor	Adaptive	Language	Personal/Social
3 months	Pulls at dress Hand predominately open Head set forward or erect Arms symmetrical Lifts head to zone 3	Retains at least briefly Ring: follows 180 degrees Rattle: glances at, in hand Cube, cup: regards more than momentarily	Coos Knows mother Blows bubbles Chuckles	Regards prolongedly Regards in midplane (long head) Vocal-social response
8 months	Sit: 1 min. erect, unsteady Stands: maintains briefly hands held Pellet: unsuccessful inferior scissors grasp	Cube: grasps 2nd cube Cup-cube: holds cube, regards cup Ring-string: secures ring	Vocalizes: single syllable as da, ba, ka	Play: bites, chews toys Play: reaches persistently for toys out of reach Ring-string: persistent
15 months	Walks: few steps, starts and stops Cubes: tower of two Book: helps turn pages	Cup and cubes: six in and out cup Formboard: places round block	Vocabulary: 4–6 words or names Book: pats picture Picture card: points to dog or own shoe	Feeding: has discarded bottle Toilet: partial toilet regulation Play: shows or offers toy to mother or examiner

SOURCE: H. Knobloch, F. Stevens, and A. Malone, *Manual of Developmental Diagnosis: The Administration of the Revised Gesell and Amatruda Development and Neurologic Examination* (New York: Harper and Row, 1980).

they provided clinicians with a rich source of information about infant behaviors and became the prototype for later infant tests.

Cattell Infant Intelligence Scale

The Cattell Infant Intelligence Scale (Cattell 1940; Cattell 1960), unlike the Gesell schedules, was specifically designed to measure the mental ability of infants. Psyche Cattell, dissatisfied with earlier infant scales, set out to improve on them. She intended her scale to be a downward extension of the Stanford-Binet Intelligence Scale. To accomplish this, she used many items from the Gesell Schedules (Whatley 1985). However, personal-social items and gross motor items were eliminated in the belief that they were incidental to mental development in infancy. In addition, Cattell developed more objective procedures for administering and scoring test items.

The Cattell test covers the age range from two to thirty months. At each test level, there are five test items and several alternative items. For the first twelve months, items are grouped into monthly intervals. From twelve to twenty-four months, items are spaced at two-month intervals, and from twenty-four to thirty months, at three-month intervals. From twenty-two to thirty months, Stanford-Binet items are included along with other test items. The Cattell scoring procedure is similar to that of the Stanford-Binet. A basal age is determined initially, and test administration proceeds from there until the infant fails to achieve all the test items at a specific age level; an IQ score is then derived.

Studies of the reliability and validity of the Cattell test revealed disappointing predictive validity scores for infants below two years in age (Escalona and Moriarity 1961). In fact, the predictive coefficients obtained in the early months of life are comparable to other infant tests (Freeman 1962). This led researchers to conclude that the Cattell test is not an adequate downward extension of the Stanford-Binet (Thomas 1970).

Nonetheless, the Cattell test did provide clinicians with an increased understanding of infant mental functions. Currently, however, the test is viewed as limited because of its dated standardization sample, which is unrepresentative of the socioeconomic and ethnic population distribution in the United States.

Bayley Scales of Infant Development

The Bayley Scales of Infant Development first appeared in 1933, when Nancy Bayley published a mental scale, later followed by a motor scale. The scales were based on research from a longitudinal study of infants called the Berkeley Growth Study (Bayley 1933). Bayley borrowed initially from Gesell's schedules and continued to improve the assessment over the next forty years. Standardization of the revised test was done with 1,262 normally developing infants. The 1969 revised scales remained the best standardized infant test available until the 1993 revision and restandardization of the Bayley scales (Bayley 1969; Bayley 1993).

The BSID measures infant development from two months to thirty months. Test items are arranged in order of age placement. Many items can be scored by incidental observation, and the order of item presentation is flexible. Test administration takes approximately forty-five minutes.

The Bayley Scales of Infant Development–Second Edition (BSID-II) retained the mental and motor scales from the original test, with a major revision of the behavior rating scale. The majority of items on the original mental and motor scales was retained, although some items were revised and others were added. Administration of the BSID-II is similar to that of the BSID; however, item "sets" are administered, based on the chronological age of the child. Basal and ceiling levels are established within item sets (Nellis and Gridley 1994). The scales measure development in infants from one to forty-two months old.

The BSID-II consist of three major subscales:

1. *The Mental Scale:* The scale has 178 items, including measures of language, object permanence, problem-solving skills, perceptual-motor integration, imitation, and visual and auditory attention. A mental developmental index (MDI) is derived from the raw score (total number of items passed above and below the basal level).
2. *The Motor Scale:* The scale has 111 gross motor and fine motor items including sitting, walking, grasping objects, and eye-hand/foot coordination. The scores yield a psychomotor developmental index (PDI).
3. *Infant Behavior Record:* This record is completed by the examiner following the assessment and provides a description of the infant's observed behavioral traits. Included in the record are assessments of state of arousal affect, sensitivity to test materials, motor control, activity level, social responsiveness, interest in test items, energy, and approach to or withdrawal from stimulation. The examiner asks two questions of the infant's caregiver: Was the test typical in terms of the infant's affect and activity level? To what extent did the child's performance reflect actual abilities?

Table 4.3 presents sample items from the BSID-II.

Although Bayley's original intent was to design an assessment that would in the early years of an infant's life predict later intellectual performance, the test has limited value as a predictor. The scales do, however, yield useful information about current developmental status. The MDI and PDI are normalized standardized scores with a mean of 100, which allows comparisons of an infant's performance with infants of the same chronological age. It has been suggested that the Bayley scales be renormed since research with

TABLE 4.3   Sample Items from the Bayley Scales of Infant Development–II

Age	Mental Scale Item	Motor Scale Item
7 months	cooperates in games	pulls to standing position
11 months	rings bell purposely	throws ball
14–16 months	names one picture	grasps pencil at the midline
23–25 months	matches four colors	walks forward on a line
32–34 months	compares sizes	walks upstairs alternating feet

SOURCE: N. Bayley, *Bayley Scales of Infant Development 2* (San Antonio, TX: Psychological Corporation, 1993).

twelve-month-old infants has shown that the Bayley scales overestimate infants' cognitive abilities (Campbell et al. 1989).

The BSID has been used to identify infants and young children with mild cognitive delays but has not been as useful with infants with visual, hearing, or motor deficits (Langley 1989). Although they have not been adapted for assessing infants with handicaps, the BSID and BSID-II are commonly used in infant intervention programs to identify functional areas of developmental problems and as a base for planning interventions for exceptional infants (Bagnato and Neisworth 1981).

Battelle Developmental Inventory

The Battelle Developmental Inventory is a relatively new test designed to measure the developmental status of infants and young children (Newborg et al. 1984). The test includes 341 items in five developmental domains: adaptive, personal-social, communication, motor, and cognition. Test administration includes direct observation and interviews. The BDI differs from the Bayley scales in two important ways. First, it covers a broader age range, and its items cover the period from birth to eight years. Second, it includes modifications for administering the test to infants with handicaps. It takes from one to two hours to administer the BDI.

As with the Bayley scales, the standardization of the Battelle reflects current ethnic mix, socioeconomic strata, and other demographic characteristics in the United States. Reliability studies have been judged adequate, although efforts to establish content and construct validity of the test continue (Gibbs 1990).

Overall, the BDI provides a comprehensive assessment of infant and preschool developmental status, and it can be used with infants with disabilities. However, because of its breadth, the number of test items do not provide an adequate in-depth view of a child's developmental status. In addition, the lengthy test time may necessitate several test sessions with an infant.

Infant Mullen Scales of Early Learning (MSEL)

The Infant MSEL is based on a neurodevelopmental model (Mullen 1991). It is divided into five subscales: gross motor base, visual receptive organization, visual expressive organization, language receptive organization, and language expressive organization. The infant's strengths and areas of concern are scored within each scale. Age equivalents and T-scores are provided for each scale. The test range is from birth to thirty-eight months. The Infant MSEL has been standardized based on a U.S. population stratification by race, sex, parental occupation, and geographic location.

Clinicians can use individual scales within the Infant MSEL to assess competencies and areas of weakness in each domain. The test has been useful with at-risk and handicapped populations in assessing and setting intervention goals.

Ordinal Assessment of Sensorimotor Development

The Piagetian approach to infant assessment is rooted in Piaget's theory of sensorimotor development, which covers the period from birth to twenty-four months. As described earlier in this chapter, infants begin this period with simple psychosocial competencies and progress to sophisticated cognitive processes that include problem solving, object relationships, imitation, and symbolic representation. Moreover, infants' cognitive functions emerge in a hierarchical fashion, in that early states serve as the foundation for later, more sophisticated cognitive levels (Piaget 1952).

A Piagetian framework has been used for several measures of sensorimotor intelligence. Included are the Casati-Lezine Scale (Casati and Lezine 1968), the Albert Einstein Scales of Sensorimotor Development (Escalona and Corman 1966), the Uzgiris-Hunt Ordinal Scales of Psychological Development (Uzgiris and Hunt 1975a), and the OBSERVE (Observation of Behavior in Socially and Ecological Relevant and Valid Environments) scale (Dunst and McWilliam 1988).

All of these scales test increasingly complex levels of sensorimotor competence as infants progress through Piaget's six sensorimotor stages. Moreover, the scales measure sensorimotor competence in various cognitive domains such as object relations in space, imitation, means-ends schemes, object permanence, and time. Within the various domains, the scales measure performance in each stage and provide an indication of an infant's level of cognitive development. Because of their hierarchical organization and flexibility in administration, the results from Piagetian ordinal measures are considered more useful than those from traditional assessment approaches for planning cognitive interventions for infants with disabilities (Dunst 1981; Dunst and Gallagher 1983).

Uzgiris-Hunt Ordinal Scales of Psychological Development

The Uzgiris-Hunt Ordinal Scales of Psychological Development (1975), commonly called the Uzgiris-Hunt scales, consist of six subscales, each of which assesses a different cognitive area:

I.   Visual pursuit and the permanence of objects
II. Means for obtaining desired environmental events
III. Development of vocal and gestural imitation
IV. Development of operational causality
V.   Construction of object relations in space
VI. Development of schemes for relating to objects

The Uzgiris-Hunt scales were constructed to obtain a picture of infant cognitive competencies through observations of certain behavioral actions that indicate an infant has attained a particular level of cognitive functioning. These behaviors are not necessarily age related but do occur in an invariant sequence. The sequence is hierarchical in that higher levels of cognitive behaviors are derived from earlier and lower levels. The development of object permanence is a good example of a hierarchical behavioral sequence. Whereas infants will not actively search for a hidden object during Substage 1, by Substage 4, infants will retrieve an object hidden within their view. At Substage 6, they will conduct an organized search for a hidden object. They will look first in one place and then in another until the object is found. Table 4.4 shows several tasks from the Uzgiris-Hunt Subscale I used to measure visual pursuit and object permanence. Note the hierarchical order, both within and across the tasks. On each subscale, the test items consist of situations called eliciting situations, which are designed to elicit certain responses from the infant (Gorrell 1985). The test directions specify the types of toys, objects, or movements to be used and give instructions on how they are to be presented. The infant's response, known as critical behavior, is recorded from one of the choices listed in the test protocol. Since the test items are ordered in terms of level of complexity, the infant's critical action on the most difficult test item indicates level of cognitive achievement in each subscale. The six subscales are administered and scored independently. The average of the highest scores across the six subscales is the overall cognitive score for the test.

The six subscales that make up the Uzgiris-Hunt Scales are described in Table 4.5.

Dunst (1980) designed record forms based on the Uzgiris-Hunt scales for clinical assessment of infants at risk for developmental disabilities. These record forms indicate whether an infant is showing a typical or an atypical pattern of cognitive development and whether sensorimotor performance is

TABLE 4.4   Sample Items from the Uzgiris-Hunt Ordinal Scale of Psychological Development (1975)

Object Permanence

1. Noticing the disappearance of a slowly moving object
    a. Does not follow to point of disappearance
    b. Loses interest as soon as object disappears
    c. Lingers with glance on point of disapperance
    d. Returns glance to starting point after several presentations
    e. Searches around point of disappearance
    f. Other:
2. Finding an object that is partially covered
    a. Loses interest
    b. Reacts to the loss, but does not obtain object
    c. Obtains the object
    d. Other:
3. Finding an object that is completely covered
    a. Loses interest
    b. Reacts to loss, but does not obtain object
    c. Pulls screen, but not enough to obtain object
    d. Pulls screen off and obtains object

SOURCE: I. Uzgiris and J. McV. Hunt, *Assessment in Infancy: Ordinal Scales of Psychological Development* (Urbana: University of Illinois Press, 1975).

delayed. The forms are designed to yield an estimated developmental age (EDA) for each of the six subscales. An infant's performance on each of the scales can then be compared, and an overall average performance level can be estimated (Dunst, Holbert, and Wilson 1990).

A recently developed assessment strategy based on Piagetian principles measures infants' interactive competence (Dunst and McWilliam 1988). The assessment, called the OBSERVE scale, is designed to measure the level and types of interactive competencies in everyday situations. This assessment assumes that an infant's interactive abilities, such as the capacity to imitate others, manifesting attentional behaviors to others, and contingency interactions, are indicators of sensorimotor cognition. These interactive abilities are considered representative of cognition because the child adapts to the environment and initiates and controls interactions that require differentiated elaboration.

The OBSERVE test measures five interactive competencies:

1. *Attentional Interactions:* Described as attentional ability and capacity to distinguish between stimuli. Examples: smiling at a particular person, looking at an object, opening eyes wide when hearing a familiar voice.

TABLE 4.5   Test Item Examples from the Six Subscales in the Uzgiris-Hunt Scales

Scale I.   Visual Pursuit and the Permanence of Objects
Through visual scanning and attending to environmental changes or moving objects, children learn to look for objects in a systematic way. This scale measures how infants organize a visual search and how they use appropriate responses to find hidden objects.

Example (Dunst 1980)

Eliciting Context	Infant's Critical Behavior
visible displacement	secures partially hidden object
visual tracking	returns glance to position above the head after object moves out of the visual field
visual tracking	reverses searching for object in anticipation of reappearance—child seated on parent's lap

Scale II.   Means for Obtaining Desired Environmental Events
How infants achieve goals through problem solving is the major function assessed in this scale. At first, infants use physical gestures to problem solve and then move to symbolic representation via language to achieve a goal. The scale measures motor behaviors and then tool use in problem solving. At the higher scale levels, the degree of goal-directed behavior and reasoning are evaluated.

Example (Dunst 1980)

Eliciting Context	Infant's Critical Behavior
string (horizontal)	pulls string along a horizontal surface to obtain an object attached to it
stick	uses a stick as a tool to obtain an out-of-reach object

Scale III.   Development of Vocal and Gestural Imitation
Imitation skills are essential to learning to use language and to engage in complex action sequences that are not directly observed. The ability to imitate—simple gestures and sounds at first and then more complex sound patterns and gestures—is evaluated in this scale. The use of mental images in symbolic play and problem solving is also assessed.

Example (Dunst 1980)

Eliciting Context	Infant's Critical Behavior
cooing sounds	imitates cooing sounds
unfamiliar sound patterns	vocalizes in response to unfamiliar sound patterns (examples: room-room, ree-ree, ding-dong, brr, ssss, zzzz)

(continues)

TABLE 4.5   *(continued)*

Scale IV.   Development of Operational Causality
A key ability of cognition is to search for what causes an event or problem. In early infancy, an infant will accidentally move an object through random movements and not connect the action with the object's movement. Later, the infant will begin to realize that he or she caused the movement and will repeat the action to move that object. In another example, the infant of 8 months gleefully rings a bell then turns it over to look for the sound source. Anticipation in game playing with adults is another indication that infants have incorporated causality into their cognitive functioning. Assessing causality includes measuring infants' repetition of pleasurable activities and their ability to determine the cause or source of an event.

Example (Dunst 1980)

Eliciting Context	*Infant's Critical Behavior*
engages adult	pushes or pulls an adult's hand to have a behavior instigated or repeated
spectacle created by toy	attempts to activate mechanical toy following demonstration

Scale V.   The Construction of Object Relations in Space
Learning to manipulate objects in space is essential to understanding spatial relationships. Initially, infants attend to one object at a time. Over time, they move from this status to being able to manipulate several objects at once to attain goals. This scale assesses infants' progress through this transition. It measures infants' visual-auditory search for objects and their ability to recognize and use the functional side of an object and make correct judgments regarding three-dimensional spatial relationships.

Example (Dunst 1980)

Eliciting Context	*Infant's Critical Behavior*
sound localization	localizes the source of sound
combining objects	stirs with a spoon in a cup
combining objects	builds tower of two cubes

Scale VI.   Development of Schemes for Relating to Objects
Through mouthing, banging, and otherwise handling objects, infants acquire knowledge of objects and their functions. Later, they use objects symbolically in pretend play. Manipulating objects to use them functionally is measured in this scale.

Example (Dunst 1980)

Eliciting Context	*Infant's Critical Behavior*
letting go	drops or throws objects—no visual monitoring of action
showing	shows object to another person to instigate social interaction

SOURCE: C. J. Dunst, *A Clinical and Educational Manual for Use with the Uzgiris and Hunt Scales of Infant Psychological Development* (Austin, TX: Pro-Ed Corporation, 1980).

2. *Contingency Interactions:* Responses, usually repetitive, used to initiate and control environmental events. These are often interesting and reinforcing for the infant. Examples: kicking a mobile to make it move, rolling a ball, smiling/vocalizing to get someone's attention.
3. *Differentiated Interactions:* Infant's ability to modify and coordinate behaviors in a way that moves toward conventional socialized behaviors. These are often trial-and-error actions. Examples: locomotion to obtain a desired object, pointing, attempts to take off or put on clothes.
4. *Encoded Interactions:* Refers to the ability to use conventionalized forms of behaviors that reflect a culturally bound set of rules. Examples: verbal communication and pretend play, such as putting a doll to bed.
5. *Symbolic Interactions:* Child's ability to use words, drawings, sign language, and pretend play to communicate information. The use of symbolism characterizes this capability. Examples: symbolic behaviors, describing an encounter that happened previously.

Criterion-Referenced Assessments

Criterion-referenced assessments are assessments based on content that is defined in terms of some specific performance skills against which an individual child's performance can be determined (Lynch 1996). Criterion-referenced measures usually have an extensive number of content items. Criterion-referenced assessments incorporate tasks drawn from norm-referenced assessments as well as items that assess functional skills such as feeding and toileting. Children are measured on their ability to meet the criteria of mastering items. Based on their performance, they are judged to be proficient or nonproficient at performing the task. For example, a criterion might be set that says if the child masters 80 percent of the test items, he or she reaches the criterion of success.

Criterion-referenced tests contain a number of task items that reflect the developmental skills expected of an infant at a certain age. Unlike norm-referenced tests that assess the developmental level of infants as compared to same-age peers, the criterion-referenced assessment measures an infant's performance on particular skills. A criterion of performance is set for passing an item; for instance, an infant points to one of three colors shown or picks up an inverted cup to reach a small object. When the infant is able to reach that criterion, then the item is passed.

By using a criterion-referenced assessment, it is possible to obtain a profile of an infant's ability without comparing the infant's performance to others' performance. An advantage of criterion-referenced assessment is that overall measures of an infant's strengths and weaknesses can be obtained. This feature is particularly advantageous when reporting results to parents of disabled infants, since the infant's strengths and weaknesses can be discussed rather than the level of developmental delay.

Although criterion-referenced assessments alone are not generally used to determine infants' eligibility for intervention services, they are used sometimes in conjunction with a standardized, norm-referenced test for placement decisions. Infant intervention programs typically use criterion-referenced assessments as ongoing measures of infants' progress in attaining specific skills.

A special form of the criterion-referenced assessment is the curriculum-referenced assessment. This type of assessment is designed to match the curricular objective with the infant curriculum used in an infant intervention program. Some well-known criterion-referenced assessments include the following: the Brigance Diagnostic Inventory of Early Development (Brigance 1978), the Early Learning Accomplishment Profile for Infants (Sanford 1981), and the Carolina Curriculum for Handicapped Infants and Infants at Risk (Johnson-Martin, Jens, and Attermeier 1986). See Table 4.6 for an example of a curriculum item from the Carolina curriculum.

Summary

Over the past fifty years, the development of infant cognition has captured the interest of researchers and clinicians. The Swiss psychologist Jean Piaget identified a progression of cognitive events during infancy that brought infants from reflexive beings at birth to active problem solvers by two years of age, a period of cognitive development that Piaget termed the *sensorimotor* stage. The stage contains six substages, each of which is characterized by the infant's passing certain major cognitive milestones such as active experimentation or use of symbolic play.

The Piagetian approach has been used as a basis for assessing infants' sensorimotor intellectual behaviors (Dunst 1982). Generally, tests that employ the Piagetian framework are called ordinal scales. Ordinal scales assess infant competence in several cognitive areas. Each area is assessed independently, and the assessment items are ordered from simple to complex. The higher-level cognitive tasks are assumed to be derived from the simpler cognitive items. A widely used Piagetian assessment is the Uzgiris-Hunt Ordinal Scales of Psychological Development. It consist of six scales, each of which measure a separate cognitive domain.

Traditional infant tests also measure infant cognitive development. These tests assess the overall developmental status of infants. Normed infant behavior scales were first used in the Gesell schedules. One of the most recent traditional infant assessments is the Battelle Developmental Inventory.

TABLE 4.6   Sample Curriculum Items from the Carolina Curriculum for Handicapped Infants and Infants at Risk

---

Item

Looks to the correct place when object is hidden in 1 of 2 places.

Procedure

Place 2 crumpled cloths or 2 containers in front of the child. Take a toy and let the child hold it. Rub it against the child or otherwise get child to focus attention on it.

Place the toy under one of the covers as you talk about what you are doing (be sure child watches what you do).

Call child by name and try to get him or her to look at you; then say, "Where is the ———?" If child looks at the right cover, take it off and give the toy to him or her, rub the child with it, or do whatever is pleasing to the child.

Repeat several times, randomly changing the side under which the toy is hidden. *Do not just alternate sides.*

If child does not look at the right cover, say, "Uh-oh, that's not where it is," lift the other cover, and show the child. Lower the cover slowly, and ask again where it is. Make sure child is watching!

Evaluation

Record—if the child
(1) Looks to the correct cover under which object has been hidden after a correction by the teacher; and
(2) Looks to the correct cover without a correction.

Criterion

Child looks to correct cover 4 of 5 trials on 3 separate days

---

SOURCE: N. Johnson-Martin, K. G. Jens, and S. M. Attermeier, *The Carolina Curriculum for Infants and Toddlers with Special Needs* (Johnson-Martin, Jens, Attermeier, and Hacker, 1981).

Several traditional tests such as the Cattell Infant Intelligence Scale and the Bayley Scales of Infant Development were designed to predict later intelligence from infant measures. Although the goal of predicting intelligence was never reached, these tests nevertheless provide comprehensive assessments of infant development. Currently, investigators are examining how specific cognitive skills are related to later intelligence.

Criterion-referenced assessments assess an infant's capacity to attain specific developmental skills by using criteria. This type of assessment is most frequently used to measure the developmental progress of disabled infants in infant intervention programs.

References

Bagnato, S. J., and J. T. Neisworth. 1981. *Linking Developmental Assessment and Curricula.* Rockville, MD: Aspen.

Bailey, D. B., and H. A. Brochin. 1989. Tests and test development. In *Assessing Infants and Preschoolers with Handicaps,* edited by D. B. Bailey and M. Wolery. Columbus, OH: Merrill.

Bayley, N. 1993. *Bayley Scales of Infant Development.* 2d ed. San Antonio, TX: Psychological Corporation.

_____. 1969. *Bayley Scales of Infant Development.* New York: Psychological Corporation.

_____. 1933. Mental growth during the first three years. *Genetic Psychology Monographs* 14:1–92.

Brigance, A. H. 1978. *Brigance Diagnostic Inventory of Early Development.* North Billerica, MA: Curriculum Associates.

Brooks-Gunn, J., and M. Weinraub. 1983. Origins of infant intelligence tests. In *Origins of Intelligence,* edited by M. Lewis. New York: Plenum.

Campbell, S. K., E. Siegel, C. A. Parr, and C. T. Ramey. 1989. Evidence for the need to renorm the Bayley Scales of Infant Development based on the performance of a population-based sample of 12 month-old infants. *Topics in Early Childhood Special Education* 6:83–96.

Casati, L., and I. Lezine. 1968. *Les étapes de l'intelligence sensorimoteur.* Paris: Editions de Centre de Psychologie Appliqué.

Cattell, P. 1960. *Cattell Infant Intelligence Scale.* Cleveland: Psychological Corporation.

_____. 1940. *The Measurement of Intelligence of Infants and Young Children.* New York: Psychological Corporation.

Dunst, C. J. 1982. The clinical utility of Piagetian-based scales of infant development. *Infant Mental Health Journal* 3:259–275.

_____. 1981. *Infant Learning: A Cognitive, Linguistic Strategy.* Allen, TX: DLM Resources.

_____. 1980. *A Clinical and Educational Manual for Use with the Uzgiris and Hunt Scales of Infant Psychological Development.* Austin, TX: Pro-Ed Corporation.

Dunst, C. J., and J. L. Gallagher. 1983. Piagetian approaches to infant assessment. *Topics in Early Childhood Special Education* 3(1):44–62.

Dunst, C. J., K. A. Holbert, and L. L. Wilson. 1990. Strategies for assessing infant sensorimotor interactive competencies. In *Interdisciplinary Assessment of Infants,* edited by E. D. Gibbs and D. M. Teti. Baltimore: Paul H. Brookes.

Dunst, C. J., and R. A. McWilliam. 1988. Cognitive assessment of multiply handicapped young children. In *Assessment of Developmentally Disabled Children,* edited by T. D. Wachs and R. Sheehan. New York: Plenum Press.

Escalona, S., and H. Corman. 1966. Albert Einstein Scales of Sensorimotor Development. Albert Einstein College of Medicine, Department of Psychiatry, New York.

Escalona, S. K., and A. Moriarty. 1961. Prediction of school-age intelligence from infant tests. *Child Development* 32:597–605.

Freeman, F. S. 1962. *Theory and Practice of Psychological Testing.* 3d ed. New York: Holt, Rinehart and Winston.

Garwood, S. C., and R. R. Fewell. 1983. *Educating Handicapped Infants.* Rockville, MD: Aspen Publishers.

Gesell, A. 1925. *The Mental Growth of the Preschool Child.* New York: Macmillan.

Gesell, A., and C. S. Amatruda. 1947. *Developmental Diagnosis.* New York: Hoeber.

Gibbs, E. D. 1990. Assessment of mental ability. In *Interdisciplinary Assessment of Infants,* edited by E. D. Gibbs and D. M. Teti. Baltimore: Paul H. Brookes.

Gorrell, J. 1985. Ordinal Scales of Psychological Development. In *Test Critique.* Vol. 2. Edited by D. J. Keyser and R. C. Sweetland. Kansas City, MO: Test Corporation of America.

Heffernam, L., and F. W. Black. 1984. Use of the Uzgiris and Hunt Scales with handicapped infants: Concurrent validity of the Dunst age norms. *Journal of Psychoeducational Assessment* 2:159–168.

Johnson-Martin, N., K. G. Jens, and S. M. Attermeier. 1986. *The Carolina Curriculum for Handicapped Infants and Infants at Risk.* Baltimore: Paul H. Brookes.

Kellman, P. J., and E. S. Spelke. 1983. Perception of partly occluded objects in infancy. *Cognitive Psychology* 15:483–524.

Knobloch, H., and B. Pasamanick. 1974. *Gesell and Amatruda's Developmental Diagnosis: The Evaluation and Management of Normal and Abnormal Neuropsychologic Development in Infancy and Early Childhood.* New York: Harper and Row.

Knobloch, H., F. Stevens, and A. Malone. 1980. *Manual of Developmental Diagnosis: The Administration of the Revised Gesell and Amatruda Development and Neurologic Examination.* New York: Harper and Row.

Kopp, C. B., and R. B. McCall. 1982. Predicting later mental performance for normal, at-risk, and handicapped infants. In *Life-Span Development and Behavior.* Vol. 4. Edited by P. B. Baltes and O. G. Brin, Jr. New York: Academic Press.

Langley, M. B. 1989. Assessing infant cognitive development. In *Assessing Infants and Preschoolers with Handicaps,* edited by D. B. Bailey and M. Wolery. Columbus, OH: Merrill.

Leslie, A. 1988. The necessity of illusions: Perception and thought in infancy. In *Thought Without Language,* edited by L. Weisbrantz. Oxford, England: Clarendon Press.

Lewis, M., and M. W. Sullivan. 1985. Infant intelligence and its assessment. In *Handbook of Intelligence: Theories, Measurements, and Applications,* edited by B. B. Wolman. New York: John Wiley and Sons.

Lynch, E. W. 1996. Assessing infants: Child and family issues and approaches. In *Atypical Infant Development,* 2d ed., edited by M. J. Hanson. Austin, TX: Pro-Ed.

Mandler, J. M. 1990. A new perspective on cognitive development in infancy. *American Screentest* 78:236–243.

McCall, R. B. 1994. What process mediates predictions of childhood IQ from infant habituation and recognition memory? Speculations on the role of inhibition and rate of information processing. *Intelligence* 18:107–126.

McCall, R. B., and C. W. Mash. 1995. Infant cognition and its relation to mature intelligence. In *Annals of Child Development.* Vol. 10. Edited by R. Vasta. New York: Jessica Kingsley Publishers.

McCall, R. B., and M. S. Carriger. 1993. A meta-analysis of infant habituation and recognition memory performance as predictors of later IQ. *Child Development* 64:57–79.

McCune, L., B. Kalmanson, M. B. Fleck, B. Gazewski, and J. Sillori. 1990. An interdisciplinary model of infant assessment. In *Handbook of Early Childhood Intervention*, edited by S. J. Meisels and J. P. Shonkoff. New York: Cambridge University Press.

Meltzoff, A. N. 1988. Infant imitation and memory: Nine-month-olds in immediate and deferred tests. *Child Development* 59:217–225.

Mullen, E. M. 1991. *The Infant Mullen Scales of Early Learning: Instrument Descriptions*. Cranston, RI: T.O.T.A.L. Child.

Nellis, L., and B. E. Gridley. 1994. Review of the Bayley Scales of Infant Development. 2d ed. *Journal of School Psychology* 32:201–209.

Newborg, J., J. R. Stock, L. Wnek, J. Guidubaldi, and J. Svinick. 1984. *Battelle Developmental Inventory*. Allen, TX: DLM Teaching Resources.

Piaget, J. 1954. *The Construction of Reality in the Child*. New York: Basic Books.

_____. 1952. *The Origins of Intelligence in Children*. New York: International Universities Press.

Rossetti, L. M. 1990. *Infant-Toddler Assessment*. Boston: Little, Brown and Company.

Sanford, A. 1981. *Learning Accomplishment Profile for Infants (Early LAP)*. Winston-Salem, NC: Kaplan School Supply.

Shonkoff, J. 1983. The limitation of normative assessment of high-risk infants. *Topics in Early Childhood Special Education* 3:29–43.

Thomas, H. 1970. Psychological assessment instruments for use with human infants. *Merrill-Palmer Quarterly* 16:179–224.

Uzgiris, I., and J. McV. Hunt. 1975a. *Assessment in Infancy*. Urbana: University of Illinois Press.

_____. 1975b. *Assessment in Infancy: Ordinal Scales of Psychological Development*. Urbana: University of Illinois Press.

Whatley, J. 1985. Cattell Infant Intelligence Scale. In *Test Critiques*. Vol. 4. Edited by D. J. Keyser and R. C. Sweetland. Kansas City, MO: Test Corporation.

5

Assessing Information Processing

Indeed nothing gets into the mind save what comes through the senses—save, of course, mind itself.

—*Jerome Bruner*

Introduction

How do babies learn? When do they begin to process information? In what ways do they gather and assimilate information from the world around them? How are their perceptual and cognitive abilities involved in thinking? These questions are currently being asked by researchers proposing an innovative approach to infant assessment (Zelazo 1986). Their procedures, called the information-processing approach, represent a challenge to traditional infant assessments.

Since traditional infant assessments have poor predictive validity and rely heavily on infants' sensorimotor abilities, some investigators argue that assessment strategies that tap infants' central processing abilities may offer a more useful assessment paradigm. They argue that because traditional assessments use measures of attention, recognition memory, and habituation, they can bypass the problems of delayed expressive development, as with conventional assessments such as the Bayley scales. Therefore, measures of central processing abilities will provide better indicators of infants' mental abilities. Scientists searched for early predictors of later IQ and concluded that because of the qualitative changes in the nature of intelligence from infancy into childhood, standardized developmental assessments could not be used as predictive measures. More recently, researchers have concluded that if habituation and recognition memory performance are assessed at age one, later IQ at eight years of age can be predicted (McCall and Carriger 1993). Such measures have been found to be useful in predicting later mental performance for at-risk and handicapped infant populations.

The information-processing assessment can be especially advantageous when assessing cognitive development in infants and young children with developmental delays. For example, infants with severe motoric delays often do poorly on conventional tests because of these tests' reliance on sensorimotor performance. These tests often require that infants make coordinated movements to perform perceptual or cognitive tasks. Infants with delays may be able to perceive a visual configuration or be able to problem solve, but their intrasensory coordination may inhibit them in performing the task so much that adequate measurement of their cognitive or perceptual skills cannot be made.

The information-processing assessment method is an outgrowth of the research on infant memory and perception. Studies of infants' perceptual and cognitive capacities have yielded impressive results. Infants, for example, are able to selectively attend to environmental stimuli. They respond to visual patterns that differ in complexity and can distinguish novel from familiar visual and auditory patterns (Fantz 1964). Moreover, infants are able to visually recognize objects that they have only touched and have never seen (Rose and Wallace 1985). Finally, information-processing abilities, including attention to auditory and visual events, become increasingly sophisticated as infants mature (Brezsnyak 1994).

In this chapter, we will explore information-processing techniques used to measure the cognitive and perceptual capacities of infants. Research on infant perceptual skills will be discussed. Differences between nontraditional information-processing procedures and traditional infant assessments will be described. The usefulness of information-processing procedures with infants at risk for development will be examined.

Upon completion of this chapter, you should be able to

- Describe several procedures used to measure infants' information-processing abilities
- Contrast the differences between information-processing procedures and traditional infant assessments
- Outline the usefulness of information-processing procedures in assessing intellectual capacities of high-risk infants

Rationale for Information-Processing Procedures: Background

In recent years nontraditional infant assessment methodologies have emerged. These procedures are based on research methods used to investigate infant visual and auditory processing. Information-processing procedures generally measure infants' attentional responses to environmental stimuli. Information-processing procedures have been used to study perceptual-cognitive processing, object permanence, number perception, and speech perception (Spelke et al. 1991; Baillargeon 1993), as well as age-related changes in information-processing. More recently, these procedures have been used to assess behaviors in infants at risk for developmental delay (Ramey et al. 1996). In contrast to conventional tests of infant-toddler cognitive functioning, information-processing tests measure ways that infants recognize, comprehend, and categorize visual, tactile, and auditory information.

The study of infant information-processing abilities originated in the work of Robert Fantz in the 1950s. Fantz (1956) developed a special "looking chamber" to test the visual interest of infants. Fantz's looking chamber and variations on the chamber were subsequently used in a number of studies to observe whether infants looked at particular visual stimuli, how long they looked, and whether they preferred one stimulus over another (Fantz 1963, 1965). This procedure was labeled the visual preference technique. Findings on infants' perception of complex patterns further advanced understanding of infant visual perception (Berlyne 1958). When presented with two checkerboard patterns with different numbers of squares in their patterns, infants preferred the more complex pattern (Berlyne 1958). Other studies illustrated infants' ability to recognize facial patterns during the first seven months of life. Subsequent research demonstrated that five-month-old infants are able to make subtle discriminations among face photographs (Fagan 1972). More than anything, this research focused on infants' abilities to sort and process visual information. As a result, infants' remarkable perceptual and cognitive talents were clearly substantiated.

In the 1960s and 1970s, visual preference research proliferated (Banks and Ginsburg 1985). Researchers looked at aspects of visual stimuli that caused one pattern to be preferred over another (Karmel and Maisel 1975). Infants, for example, were found to look longer at a polygon with several angles than at one with few or many angles (Kagan 1974). Several theories were formulated to explain findings about early visual preferences (Kagan 1970; Karmel 1969). During this period, infant visual behavior was increasingly becoming being viewed as an index of neurological organization, and for the first time in history, infants were described as information-seeking organisms. Selected findings from both early and more current investigations are summarized here. Francis Horowitz et al. (1972) found that infants as young as two months in age demonstrate face perception. Two-month-old infants were found to be able to discriminate among diagrams of faces, both scrambled and unscrambled (Maurer and Barrera 1981). By the time infants are three months old, they are able to discriminate among photographs of their mothers' and fathers' faces and photos of strangers' faces (Barrera and Maurer 1981). When patterns or faces move, infants look at them longer than they do at stationary patterns (Samuels 1985). Apparently, infants use object movements to discern whether or not an object is three-dimensional (Yonas, Arterberry, and Granrud 1987). By seven months, they are able to utilize visual cues to judge depth (Granrud, Yonas, and Opland 1985). Very young infants react in a meaningful fashion to the approach of looming objects. That is, they move their arms and hands defensively, blink their eyes, and move their head backward in response to a looming situation (Yonas, Pettersen, and Lockman 1979).

The results of the voluminous research on infant visual perception indicate clearly that infants detect and process visual information. Further, their abilities to discriminate among visual properties, recognize objects from different orientations, and process visual information become increasingly sophisticated as they mature and interact with the world around them. Other research has demonstrated a continuum of learning and memory abilities originating in the neonatal period and becoming focused and more organized as infancy progresses. Arnold Sameroff and Patrick Cavanagh (1979) found that newborns as young as two to three days old could be classically conditioned. Evidence of newborn memory has been shown in demonstrations of habituation (Friedman 1972; Friedman, Bruno, and Vietze 1974). In the first few months of life, infants improve their learning and memory abilities. At five months, they show long-term retention of much of what they have learned (Fagan 1973). As they mature, infants are able to recognize details of previously seen patterns and use subtle stimuli cues for memory recognition (Olson 1976). Such findings have provided the impetus for the development of infant information-processing procedures to assess cognitive development.

Information-Processing Paradigms

The ability of infants to detect and abstract information from their environment is called information processing. This can involve memory mechanisms, attention, habituation to stimuli, and conditioning (Rosenblith 1992). Basic research on infant information processing has yielded techniques considered to hold promise as alternatives to traditional developmental measures. Information-processing methods can be used in situations where traditional test batteries are not appropriate. These procedures are relatively simple, and assessment is based for the most part on observations or recordings of infants' attentional responses. Because infants are not required to perform a particular task, these tests are thought to be better suited for infants with motoric and developmental handicaps (Sigman et al. 1992).

The idea that information-processing procedures tap central processing functions has led researchers to propose that these methods may yield more accurate indicators of later intelligence. Support for the predictive validity of information-processing procedures has come from studies of infant recognition memory (Fagan and Singer 1983; Singer and Fagan 1992; Bornstein 1989) and from the Standard-Transformation-Return (STR) procedure (Zelazo et al. 1989). Since traditional assessments have been useful for predicting intelligence only for low-functioning infants, information processing may prove useful in identifying both high- and low-functioning infants. Therefore, Peter Vietze and Deborah Coates (1986) have proposed that several information-processing paradigms would be useful as a test battery for infants at risk for mental retardation.

A number of information-processing techniques are described in this section. Habituation and conditioning are basic forms of learning used to measure early infant cognitive skills and have been useful in programming intervention strategies for at-risk infants. Visual recognition memory and the standard-transformation-return paradigm have been used to measure infants' central processing abilities.

Habituation Paradigm

A novel stimulus such as a sound, odor, or flashing light will probably get our attention. Our increased attention, called an *orienting response,* can be measured physiologically because our heart rate slows down, our pupils dilate, and there is increased muscle tension. But if the stimulus is presented over and over again, our attention to it decreases. This change, too, is reflected in changes in our heart rate, pupils, and muscle tension. The decrease in response to the repeated stimulus is known as *habituation.*

Suppose also that once we have been habituated to one stimulus, another stimulus is introduced. Our attention will again be aroused, this time in response to the new stimulus. The recovery of attention to the novel stimulus is called *dishabituation.*

The habituation paradigm has been used to measure infants' learning and memory. The process is relatively simple. Usually, either auditory or visual stimuli are used to determine habituation. Infants are repeatedly exposed to a target stimulus such as a pattern, form, face, or sound. Their attention (the orienting response) is monitored, and when their looking or attending to the first target drops (habituation) to 50 percent of their initial response, a new target is introduced. If attention is increased for the new target (dishabituation), it is inferred that the infants encoded and habituated the first stimulus and discriminated between the two stimuli.

Whereas many habituation procedures employ visual stimuli, the high-amplitude sucking procedure is a technique frequently used with auditory stimuli. In this procedure, an infant sucks on a pacifier outfitted with a pressure transducer. A novel sound stimulus is presented for as long as the infant continues to suck at a certain rate. When the sucking drops below that rate, the stimulus is discontinued and a new stimulus introduced. If the rate of sucking increases, the infant is believed to have detected the stimulus change. Measures such as the rate of response decrement, the amount of response recovery in the dishabituation phase, and the types of stimuli most likely to be habituated may yield information about infant attention and discriminative abilities.

Habituation and dishabituation have been documented in studies of newborns and infants (Slater, Morison, and Rose 1984; Von Bargen 1983).

Loud sounds presented to newborns result in decreased cardiac response over repeated trials (Bartoshuk 1962). Newborns have been shown to habituate to visual stimuli such as checkerboard patterns. Newborns older than three days habituate faster than newborns younger than three days (Friedman and Carpenter 1971).

Infant habituation studies have shown that habituation rates differ depending on several factors. Individual differences in the rate of habituation can be influenced by the type of stimulus presented and the infant's characteristics. Infants who habituate quickly at three months tend to be fast habituators when retested at six months (Colombo et al. 1987). And an infant's arousal state affects habituation (Lewis and Goldberg 1968). The quiet alert state is necessary for habituation to occur. Maturation also affects habituation. Newborns' habituation rates are slower than the habituation rates of three-month-olds, whose rates in turn are slower than the rates of six-month-olds (Mayes and Kessen 1989; Bornstein 1985). Finally, male and female infants differ in their response to the repetition of stimuli. Female infants need more stimuli repetitions before they stop responding (Cornell and Strauss 1973).

Differences in rates of habituation have been demonstrated with infants who have experienced high-risk prenatal or perinatal conditions. Barry Lester (1975) found that infants malnourished prenatally have slow response decrements and do not habituate as early as normal infants. Other researchers have found that habituation rates are correlated with disorganized states, illness, and perinatal risk factors (Moss et al. 1988).

The infant habituation paradigm has been used in assessing attention in normal infants and has been proposed as a useful technique to assess information processing in infants who are likely to be cognitively delayed (Cohen 1981; Cohen and Younger 1983; Vietze 1986).

The habituation-dishabituation paradigm was employed to assess possible differences in habituation between normal infants and infants with Down syndrome (Cohen 1981). When presented with visual patterns that differed in color and form, the two groups differed in overall fixation time and in habituation and dishabituation. Infants with Down syndrome did not habituate at nineteen weeks; at twenty-three weeks, they habituated but did not differentiate between two visual patterns; and at twenty-eight weeks, they habituated and dishabituated. In contrast, normal infants at all three ages habituated to the first visual stimulus and dishabituated when a novel stimulus was introduced. Results similar to those for infants with Down syndrome were obtained when visual habituation and dishabituation were measured with lower-class infants with biological or environmental risk factors. These findings point to the promise of the habituation paradigm in assessing infants at risk for development.

Conditioning Paradigm

Conditioning is one of the oldest assessment procedures used to measure infants' learning. The question as to whether newborns and young infants learn has been answered affirmatively via conditioning studies. Conditioning procedures have been used effectively to measure learning in individual infants. Because of the control that is possible in conditioning, the procedure is sensitive in detecting the abilities of individual infants. Conditioning methods are widely employed in infant intervention programs as an intervention tool for infants with disabilities. However, because of the cost, time, and complexities associated with its administration, conditioning is not generally used as an assessment of cognitive abilities.

Conditioning is the process whereby an association is learned between two events. The association results in a change in behavior. That change in behavior is the element that is measured to determine whether learning has taken place. There are two common types of conditioning, *classical* and *operant*. Both are considered basic forms of learning. Infants have been shown to be capable of using both of these conditioning paradigms.

Classical Conditioning.   Classical conditioning is the learning of an association between two unrelated events. In classical conditioning, there must be an unconditioned stimulus (UCS) that evokes a response called the unconditioned response (UCR). In the case of infancy, a puff of air in the infant's eye results in a blink. When the UCS is repeatedly paired with a new stimulus, called the conditioned stimulus (CS), an association between the two stimuli is learned. When the CS alone is presented, it will then elicit a response similar to the UCR, called the conditioned response (CR). In our example, if a puff of air (UCS) is made to occur at the same time as a low soft tone (CS) is presented, over time the tone alone will elicit an eye blink (CR).

Ivan Pavlov (1927) first discovered the phenomenon through systematic environmental manipulation with dogs. He discovered that previously neutral stimuli, for example, a bell ringing, could be paired with the salivary response in hungry dogs when food was presented to them. After several pairings of the UCS (food) and CS (bell), the dogs would salivate (CR) at the sound of the bell. Classical conditioning was studied in human infants to determine whether they are capable of learning associations between certain stimuli (Fitzgerald and Brackbill 1976). One of the earliest studies of classical conditioning in infants was conducted by Dorothy Marquis in 1931. She attempted to condition the feeding response of neonates two to nine days old by pairing a buzzer with the sight of the feeding bottle. In a later study, classical conditioning was attempted with fetuses in utero (Spelt 1948). Despite the experimenters' reports of newborn and fetal conditioning, the studies have been called into question because they lacked adequate controls (Sameroff 1972). More recent evidence of neonatal conditioning has been demonstrated using better-controlled experimental conditions (Blass, Ganchrow, and Steiner 1984; Cantor, Fishchel, and Kaye 1983). These reports indicate that classical conditioning in the neonatal period can take place, though within limited conditions. As infants develop, their behavioral repertoire and responsiveness allow them to be more easily conditioned.

Although most of the research on classical conditioning in human infants has been directed at the earliest age possible for conditioning, infants past the newborn stage can be classically conditioned. Infants have been shown to associate several stimuli and regulate their heart rate depending on the stimuli presented to them (Fitzgerald and Porges 1971). Hans Papousek (1967) compared the speed of learning among infants of different ages. Five-month-old babies conditioned faster than three-month-olds and newborns. Other conditioning studies have provided evidence of temporal conditioning, that is, the use of time passage as a cue to elicit a conditioned response (Brackbill 1967).

Operant Conditioning.   Operant conditioning has to do with an emitted spontaneous response being followed by consequences that increase or decrease the likelihood that the response will be repeated. A positive reinforcer makes it more likely that the response will occur again. Consequently, those behaviors resulting in pain or negative outcomes are less likely to be repeated. Parents have long known that their infants' behaviors can be shaped or modified by reinforcing them. A baby girl smiles at her father, and her father smiles back. His response, a positive reinforcer, is likely to elicit even more smiling from his baby.

Operant conditioning of newborns and older infants has been well documented. Operant techniques have been useful in demonstrating early memory development in infants between two and six months old (Hill, Borousky, and Rovee-Collier 1988). Sameroff (1968) used operant techniques to modify the early sucking response in newborns. Newborns were also conditioned to turn their heads in response to sucking on a non-nutritive nipple (Sameroff and Cavanagh 1979). Compared to newborns, older infants are more easily conditioned and have a greater variety of responses that can be conditioned.

Operant conditioning procedures have been used with infants between two and four months old to increase vocalizations, smiling, sucking, and head turning (Watson 1968; Siqueland 1964; Zelazo and Komer 1971). The vocal and facial responses of adults have been found to be powerful reinforcers of infants' social and nonsocial behaviors. Older infants condition more rapidly than younger infants. They also condition more easily to a novel rather than familiar stimulus (Koch 1968). When infants have control of the contingent reinforcement, they condition more easily. Infants who have learned that their sucking response will bring a blurred picture into focus quickly determine the minimum amount of sucking needed to keep the picture in focus (Siqueland and DeLucia 1969).

Although operant conditioning in infancy has not been linked to later IQ, the operant paradigm has provided important insights about how infants learn and remember. Operant conditioning situations provide infants with the opportunity to learn that they can make something happen. They find that their actions bring about predictable results and that they can exert control over their environment.

Visual Recognition Memory

Visual recognition capabilities in infants have been well documented (Fagan 1984). In this procedure, an infant is shown two identical stimuli, side by side. Following a familiarization period of about twenty seconds, the familiar stimuli is paired with novel stimuli. When shown a novel and a familiar visual stimulus, infants prefer to look at the novel one. The idea is that infants recognize the familiar stimulus and give their attention to the new one. The process is termed *visual recognition memory*, since infants are thought to remember having seen the original stimulus. Research on visual recognition memory has attempted to link infants' responses to novelty to their intelligence later in life (Fagan and Singer 1983; Fagan and Mc-Grath 1981).

Assessment of recognition memory uses several procedures based on visual preference. In each procedure, visual stimuli are shown to an infant and the infant's visual fixation time is measured. One procedure is based on the habituation-dishabituation paradigm. The infant is repeatedly exposed to a visual target. Typically, habituation occurs, and when a novel visual target is introduced, the infant's visual attention to the target increases, or dishabituates. The recovery of the attentional response indicates recognition of the novel stimulus.

The paired-comparison assessment consists of a familiarization and a novelty phase. In the familiarization phase, two identical patterns are shown to an alert infant. For example, two identical bull's-eye patterns might be presented. During the novelty phase, two patterns are again presented. However, one of them is a new pattern, and the other is the familiar pattern shown previously. In this situation, the bull's-eye pattern would be shown simultaneously with another pattern, perhaps a cross. The length of time the infant spends looking at each pattern is recorded. It is inferred that longer visual fixation times for the novel pattern indicate recognition memory.

The recognition memory paradigm was used to compare the performance of preterm and full-term infants at six and twelve months of age (Rose, Feldman, and Wallace 1988). Preterm infants were shown to need longer exposure time to the original stimuli and had difficulty sustaining attention to the stimuli, compared to full-term infants. Preterm infants who were at high risk because of respiratory illness at birth were found to have greater deficits in attending behavior (Rose 1989).

Visual recognition memory is measured by infants' tendency to look at a novel visual stimulus rather than at a previously viewed stimulus. Studies of infant novelty preferences have shown that from birth, infants are able to discriminate visual patterns (Werner and Siqueland 1978) and that with maturation, recognition memory becomes more sophisticated. Joseph Fagan (1971) found that at five months old, infants were able to recognize several stimuli that had been presented in a single previous test session. Infants between four and six months were able to recognize a visual pattern despite a change in its orientation (Fagan 1976).

By the time they are one year old, infants can use information obtained through manipulating an object in order to visually recognize the object (Gottfried, Rose, and Bridger 1978). Long-term retention of recognition memory has been demonstrated in a number of studies. Infants between five and six months old were able to recognize patterns they had been shown two days previously (Fagan 1973). Infants of seven months showed up to a two-week retention of abstract patterns (Topinka and Steinberg 1978).

Emerging evidence suggests that differences in visual recognition memory occur among at-risk and normal infants. Normal infants and infants with Down syndrome were compared at thirteen, twenty-four, and thirty-six weeks of age (Miranda and Fantz 1974). The normal infants showed superior recognition memory at all three ages. In other studies of recognition memory, the overall performance of normal infants was superior to premature infants (Caron and Caron 1981; Rose 1983), to failure-to-thrive infants (Singer et al. 1983), and to infants exposed to teratogens (Jacobson 1984). Similarly, infants of diabetic mothers, infants with potential central nervous system damage, and infants with growth retardation were found to have less recognition memory capacity than normal infants (Fagan and Singer 1983).

The possibility that recognition memory can be a measure of intellectual ability has been supported by research. Recognition memory was found to develop earlier in infants of highly intelligent parents than in infants of parents of average intelligence (Fantz and Nevis 1967). Several researchers have tested the assumption that there is continuity between early visual recognition memory and later intelligence. Fagan and McGrath (1981) examined whether infant visual recognition memory was related to later intelligence. Longer visual fixation on novel stimuli at four to five months old was found to be positively correlated with verbal IQ at five and seven years.

Fagan and Singer (1983) compared the predictive validity of the Bayley Scales of Infant Development and recognition memory for intelligence later in childhood. Measures of recognition memory at seven months had a higher correlation with scores on the Stanford-Binet Intelligence Scale at three years than did measures of performance on the Bayley scales. Several other studies of the relationship between tests of infant visual recognition memory and later intelligence have shown significant associations between early preferences for visual novelty and later intelligence (Yarrow et al. 1975; Fagan 1981; Lewis and Brooks-Gunn 1981; Bornstein and Sigman 1986). The relation of infant attention and memory to later cognition was examined by Rose et al. (1989). Novelty scores averaged over nine visual recognition problems administered to seven-month infants significantly predicted the Bayley Mental Development Index (Bayley MDI) and the IQ of preterm infants at ages one, one and one-half, two, three, four, and five and the IQ of full-term infants from ages two to five. These results led Fagan and his associates to conclude that procedures used to measure infant visual recognition could be used to assess infants' abilities to remember, discriminate, and categorize information. The Fagan Test of Infant Intelligence (Fagan and Shepherd 1987) was developed as a method of identifying delayed cognitive development. Based on the previous research on early novelty preference, the test measures infants' visual fixations on novel stimuli.

The basic test procedure consists of showing an infant a stimulus such as a picture of a human face. The stimulus is presented until the infant has looked at it for a standard length of time, which means that the actual time of presentation of the stimulus may vary depending on the age of the infant. A trained observer watches through a peephole and records the length of visual fixation time. Once the standard viewing time has been reached, the infant is moved to a second viewing apparatus where the previously shown visual stimulus is paired with a novel stimulus. These stimuli are presented simultaneously for a standard test period that ranges from four to ten seconds. The position of each picture is switched midway during the test to control for position viewing preferences. The amount of viewing time devoted to each picture is recorded. A novelty score is derived by dividing the amount of fixation time on the test novel stimulus by the total fixation time on both the novel stimulus and the familiar stimulus, a figure that is then multiplied by 100.

The test was originally designed to assess infants between three and seven months old. It consists of twelve novelty problems, three of which are administered at twelve weeks, two at sixteen weeks, four at twenty-two weeks, and three at sixty-nine weeks. Used as a screening device, the Fagan test has been shown to have concurrent validity, since normal infants performed better on the test than did infants at risk for cognitive delay (Fagan and Singer 1983).

The predictive validity of the screening device was examined by Fagan et al. (1986). The sample used consisted of sixty-two infants suspected of being at risk for mental retardation. The validity for predicting normal cognitive development was 96 percent, and it was 55 percent for predicting infants' cognitive delay. Continued refinement of the Fagan tests focused on determining individual differences in visual information processing, the use of the visual novelty response with multiply-handicapped infants (McDonough and Cohen 1982), and development of an upward age extension of the test. In 1992, a standardized test, *The Fagan Test of Infant Intelligence,* was published (Fagan and Detterman 1992). According to the authors, the test can be used to predict cognitive delays in later childhood.

Several concerns were raised about the Fagan Test of Infant Intelligence, specifically questioning the adequacy of the sample used in standardizing the test (Benasich and Bejar 1992). Despite this limitation, the authors nevertheless point to the clinical usefulness of using information-processing procedures in measuring infant cognition and perception.

Standard-Transformation-Return Procedure

The Standard-Transformation-Return procedure was designed to test infants' information-processing ability during a sequential auditory or visual event (Zelazo 1979). In the "standard" phase, a given event is repeated in order for the infant to form an expectancy for the event. The event is usually either auditory or visual. An example of a visual event is the car-doll sequence. Here, a small car is rolled down a ramp and pushes over a Styrofoam doll at the bottom of the ramp. The "transformation" phase presents the infant with a slightly discrepant event. The toy car is rolled down the ramp, but the doll does not fall over. This is repeated for three or four trials, and then the car rolls down the incline and again knocks down the doll. The reappearance of the standard is called the "return" phase.

In a given STR test, five dynamic sequential events are presented—three auditory and two visual stimuli. An example of an auditory sequence is the repetition of a short phrase such as "Wave bye-bye." This is repeated several times, and after several trials, the phrase changes to "Throw me a kiss." After several trials, the infant again hears the original phrase.

The procedure takes place in a darkened theater, with the infant sitting on the parent's lap and facing a small lit stage. Observers watch and code the infant's responses and behaviors. The infant's capacity to respond to and process the sensory input is measured via behavioral and psychophysiological responses. The speed of the processing of the visual and auditory information is measured in the STR paradigm. Clusters of behaviors shown to reliably signal recognition of discrepant events are recorded (Reznick and Kagan 1982; Zelazo et al. 1974). Behavioral measures include pointing toward the stage, vocalizations, smiling, turning to the parent, clapping, and pointing. Searching behavior during presentation of an auditory sequence is assessed by noting eye widening, head movement, and quieting.

Heart rate is also measured through an electrocardiogram (EKG). From the infant's pattern of behavioral and physiological responses to the events in the test episode, information-processing abilities are inferred. In the car-doll sequence, for example, the standard trials allow the infant to watch a complex visual event. The transformation trials present discrepant information, whereas the return trials provide the opportunity for the infant to "remember" the original event, that is, the car rolling down the ramp and knocking over the doll. An infant watching the return trials might smile, vocalize, and show a heart-rate deceleration. The use of multiple response measures expands the opportunity to assess different styles of recognition of an event. By observing and measuring infants' responses in this procedure, it is possible to obtain recognition measures from infants and young children with handicapping conditions that might limit their responses on traditional infant tests. For example, an infant boy with severe cerebral palsy might smile, vocalize, move, and show a heart-rate change when observing the third presentation of the car sequence, indicating that he "solved" the puzzle.

An experimental validation of the STR procedure was supported in the results of a study of children with developmental delays of unknown etiology (Zelazo and Kearsley 1989). The sample of children had four- to five-month delays on the Bayley Mental Development Index. The STR procedure was used to distinguish infants with age-appropriate central processing ability from those with impaired processing. At the time of testing, children were twenty-two or thirty-two months old, and following the test, a ten-month treatment plan designed to stimulate expressive language and play was implemented. It was hypothesized that children with intact central processing abilities would show greater improvement in response to the treatment plan than children with impaired processing ability. Longitudinal follow-ups confirmed the predicted results and supported the validity of the test of central processing.

The STR test procedure is dynamic and measures infants' abilities to actively process information (Zelazo 1979). Further, the procedure itself is designed to capture the interest and attention of infants rather than trying to entice them to comply with a test situation. Finally, the STR paradigm may have potential as a useful clinical tool and alternative assessment approach for infants with handicaps.

Comparison with Traditional Tests

Heather, a six-month-old infant girl, was born with cerebral palsy. She has poor motor control and limited use of her upper limbs. Recently, at a developmental clinic, she was given the Bayley Scales of Infant Development. Both her Mental Development Index and Psychomotor Development Index scores were significantly below the average expected of her chronological age equivalent. Both her physician and mother think that her cognitive abilities are higher than indicated on the examination.

This case example highlights one of the problems of using only standardized traditional tests on infants with motor problems.

Clinicians are increasingly concerned that infants at risk for cognitive disabilities are not being detected by traditional screening and assessment measures (Caron, Caron, and Glass 1983). Although there is agreement that early biological perinatal risk factors such as prematurity, intraventricular hemorrhage, and respiratory distress syndrome are often preconditions of subsequent intellectual dysfunction, the majority of learning-disabled children appear to have normal infant histories (Scott and Masi 1979). So, too, the bulk of newborns who have identified obstetrical risk factors do not become developmentally disabled in childhood. It appears that efforts to identify infants in jeopardy of childhood cognitive disabilities have not met with uniform success.

Traditional psychometric assessments of infants and toddlers have low predictive validity (Brooks and Weinraub 1976; McCall 1976). Scores on traditional cognitive tests such as the Bayley scales and Piagetian scales are poor predictors of later intellectual functioning. Studies indicate that when conventional infant tests are administered to infants less than two years old, their scores do not accurately predict later cognitive functioning for normal infants or for infants considered at risk for developmental delays (Kopp and McCall 1982). Typically, cognitive problems are not identified until children enter school.

Traditional tests such as the Bayley Scales of Infant Development have pronounced limitations when used with infants with developmental disabilities. Zelazo and his colleagues argue that although this infant population is in greatest need of assessment, traditional tests actually work against such infants (Zelazo and Kearsley 1982; Zelazo 1979). Infants with disabilities often do not perform well on conventional measures because their disabling conditions can seriously limit their performance on tasks that require sensory motor integration, coordinated movements, or speech—and such tasks comprise the majority of items on conventional measures. The Gesell schedules and Bayley scales, for example, rely heavily on an infant's ability to imitate, make speech sounds, and use integrated fine and gross motor movements. Thus, infants with cerebral palsy or other neuromotor deficits may be assessed as having low intellectual competence, when in fact their neuromotor behaviors preclude optimal performance. In recognition of this, other means of assessing cognitive ability have been developed.

In the information-processing approach, measures of attention, such as smiling, vocalizing, and heart-rate changes while looking at a visual stimulus, are typically used. Because information-processing procedures can circumvent the limitations of confounding performance problems encountered in conventional tests, they hold promise as improved measures of infants' mental ability. This approach allows assessment of infants' central processing, yet it bypasses the problems of developmental delay that may depress scores of mental activity (Zelazo and Weiss 1990). With such indices, an infant's attention and ability to process information can be inferred free from reliance on neuromotor behaviors or expressive language.

Critique of Information-Processing Assessment Paradigm

The application of information-processing procedures to assess the cognitive abilities of infants is being considered as a viable alternative to conventional developmental tests (Benasich and Bejar 1992; Rose et al. 1991). One concern has been that traditional infant assessments do not sample the same kind of tasks, for instance, memory, perceptual discrimination, and categorization, that are measured on later intelligence tests. Thus, the processes related to intelligence are not being tapped in traditional tests. Information-processing paradigms offer the possibility of measuring mental processes related to later intelligence.

Information-processing procedures come directly from the basic research on infant perceptual-cognitive development. Although these methods have potential as alternative assessments, concerns have been raised about their use of valid indicators of mental processing (Sophia 1980; Reznick and Kagan 1982). One issue is the use of measures of attention to infer central processing. At different ages in infancy, different stimuli elicit attentional responses. Investigators point out that the use of patterns of response measures such as visual fixation time, heart-rate changes, smiling, and other behaviors can reduce the problems inherent in using one single attention measure (Zelazo and Weiss 1990).

Another issue is that probably no single information-processing technique is the definitive assessment instrument. Memory of, attention to, and recovery of interest in repetitive or discrepant events are all indicators of central processing. These are measured using different procedures. Nevertheless, in a meta analysis of the literature on infant habituation and recognition memory, both procedures showed significant predictive correlation with later childhood intelligence (McCall and Carriger 1993). This suggests that these abilities may be essential components of the basic perceptual-cognitive abilities related to later IQ.

Since information-processing techniques were developed to answer research questions rather than to assess infants, more research and refinements are necessary before they can be used as clinical screening and assessment instruments. Vietze and Coates (1986) suggest several steps in constructing an information-processing test. First, available procedures should be examined for their appropriateness as an assessment for at-risk infants. Next, the procedures should be used with populations of infants at risk for developmental disabilities to determine the utility and limits of the procedures. Then, longitudinal studies of the predictive validity of information-processing methods for later intelligence should be done. Techniques that do not discriminate between normal and at-risk infant populations should be eliminated. The assessment should be field-tested to determine age-appropriate responses.

Summary

Assessing the ways that infants process information contributes to our understanding of the mental processes involved in perception, attention, memory, and categorization. Whereas traditional infant tests are heavily reliant on sensorimotor tasks, the information-processing approach offers an alternative look at central processing abilities of infants.

The information-processing assessment approach comes from the research on the perceptual and attentional capacities of infants. The visual attention and visual preference research of the 1950s and 1960s established the remarkable capabilities of infants. Subsequent studies have traced the development of information processing through infancy and have also shown infants to be active seekers and organizers of information in their environment.

Information-processing paradigms measure mental activity. Because the measures used are infants' passive responses, such as looking, smiling, eye widening, and heart rate, information-processing procedures are considered potentially better indicators of central processing skills of infants with motoric impairments and severe developmental handicaps. Their use as a clinical screening instrument for infants at risk is still in the experimental stage.

Several information-processing procedures have been extensively studied with infants. The habituation-dishabituation paradigm measures decrement of response to a repeated stimulus and recovery of attention with a new stimulus. Visual recognition memory has been used to determine recognition of a novel stimulus when paired with a familiar stimulus. The Fagan Infant Intelligence Test uses recognition memory to assess infant cognition. Classical conditioning and operant conditioning have been demonstrated with newborns and infants. Although these basic learning paradigms have provided information about how infants learn, they have been used in intervention strategies rather than in assessment. The Standard-Transformation-Return procedure is currently being examined as a measure of infants' responses to sequential visual and auditory events.

Infant information-processing procedures hold promise as alternative assessments to traditional developmental assessments. Because they are thought to tap central processing rather than sensorimotor tasks, they may be useful in early identification of cognitive problems.

References

Baillargeon, R. 1993. The object concept revisited: New directions in the investigation of infants' physical knowledge. In *Visual Perception and Cognition in Infancy*, edited by C. E. Granrud. Hillsdale, NJ: Lawrence Erlbaum Associates.

Banks, M. S., and A. P. Ginsburg. 1985. Infant visual preferences: A review and new theoretical treatment. In *Advances in Child Developmental Behavior*. Vol. 19. Edited by H. W. Reese. New York: Academic Press.

Barrera, M., and D. Maurer. 1981. Recognition of mother's photographed face by the three-month-old infant. *Child Development* 52:714–716.

Bartoshuk, A. K. 1962. Human neonatal cardiac acceleration to sound: Habituation and dishabituation. *Perceptual and Motor Skills* 15:15–27.

Benasich, A. A., and I. I. Bejar. 1992. The Fagan Test of Infant Intelligence: A critical review. *Journal of Applied Developmental Psychology* 13:153–171.

Berlyne, D. E. 1958. The influence of the albedo and complexity of stimuli on visual fixation in the human infant. *British Journal of Psychology* 49:315–319.

Blass, E. M., J. R. Ganchrow, and J. E. Steiner. 1984. Classical conditioning in newborn humans 2–24 hours of age. *Infant Behavior and Development* 7:223–235.

Bornstein, M. H. 1989. Stability in early mental development: From attention and information processing in infancy to language and cognition in childhood. In *Stability and Continuity in Mental Development*, edited by M. H. Bornstein and N. A. Kaasnegar. Hillsdale, NJ: Lawrence Erlbaum Associates.

_____. 1985. Habituation of attention as a measure of visual information processing in human infants: Summary, systematization and synthesis. In *Measurement of Audition and Vision in the First Year of Postnatal Life: A Methodological Overview*, edited by G. Gottlieb and N. A. Krasnegor. Norwood, NJ: Ablex.

Bornstein, M. H., and M. D. Sigman. 1986. Continuity in mental development from infancy. *Child Development* 57:251–274.

Brackbill, Y. 1967. Developmental studies of classical conditioning. *Proceeding, 75th Annual Convention, American Psychological Association* 2:155–156.

Brezsnyak, M. 1994. Reliability and stability of visual expectations and reaction time from two to three months. *Infant Behavior and Development* 17:537.

Brooks, J., and M. Weinraub. 1976. A history of infant intelligence testing. In *Origins of Intelligence*, edited by M. Lewis. New York: Plenum Press.

Cantor, D. S., J. E. Fishchel, and H. Kaye. 1983. Neonatal conditionability: A new paradigm for exploring the use of interceptive cues. *Infant Behavior and Development* 6:403–413.

Caron, A. J., and R. F. Caron. 1981. Processing of relational information as a measure of cognitive functioning in nonsuspect infants. In *Infants Born at Risk: Psychological, Perceptual, and Cognitive Processes*, edited by T. Field and A. Sostek. New York: Grune and Stratton.

Caron, A. J., R. F. Caron, and P. Glass. 1983. Responsiveness to relational information as a measure of cognitive functioning in nonsuspect infants. In *Infants Born at Risk: Physiological, Perceptual, and Cognitive Process*, edited by T. Field and A. Sostek. New York: Grune and Stratton.

Cohen, L. 1981. Examination of habituation as a measure of aberrant infant development. In *Preterm Birth and Psychological Development*, edited by S. L. Friedman and M. Sigman. New York: Academic Press.

Cohen, L., and B. A. Younger. 1983. Perceptual categorization in the infant. In *New Trends in Conceptual Representation*, edited by E. Scholnick. Hillsdale, NJ: Lawrence Erlbaum Associates.

Colombo, J., D. W. Mitchell, M. O'Brien, and F. D. Horowitz. 1987. The stability of visual habituation during the first year of life. *Child Development* 58:474–487.

Cornell, E. H., and M. S. Strauss. 1973. Infants' responsiveness to compounds of habituated visual stimuli. *Developmental Psychology* 9:73–78.

Fagan, J. F. 1984. Infant memory. In *Advances in the Study of Communication and Affect*. Vol. 9. Edited by M. Moscovitch. New York: Plenum Press.

_____. 1981. Infant memory and the prediction of intelligence. Paper presented at the Society for Research in Child Development meeting, Boston, April 4, 1981.

_____. 1976. Infants' recognition of invariant features of faces. *Child Development* 47:68–78.

_____. 1973. Infants' delayed recognition memory and forgetting. *Journal of Experimental Child Psychology* 16:424–450.

_____. 1972. Infants' recognition memory for faces. *Journal of Experimental Child Psychology* 14:453–476.

_____. 1971. Infants' recognition memory for a series of visual stimuli. *Journal of Experimental Child Psychology* 11:244–250.

Fagan, J. F., and D. K. Detterman. 1992. *The Fagan Test of Infant Intelligence: Training Manual*. Cleveland: Infantest Corp.

Fagan, J. F., and L. T. Singer. 1983. Infant recognition memory as a measure of intelligence. In *Advances in Infancy Research*. Vol. 2. Edited by P. Lipsitt. Norwood, NJ: Ablex.

Fagan, J. F., and S. K. McGrath. 1981. Infant recognition memory and later intelligence. *Intelligence* 5:121–130.

Fagan, J. F., and P. A. Shepherd. 1987. *The Fagan Test of Infant Intelligence Training Manual*. Vol. 4. Cleveland: Infantest Corporation.

Fagan, J. F., L. T. Singer, J. E. Montie, and P. A. Shepherd. 1986. Selective screening device for early detection of normal or delayed cognitive development in infants at risk for later mental retardation. *Pediatrics* 78:1021–1026.

Fantz, R. L. 1965. Visual perception from birth as shown by pattern selectivity. *Annals of the New York Academy of Sciences* 118:793–814.

_____. 1964. Visual experience in infants: Decreased attention to familiar patterns relative to novel ones. *Science* 146:668–670.

_____. 1963. Pattern vision in newborn infants. *Science* 140:296–297.

_____. 1956. A method for studying early visual development. *Perceptual and Motor Skills* 6:13–15.

Fantz, R. L., and S. Nevis. 1967. The predictable value of changes in visual preference in early infancy. In *The Exceptional Infant*. Vol. 1. Edited by J. Hellmuth. Seattle: Special Child Publications.

Fitzgerald, H. E., and S. W. Porges. 1971. Infant conditioning and learning research. *Merrill-Palmer Quarterly* 17:79–117.

Fitzgerald, H. E., and Y. Brackbill. 1976. Classical conditioning in infancy: Development and constraints. *Psychological Bulletin* 83:353–376.

Friedman, S. 1972. Habituation and recovery of visual response in the alert human newborn. *Journal of Experimental Child Psychology* 13:339–349.

Friedman, S., and G. C. Carpenter. 1971. Visual response decrement as a function of age of human newborn. *Child Development* 42:1967–1973.

Friedman S., L. A. Bruno, and P. Vietze. 1974. Newborn habituation to visual stimuli: A difference in novelty detection. *Journal of Experimental Child Psychology* 18:242–251.

Gottfried, A. W., S. A. Rose, and W. H. Bridger. 1978. Effects of visual, haptic and manipulating experiences on infants' visual recognition memory of objects. *Developmental Psychology* 14:305–312.

Granrud, C. E., A. Yonas, and E. A. Opland. 1985. Infants' sensitivity to the depth cue of shading. *Perception and Psychophysics* 37:415–419.

Hill, W., D. Borousky, and C. Rovee-Collier. 1988. Continuities in infant memory development. *Developmental Psychobiology* 21:43–62.

Horowitz, F. D., L. Y. Paden, K. Bhana, and P. Self. 1972. An infant control procedure for studying infant visual fixations. *Developmental Psychology* 7:90.

Jacobson, S. W. 1984. Use of Fagan's recognition memory test in detection of teratogenic risk. In J. F. Fagan (chair), New Directions in the Study of Infant Intelligence, symposium held at the Gatlinburg Conference on Research in Mental Retardation and Developmental Disabilities, Gatlinburg, TN, March.

Kagan, J. 1974. Discrepancy, temperament and infant distress. In *The Origins of Fear*, edited by M. Lewis and L. A. Rosenblum. New York: Wiley.

_____. 1970. Attention and psychological changes in the young child. *Science* 170:826–832.

Karmel, B. Z. 1969. The effect of age, complexity and amount of contour density on pattern preferences in human infants. *Journal of Experimental Child Psychology* 7:339–354.

Karmel, B. Z., and E. B. Maisel. 1975. A neuronal activity model for infant visual attention. In *Infant Perception: From Sensation to Cognition. Basic Visual Processes.* Vol. 1. Edited by L. B. Cohen and P. Salapatek. New York: Academic Press.

Koch, J. 1968. Conditioned orienting reactions to persons and things in two- to five-month-old infants. *Human Development* 11:81–91.

Kopp, C. B., and R. B. McCall. 1982. Predicting later mental performance for normal at-risk and handicapped infants. In *Life-Span Development and Behavior.* Vol. 14. Edited by P. B. Baltes and O. G. Brien. New York: Academic Press.

Lester, B. 1975. Cardiac habituation of the orienting response to an auditory signal in infants of varying nutritional states. *Developmental Psychology* 11:432–442.

Lewis, M., and J. Brooks-Gunn. 1981. Visual attention at three months as a predictor of cognitive functioning at two years of age. *Intelligence* 5:131–140.

Lewis, M., and S. Goldberg. 1968. Habituation difference to tactile stimulation for waking and sleeping infants. *Psychophysiology* 4:498–499.

Mayes, L. C., and M. Kessen. 1989. Maturational changes in measures of habituation. *Infant Behavior and Development* 12:437–450.

Maurer, D., and M. Barrera. 1981. Infants' perception of natural and distorted arrangements of a schematic face. *Child Development* 52:196–202.

McCall, R. B. 1976. Toward an epigenetic conception of mental development in the first three years of life. In *Origins of Intelligence: Infancy and Early Childhood*, edited by M. Lewis. New York: Plenum Press.

McCall, R. B., and M. S. Carriger. 1993. A meta-analysis of infant habituation and recognition memory performance as predictors of later IQ. *Child Development* 64:57–79.

McDonough, S. C., and L. B. Cohen. 1982. Attention and memory in cerebral-palsied infants. *Infant Behavior and Development* 5:347–353.

Miranda, S. B., and R. L. Fantz. 1974. Recognition memory in Down's syndrome and normal infants. *Child Development* 45:651–660.

Moss, M., J. Colombo, D. W. Mitchell, and F. D. Horowitz. 1988. Neonatal behavioral organizational visual processing at three months. *Child Development* 59:1211–1220.

Olson, G. M. 1976. An information processing analysis of visual memory and habituation in infants. In *Habituation: Perspectives from Child Development, Animal Behavior, and Neurophysiology*, edited by T. J. Tighe and R. N. Leaton. Hillsdale, NJ: Lawrence Erlbaum Associates.

Papousek, H. 1967. Conditioning during postnatal development. In *Behavior in Infancy and Early Childhood*, edited by Y. Brackbill and G. C. Thompson. New York: Free Press.

Pavlov, I. 1927. *Conditional Reflexes*. London: Oxford University Press.

Ramey, C. T., B. J. Breitmayer, B. D. Goldman, and A. Wakely. 1996. Learning and cognition during infancy. In *Atypical Infant Development*, edited by M. J. Hanson. 2d ed. Austin, TX: Pro-ed Corporation.

Reznick, J. S., and J. Kagan. 1982. Category detection in infancy. In *Advances in Infancy Research*. Vol. 2. Edited by L. Lipsitt. Norwood, NJ: Ablex.

Rose, S., and I. Wallace. 1985. Cross-model and intra-model transfer as predictors of mental development in full-term and pre-term infants. *Developmental Psychology* 56:843–852.

Rose, S. A. 1989. Measuring infant intelligence: New perspectives. In *Stability and Continuity in Mental Development*, edited by M. H. Bornstein and N. A. Krasnegor. Hillsdale, NJ: Lawrence Erlbaum Associates.

———. 1983. Differential rates of visual information processing in full term and preterm infants. *Child Development* 54:1189–1198.

Rose, S. A., J. F. Feldman, I. F. Wallace, and C. McCarton. 1991. Information processing at 1 year: Relation to birth status and developmental outcome during the first 5 years. *Developmental Psychology* 27:723–737.

———. 1989. Infant visual attention: Relation to birth status and developmental outcome during the first 5 years. *Developmental Psychology* 25:560–576.

Rosenblith, J. 1992. *In the Beginning: Development from Conception to Age Two*. 2d ed. Newbury Park, CA: Sage Publications.

Sameroff, A. J. 1972. Learning and adaptation in infancy: A comparison of models. In *Advances in Child Development*. Vol. 7. Edited by H. W. Reese. New York: Academic Press.

———. 1968. The components of sucking in the human newborn. *Journal of Experimental Child Psychology* 6:607–623.

Sameroff, A. J., and P. J. Cavanagh. 1979. Learning in infancy: A developmental perspective. In *Handbook of Infant Development,* edited by J. D. Osofsky. New York: Wiley.

Samuels, C. A. 1985. Attention to eye contact opportunity and facial motion by three-month-old infants. *Journal of Experimental Child Psychology* 40:105–114.

Scott, K. G., and W. Masi. 1979. The outcome from and utility of registers of risk. In *Infants Born at Risk,* edited by T. Field, A. Sostek, S. Goldberg, and H. Shuman. Jamaica, NY: Spectrum.

Sigman, M. D., S. E. Cohen, L. Beckwith, R. A. Sarnow, and A. H. Parmelee. 1992. The prediction of cognitive abilities at age 8 and 12 years of age from neonatal assessments of preterm infants. In *The Psychological Development of Low-Birthweight Children.* Advances in Applied Developmental Psychology, vol. 6. Edited by S. C. Friedman and M. D. Sigman. Norwood, NJ: Ablex.

Singer, J., and J. Fagan. 1992. Negative affect, emotional expression and forgetting in young infants. *Developmental Psychology* 26:745–751.

Singer, L. T., D. Drotar, J. F. Fagan, L. Devost, and R. Lake. 1983. The cognitive development of failure to thrive infants: Methodological issues and new approaches. In *Infants Born at Risk: Physiological, Perceptual, and Cognitive Processes,* edited by T. Field and A. Sostek. New York: Grune and Stratton.

Siqueland, E. R. 1964. Operant conditioning of head turning in four-month-old infants. *Pschonomic Science* 1:223–224.

Siqueland, E. R., and C. A. DeLucia. 1969. Visual reinforcement of nonnutritive sucking in human infants. *Science* 165:1144–1146.

Slater, A. V., V. Morison, and D. Rose. 1984. Habituation in the newborn. *Infant Behavior and Development* 7:183–200.

Sophia, C. 1980. Habituation is not enough. Novelty preferences, search and memory in infancy. *Merrill-Palmer Quarterly* 26:239–256.

Spelke, E. S., K. Breinlinger, J. Macomber, and K. Jacobson. 1991. Origins of knowledge. *Psychological Review* 99:605–632.

Spelt, D. 1948. The conditioning of the human fetus in utero. *Journal of Experimental Psychology* 38:375–376.

Topinka, C. V., and B. Steinberg. 1978. Visual recognition memory in 3½ and 7½ month-old infants. Paper presented at the International Conference on Infant Studies, Providence, RI, March.

Vietze, P. M. 1986. Using information processing strategies for early identification of mental retardation. *Topics in Early Childhood Special Education* 6:72–85.

Von Bargen, D. M. 1983. Infant heart rate: A review of research and methodology. *Merrill-Palmer Quarterly* 29:115–150.

Watson, J. S. 1968. Operant fixation in visual preference behavior in infants. *Psychonomic Science* 12:241–242.

Werner, J. S., and E. R. Siqueland. 1978. Visual recognition memory in the preterm infant. *Infant Behavior and Development* 1:79–94.

Yarrow, L. J., R. P. Klein, S. Lomonaco, and G. A. Morgan. 1975. Cognitive and motivational development in early childhood. In *Exceptional Infant.* Vol. 3. Edited by B. X. Friedlander, G. M. Sterritt, and G. E. Kirk. New York: Brunner/Mazel.

Yonas, A., L. Pettersen, and J. Lockman. 1979. Young infant's sensitivity to optical information for collision. *Canadian Journal of Psychology* 33:268–276.

Yonas, A., M. E. Arterberry, and C. E. Granrud. 1987. Four-month-old infants' sensitivity to binocular and kinetic information for three-dimensional-object shape. *Child Development* 58:910–917.

Zelazo, P. R. 1986. An information processing approach to infant-toddler assessment and intervention. In *Theory and Research in Behavioral Pediatrics*. Vol. 3. Edited by H. Fitzgerald, B. Lester, and M. Yogman. New York: Plenum.

_____. 1979. Reactivity to perceptual-cognitive events: Applications for infant assessment. In *Infants at Risk: Assessment of Cognitive Functioning*, edited y R. B. Kearsley and I. Sigel. Hillsdale, NJ: Lawrence Erlbaum Associates.

Zelazo, P. R., J. R. Hopkins, S. N. Jacobson, and J. Kagan. 1974. Psychological reactivity to discrepant events: Support for the curvilinear hypothesis. *Cognition* 2:385–395.

Zelazo, P. R., and M. J. Komer. 1971. Infant smiling to nonsocial stimuli and the recognition hypothesis. *Child Development* 42:1327–1339.

Zelazo, P. R., and M. J. Weiss. 1990. Infant information processing: An alternative approach. In *Interdisciplinary Assessment of Infants: A Guide for Early Intervention Professionals*, edited by E. D. Gibbs and D. M. Teti. Baltimore: Paul H. Brookes.

Zelazo, P. R., M. Weiss, A. Papageorgiou, and D. Laplante. 1989. Recovery and dishabituation of sound localization among normal, moderate and high-risk newborns: Discriminant validity. *Infant Behavior and Development* 12:321–340.

Zelazo, P. R., and R. B. Kearsley. 1989. Validation of an information processing approach to infant-toddler assessment.

_____. 1982. Memory formation for visual sequences: Evidence for increased speed of processing with age. *Infant Behavior and Development* 5:263 (abstract).

6

Play Assessment

You are troubled at seeing him spend his early years in doing nothing. What! Is it nothing to be happy? Is it nothing to skip, to play, to run about all day long? Never in his life will he be so busy as now.

—*Jean-Jacques Rousseau*

Introduction

Remember the pleasurable childhood hours you spent playing? As children, we became princes and princesses, made believe in makeshift tents or tree houses, and learned how to play pickup sticks and kickball. These experiences helped to shape who and what we would become as adolescents and later as adults. As Rousseau knew, we were not busy doing nothing.

What you probably don't remember is how you played as an infant. But you did play, maybe not in tree houses and in games of pickup sticks and kickball, but certainly in variations of those activities. You explored objects through touching and mouthing. Later, you banged and shook objects and used them as tools or to imitate adult activities. Your play also involved interactions with others, and this, too, progressed from simple interactions such as looking at or touching someone else to complex interactive sequences that included game playing. Infant-caregiver interactions will be examined in the next chapter. In this chapter, we will address the assessment of infant play with objects and the relationship of infant play to infant development.

Developmental psychologists now believe that infant play reflects infants' cognitive abilities and has an integral role in promoting infant competence (McCall 1974; Piaget 1952). Through play, infants discover that they can affect their environment, for example, that they can make a ball move by pushing it or cause adults to smile by looking at them. They learn about space and time and about qualities such as hard or soft by playing with objects. Their intellectual functions are fostered through problem solving, systematic exploration, decisionmaking, and use of symbolic representation (Athey 1984; Johnson, Christie, and Yawkey 1987).

Observing infants at play is the basis of play assessment. In fact, play is the context for measuring social, emotional, language, and cognitive development. Typically, assessors look at the stages of play and changes in the complexity of play. The developmental consistencies between play and language or cognition provide information about the developing infant (Terrell and Schwartz 1988).

Since play is considered so central to the cognitive development of infants, the development of infant play has been systematically examined by researchers (Belsky and Most 1981; Rubin, Fein, and Vandenberg 1983; Smith and Vollstedt 1985). This research has shown that regular developmental patterns characterize infant play and, recently, that assessing infant play is a legitimate way to measure infants' acquisition of cognitive skills, social abilities, and language function (Bond, Creasey, and Abrams 1990).

In this chapter, we will first review the development of infant play. Next, we will examine the functions of play, play characteristics, and the ways that play influences cognitive, social, and emotional development throughout infancy. Finally, we will explore some assessment methods currently used to measure infant play skills.

Your study of this chapter should enable you to

- Describe the development of infant play
- Describe the ways that infant play enhances development during infancy
- Outline the general methods used to assess play
- Describe several play assessments

Play Characteristics

Play is what infants and young children do. They spend most of their waking hours playing. Adults watching infants play can generally recognize play behavior, although some play is subtle and not easy to identify. Defining play is, however, more difficult. That is because there is such a variety of play behaviors. Play begins in early infancy and takes very different forms as the infant develops. Play can be solitary or involve games with others.

Generally, it is agreed that play involves pleasurable activities for the infant (Rogers and Sawyer 1988). Play has been described as a variety of observable behaviors within specific contexts (Rubin, Fein, and Vandenberg 1983). In this chapter, *play* is defined as the broad array of activities that are intrinsically motivated and that result in positive affect.

To get a feeling for the complexity of defining play, look at the following examples:

- A baby girl grasps a rattle, looks at it, and puts it in her mouth.
- A mother claps her hands together, while smiling at her ten-month-old boy. He smiles and claps his hands.
- An eighteen-month-old infant picks up a toy phone and says, "Hi."

- A thirteen-month-old infant puts a small plastic cup inside a larger one.

Now consider these questions. Are all of these examples of play? Why? What characteristics do they share? If you identified attention to objects or to others, internally generated actions, spontaneous behavior, and positive affect you would be in agreement with researchers. A number of play characteristics have been proposed by researchers (Fewell and Kaminski 1988; Wolery and Bailey 1989; Fein and Apfel 1979). Some general play characteristics agreed upon by these authors include flexibility, spontaneity, intrinsic motivation, active attention, and pleasurable consequences.

Play has been categorized by several researchers (Rossetti 1990). One model of play defines it as having three categories: social, cognitive, and miscellaneous (Mindes 1982). Each category includes subcategories with increasing levels of developmental sophistication. Social play begins with solitary play, in which the infant plays alone and is focused on individual play. This is followed by parallel play, where the child plays beside other children rather than with them. The next substage is group play—associative play in which the child plays with other children but does not engage in identical play activities. The final substage is cooperative play, where the child plays organized activities within a group. In the category of cognitive play, the child moves from functional play, which involves repetitive actions, to constructive play, in which play materials are used to create something. The substage dramatic play follows, and that involves pretend play. The final substage is games with rules. The miscellaneous play category includes these substages: unoccupied behavior, onlooker behavior, and reading.

Piaget (1952) described three types of play: practice play, which involves motor activities on objects; symbolic play; and games with rules. Four cognitive types of play have been elaborated, including sensorimotor or functional play, constructive play, dramatizing play, and games with rules (Smilansky 1968). Other researchers expanded the types of play to include physical play, game playing, constructive play, and pretend play. One investigator described a hierarchy of infants' object play (Wehman 1977). Each level represents a more complex cognitive behavioral sequence. Donald Bailey and Mark Wolery (1984) organized Wehman's sequence into six levels:

Level I. Repetitive manual manipulation or oral contacts. Mouths objects, repeats actions on objects.

Level II. Pounding, throwing, pushing, pulling. Increases gross motor actions on objects.

Level III. Personalized toy use. Uses toys to perform actions on own body, such as feeding self.

Level IV. Manipulation of movable parts of toys.

Level V. Separation of parts of toys.

Level VI. Combinational use of toys. Infant uses and combines different play objects together.

Importance of Play

Infants play because it is fun. Not only is play enjoyable, but it also contributes to infants' knowledge of the world around them. They learn by playing. Play promotes appropriate social interactions, language use, and physical development (Garvey 1977). It has been suggested that play leads development (Fromberg 1987). Let us look at several developmental domains and their relationship to play during infancy.

Influence on Cognitive Functions

Until recently, play was thought to be purposeless. Infants manipulated objects, moved their bodies, and played games with their parents. Adults saw this as fun, not thinking. Play activities did not appear to have any meaning beyond simple enjoyment. In 1952, however, Piaget suggested that infants' early actions on the environment are the basis for the development of cognition. During play, infants' interactions with the environment provide the practice needed for mastery, which in turn influences cognitive competence. Infants begin to understand cause and effect and assume responsibility for making things happen. Today, Piaget's views on the relationships of play to cognitive development are widely accepted.

Investigators have designed play behavior assessments based on Piaget's research (Piaget 1962; McCune et al. 1990). Play behavior is observed using a standard set of toys, and the sample is assigned to one of Piaget's five sensorimotor stages (McCune 1986). These observations allow the assessor to observe the child's interaction with toys and play partners as well as to obtain a measure of the representational play skill (Nicolich 1977).

Infant play promotes other cognitive functions. The ability to discriminate between relevant and irrelevant information is acquired through using different types of toys or objects. The discovery that objects exist in time and space is acquired in object play. Exploratory behavior is enhanced through play. Systematic exploration enhances investigative play and reduces distractibility (Rosenblatt 1977). Moreover, it has been suggested that infant play promotes creativity through the application of play skills in a variety of different ways (Athey 1984; Zelazo and Kearsley 1980). Higher levels of play, such as symbolic play with objects or pretend play, foster classification skills and sequential memory as well as the ability to plan and reason (Rubin and Maioni 1975; Saltz and Johnson 1977; McCune-Nicolich and Fenson 1984; Slade 1987a, 1987b).

Influence on Mastery Motivation

Play provides optimal opportunities for infants to experience their effect on their environment. Their manipulation of objects allows practice in problem solving (Sharp 1970). Through problem solving, infants begin to expand their behavioral repertoire for solving new problems. One important outcome of this process is *mastery motivation*, which is simply staying with a task or persisting until the problem is solved (Yarrow et al. 1983).

Mastery motivation is viewed as a key component of cognition and as essential to the development of infant competence (Brockman, Morgan, and Harmon 1988). Persistence in solving a problem posed by play materials results in goal achievement, which in turn leads to feelings of self-efficacy as well as control over the environment. Having experienced success with a problem, infants are more likely to seek new challenges. In play, they will then persist until the task is completed. This characteristic of task persistence continues through adulthood.

Expressions of positive feelings resulting from mastering a problem can be observed during infant assessments or play. An infant of eighteen months who places all the pegs correctly in a peg board will usually look up at the examiner or at a parent and smile, as if to say, "Didn't I do a good job!"

Influence on Social-Emotional Development

Play and social-emotional development are closely intertwined. As infants play, they learn about themselves and others, which promotes the subsequent development and refinement of social skills. They acquire social cognition, or the ability to think about their social world (Rubin 1980), and as their social interactions become more sophisticated, infants' play becomes more complex (Musselwhite 1986).

Play is a valuable resource for the development of social skills. Through play with their parents, infants begin to regulate their responses in accordance with their parents' responses. Timing, mutuality, and intensity of affect are all governed through parent-infant interaction sequences (Stern 1985). Moreover, parent-infant interactions can foster a sense of humor in infants, resulting, for example, from such interactions as adults making funny faces in response to them or carrying out unexpected actions during a game. Dante Cicchetti and Alan L. Sroufe (1976) have found that children's cognitive levels are related to their sense of humor.

By playing, infants gradually become aware of who they are and develop a sense of their own individuality. They come to discover the consequences of their actions on others. One of the first lessons learned by infants is that they can elicit responses from adults by crying or moving. This cause-and-effect relationship is called *contingency*. Early contingent experiences influence later cognitive development. Leila Beckwith (1985) proposed that the self-regulation learned through parent-infant play fosters secure attachment in the development period between twelve and eighteen months.

Social skills are practiced and tested with pretend play. It is possible for twenty-one-month-old infants to practice social roles by pretending, for example, to be a parent while they put their doll to bed. Toddlers also practice what might be socially acceptable in different situations. Similarly, they also try out a variety of emotional responses when playing. In pretend games, young children may display aggression, happiness, joy, anger, and sadness. Through practice, they learn emotional control in specific contexts as well as ways for these emotions to be appropriately expressed (Greenspan and Porges 1984).

Influence on Physical and Motor Skills

During infancy, play contributes to the development of physical skills and influences fine and gross motor development. Much is involved. Muscle tone and strength improve through play. The repetitive movements and body actions typical of play in very young infants result in smoother movement patterns. In this case, practice makes perfect. Moreover, it is a circular situation. As infants become stronger and more coordinated, their play improves. And as their play improves, infants become even stronger and more coordinated.

Immediately after birth, infants begin to respond to the movements of objects around them and to being moved themselves. As they play with objects, they learn to control their own bodies. The sensory feedback that occurs as a result of touching or kicking objects improves eye-hand coordination and fine motor abilities. Overall motor functioning is enhanced with accurate awareness of the body's relationship to other objects in space (Hall 1990).

Influence on Language Development

Play is also believed to influence the development of communication and language skills. During early infant-parent play, infants become more responsive to their parents' cues and begin to express themselves nonverbally through facial expressions and gestures. They emit sounds in response to the actions of others. Parents often emit different rhythms of speech sounds to their infants or say the name of objects as they play together. The result is that infants begin to associate certain sounds with objects.

When their play advances from action to symbolic representation, older infants begin to practice the rules of language usage (McCune-Nicolich, 1981). A twenty-four-month-old child, for example, will experiment with sounds and words in play. Infants will play with language itself, making rhymes, saying nonsense phrases, and varying sound intonations. This practice helps them to become competent communicators. A number of researchers have noted the similarities in the use of symbols in language and in pretend play (Athey 1984; Sachs 1980).

The linkage of play activities with language skills was investigated in 1980 (Westby 1980). Through play assessment, a child's concurrent language abilities can be measured. Seven stages of symbolic play activities were identified. At each stage, the expected language behaviors were identified.

Assessing Infant Play

Usefulness of Play Assessments

Analysis of infant play is now thought to reflect cognitive functioning and mastery motivation. Consequently, various strategies for measuring infant play have been developed to assess infant competence (Clune, Paollella, and Foley 1979). In the past decade, play has increasingly become a vehicle for the measurement of behavior in infants with handicaps.

Although the play behaviors of infants with disabilities follow developmental trends similar to those of nonhandicapped infants, there are qualitative play differences. These differences depend on the severity level of the disability. However, symbolic play, play spontaneity, exploratory play, and attention are all affected (Rogers 1986). Play assessments have proven to be useful in documenting differences in play within handicapped infant populations. Because play assessments allow for greater flexibility and can be administered in naturalistic settings, they are considered to be more useful than traditional assessments in assessing the competencies of atypical infants (Gibbs 1990).

Many young children with handicaps are language delayed, thus it is often difficult, if not impossible, to assess their cognitive abilities using traditional developmental assessments. Assessments of play that measure symbolic play provide a language-free and more accurate assessment of cognitive development for infants and toddlers with language impairment (Cicchetti and Wagner 1990).

Assessment Methods

Two general strategies are used for assessing infants' object play. Observing free play in a naturalistic setting or in a more structured setting that contains specified toys is a common technique. A second strategy uses demonstration and prompts to elicit play behaviors. Here, the examiner models particular play behaviors or verbally prompts the infant to use a play behavior. Both types of assessment classify play behaviors according to the complexity of play, individual play differences, and motivational play level.

In free-play tests, infants are observed playing with objects without adult intervention (Rubenstein and Howes 1976). Infants are free to select toys of their choice and play with them in whatever way they like. In structured free-play observations, specific toys or objects are made available to the infant. For example, in one study of play behaviors of infants between seven and twenty months, a metal tea set, a large bucket, a male doll, a female doll, and wooden blocks were used as the play objects (Fenson et al. 1976).

Structured free-play usually takes place in a carefully arranged observation room that is free of distractions. The use of structured settings allows for greater toy standardization and more control over environmental differences such as the number and type of available toys or the play space itself. One investigation found, for example, that the amount of play space affects play (Rubin and Howe 1985).

Three sets of measures assessing cognitive, affective-motivational, and social domains of free-play behavior can be obtained from both structured and unstructured free-play situations (Cicchetti and Wagner 1990). The first measure is the maturity of a child's *object and social play*. The second measure is the developmental progression in the maturity and complexity of *symbolic play*. The third set of measures is of the child's affective *motivational play* style. These measures provide information about the developmental organization of young children.

Using naturalistic settings for assessing play has its advantages. It provides samples of play behaviors in an infant's daily surroundings such as the home environment. Infants can be observed across a number of familiar environments that can be assessed in terms of their cognitive-stimulating properties. A naturalistic observation, however, may be more difficult than an observation in a structured setting, since it is often not possible to control distractions or the environment itself.

Modeling and prompts are used in several play assessments (Belsky and Most 1981; Fewell 1986). Modeled play assessments use a succession of prompts or actual modeling of play behaviors to encourage more complex levels of toy play. This assessment strategy, also known as elicited play assessment, allows the examiner to determine the prompt level and mechanisms needed to elicit various levels of infants' play. By modeling a task, it is possible to observe infants' persistence or mastery motivation in completing the task. Comparisons of the level and quality of play can be made between free play and modeled play (Belsky, Garduque, and Hrncir 1984).

Both the free-play and elicited play assessment methods yield valuable information about play behaviors and the relationship of play to infant cognitive functioning. Each assessment strategy has strengths and weaknesses. However, the choice of one strategy over another will depend on the assessment goals. In some instances, assessments may combine observation of free-play as well as modeled play strategies.

Procedures have been developed to assess infants' free play and elicited play and their play strategies. In the following section, we will review several examples of both types of assessments and describe some assessments currently being developed for clinical use.

Assessment Procedures

Rubenstein and Howes Play Assessment.   This scale is a free-play measure of infants' and toddlers' play in naturalistic settings. It was originally designed to investigate the effects of peers on the interaction of toddlers with toys and with their mothers (Rubenstein and Howes 1976). Subsequently, the scale has been used in several research investigations on the relationship of play to cognitive functions (Howes and Stewart 1987).

In this procedure, infants are observed in solitary free play, and the level of play behaviors is coded using a 5-point scale that indicates developmental play levels. These include

1. Oral play, such as mouthing objects
2. Passive tactile contact, for example, holding an object or toy
3. Active toy manipulation
4. Using the unique properties of a toy
5. Imaginative play

It has been suggested that the Rubenstein-Howes Play Scale is appropriate for ages eight to thirty months (Bond, Creasey, and Abrams 1990). In a longitudinal study conducted in 1984, these authors examined the utility of the Rubenstein-Howes scale in assessing the play behavior of twelve- to eighteen-month-old infants, and they found that increases in infants' age were accompanied by higher levels of play behaviors (Bond et al. 1984).

Belsky and Most Free Play Assessment.   The Belsky and Most (1981) Free-Play Scale is designed to measure play development from infancy to toddlerhood. Based on the developmental progression of play described by Piaget (1952), the scale includes twelve behavior sequences arranged in order of developmental progression. The infant is observed in the home setting with a set of standardized toys. The observer records the infant's most competent play level, using ten-second intervals over a thirty-minute observation period.

The scale encompasses an age range of between eight and thirty-six months and divides play into three categories or levels: (1) simple or low-level play, (2) functional play, and (3) high-level pretense play. The twelve-step sequence of play includes

Simple or Low-Level Play

1. Mouthing: Indiscriminate mouthing of objects.
2. Simple manipulation of objects: Excludes banging and shaking objects.

Functional Play

1. Functional: Includes manipulation that is appropriate for an object, for example, ringing a bell or rolling a toy car on its wheels.
2. Relational: Bringing together two or more pieces of material in a manner unintended by the manufacturer.
3. Functional-Relational: Bringing together two or more objects or pieces of material in an appropriate way. Included would be such things as putting a form in a form board or placing a toy phone on the hook.
4. Enactive naming: Approximating pretense activity without actually completing the pretense behavior, for example, putting a brush to a doll's hair without making brush motions.

High-Level Pretense Play

1. Pretense behaviors directed toward self: Pretense is directed toward self and the pretense behaviors are evident. A good example is an infant raising a cup to the lips and making drinking sounds.
2. Pretend other: Pretense behaviors are directed toward others.
3. Substitution of objects for one another in a creative way: A typical instance is a young child feeding a teddy bear with a bottle.
4. Linking pretend sequences: A child, for example, might take a drink from a cup, then give a doll a drink, and finally, pretend to refill the cup from a bottle.
5. Sequence pretend substitution: An object substitution is used in a pretend sequence. At first, for example, a child might feed a doll with a spoon, then with a ruler.
6. Double substitution: In a pretend sequence, two objects are substituted within a single pretend act. At this level, children might use a stick as a car, then place the stick inside a cardboard box that they pretend is a garage.

In a cross-sectional study of play behaviors of normal infants between seven and twenty-one months old, Belsky and Most (1981) found that their twelve-step play procedure accurately described their subjects' developmental sequence of play. The frequency of mouthing and simple toy manipulation decreased with age, while several types of pretense play increased linearly across the age period.

Another scale, the Belsky and Most Development of Play Scale, was used to assess whether infants would play in a more complex fashion when with a familiar peer than with their mother (Turkheimer, Bakeman, and Adamson 1989). Fourteen infants were videotaped at play at twelve, fifteen, and eighteen months old. Play was found to be more sophisticated with mothers than with peers, as compared to when the infant played alone. This suggests that active and involved mothers promote symbolic and fantasy play.

Belsky and Most (1981) point out that their assessment may provide more information about infants' cognitive functions than standardized tests do. In contrast to standardized tests, the free-play situation allows infants to define the problem and persevere according to their own motivational level. Such individual motivational differences may account for the cognitive style differences observed first in infancy and subsequently in later developmental periods. Further, analysis of free play can provide information about the ways that an infant's environment can be structured to enhance early exploratory activities and later, to enhance more complex and cognitive-demanding play routines.

McCune-Nicolich Play Assessment.   The McCune-Nicolich play assessment (1983) uses a free-play analysis to measure symbolic play behaviors in older infants and toddlers (of fifteen to thirty-six months). Based on Piaget's stages of symbolic play, pretend play is analyzed at five play levels.

> Level I. Presymbolic schemes: Child through gesture shows understanding of object use with no pretending. Examples: Picks up a cup and puts it to the lips; gives a broom a sweep on the floor.
> Level II. Autosymbolic schemes: Symbolic play is directly related to own body. Example: Child pretends to drink from an empty cup.
> Level III. Single symbolic games: Symbolic play is extended beyond child's own actions. Child pretends making actions of other people or objects. Examples: Child gives doll a drink; combs father's hair.
> Level IV. Combination symbolic games: One pretend action is related to another or to several receivers of action. Examples: Child combs own hair, then doll's, then mother's; child pretends to heat water on a toy stove, pour into cup, then gives doll a drink.
> Level V. Planned symbolic games: Child indicates that pretend acts are planned before doing the act. Example: Child says "tea," then pretends to pour into cup and feeds doll.

This assessment is conducted in the infant's home. The infant's free play with a standardized set of toys is observed for a thirty-minute period. The observer records the type of symbolic play from the time the infant begins to play with an object until attention to the object lags.

The assessment procedure is described in *A Manual for Analyzing Free Play* (McCune-Nicolich 1983). This protocol has been used in several empirical studies of Piaget's hypothesized progression of symbolic play (Power, Chapieski, and McGrath 1985; Slade 1987a). Developmental trends in symbolic play have been found to support Piaget's theorized play stages.

Fewell's Play Assessment Scale.   Fewell's Play Assessment Scale (Fewell 1986) is an example of a modeled play assessment used to assess elicited object play in infants from two to thirty-six months old. Infants are observed interacting with a series of toys presented in sets of increasing difficulty. The procedure is conducted using two conditions. In the first condition, the infant's spontaneous play with toys is recorded. Forty-five types of play, such as mouthing objects or using one object for several different purposes, are listed as scale items. The observer notes both the type of play and number of times the play type occurred during the observation period. In the second condition, play is elicited first with verbal cues, then by physical modeling, and finally by verbal and model prompts. The highest level of assistance needed is recorded.

The usefulness of the Fewell play assessment scale was assessed using a group of toddlers with multihandicaps (Fewell and Rich 1987). The assessment accurately assessed the children's cognitive, social, and communication skills. Fewell (1986) has suggested that the prompt-level data obtained from the second condition of the scale provide useful information for planning instructional programming for infants and toddlers with disabilities.

Executive Capacity Procedure in Infant Play. The Executive Capacity Procedure assesses infant competence through elicited play (Belsky, Garduque, and Hrncir 1984). Following a ten-minute free-play observation, a competence episode is initiated by the examiner, who attempts to elicit higher levels of play through three successive coaching methods. First, verbal prompts are used to encourage more sophisticated play with a toy. If the child does not engage in the higher play, the examiner then models the behavior. Finally, a combination of verbal and modeling prompts is used if modeling alone does not produce the desired play.

Scoring on both the free-play and competence observations is based on Belsky and Most's (1981) free-play assessment. Three scores are obtained: (1) performance, or the highest play level reached in the free-play episode; (2) competence, or the highest level of elicited play in the competence episode; and (3) executive capacity, defined as the difference between performance and competence.

The executive capacity score is designed to measure mastery motivation, which involves self-initiated and goal-directed activity. Mastery motivation is thought to underlie cognitive competence (Brockman, Morgan, and Harmon 1988). Belsky, Garduque, and Hrncir (1984) maintained that infants who are highly motivated would need little prompting to master a task. As a result, there would be little difference between performance and competence. However, a longitudinal study of infants' executive capacity found that although higher levels of spontaneous mastery during free play was indicative of increased cognitive abilities six months later, infants' executive capacity at twelve months old was not predictive of their executive competence at eighteen months (Hrncir, Speller, and West 1985).

Mastery Motivation Assessment.   Mastery motivation is considered a necessary component for the development of cognitive competence. In 1959, Robert White proposed the idea that infants' competence is attained through self-directed efforts motivated by curiosity and the need to exercise control over the environment. Because of the child's feelings of self-efficacy and control, the very process of mastering the environment is rewarding (White 1959). The idea that intellectual competence reflects mastery motivation spurred subsequent research investigations as well as the development of assessment procedures to measure mastery motivation in infants (Morgan and Harmon 1984).

Leon Yarrow and his associates systematically examined the relationship between achievement of test items believed to assess mastery motivation on the Bayley Scales of Infant Development and later scores on the Stanford-Binet (Yarrow et al. 1975). Infant scores on clusters of Bayley items, such as reaching and goal-directedness, were found to predict later Stanford-Binet scores, whereas the overall Bayley Mental Development Index score did not. Recent studies have shown a correspondence of Bayley MDI scores with mastery scores in twelve-month-old infants (Yarrow et al. 1982; Jennings, Yarrow, and Martin 1984). These results indicate that mastery motivation is important for promoting infant competence.

The development of mastery motivation procedures that included free-play and elicited play measures was subsequently carried out by Yarrow et al. (1983). These procedures have been shown to have high interrater reliability and provide evidence of reliability and validity.

In the structured free-play mastery-task situation, (Brockman, Morgan, and Harmon 1988) an interesting task is given to an infant, and depending on the infant's age, the observer records the efforts required to complete the task. Some examples of tasks include exploring a complex object, playing with parts of a busy box, putting pegs in a hole, completing a complex form board, using a toy cash register, and playing with a surprise pop-up toy.

Mastery motivation measures vary depending on the assessment. Generally, however, two measures are used: mastery pleasure (T) and task persistence (T). Mastery pleasure refers to the number of positive affective signals given, for instance, smiling or hand clapping following successful task completion. During each task, the observer records the most frequent motivational behavior shown by the infant during a fifteen-second interval. Both task persistence and positive affect behaviors are recorded. Scoring the assessment consists of summing the total number of T's on task persistence and T's on mastery pleasure for each task. Persistence is measured by the amount of time the child stays with the task.

Assessment of mastery motivation in free-play situations focuses on infants' manipulation and use of objects in appropriate or symbolic ways

(Glicker, Couchman, and Harmon 1981; Morgan, Harmon, and Bennett 1976). Mastery motivational differences between preterm and full-term infants have been found with this assessment (Harmon and Culp 1981). Preterm infants were less active and exploratory compared to full-term infants. Contrasted to their twelve-month-old full-term counterparts, preterm infants exhibited lower levels of persistence with tasks.

An example of a method of mastery motivation assessment appears in an adaptation of one of the three rating scales from the Bayley Infant Behavior Record (Maslin and Morgan 1984). The infant's behavior is rated during administration of the Bayley scales and free play. The scale consists of nine ratings that address the infant's persistence in trying to reach a goal. The rating yields an overall rating of goal-directedness. The nine-point rating scale of goal-directedness includes the following:

1. No evidence of directed effort or purposeful activity.
2. Makes an occasional attempt at goal-directed action but does not repeat attempts.
3. Makes some attempts to attain a goal with some repetition but does not show interest in carrying attempts to completion.
4. Attempts at goals are more frequent but generally lack sustained persistence; does not continue if initial attempt fails.
5. Usually makes an initial attempt to attain a goal and shows some repetition of efforts; however, quits fairly soon if not successful.
6. Makes initial attempts to attain goals with moderate persistence; however, gives up if task requires repeated efforts. Usually does not repeat solutions of tasks.
7. Initial attempts are followed by moderate to high persistence, even if task is somewhat difficult. Repeats solutions of some tasks.
8. Persistence in attaining goals is high, even when task is challenging, but without the marked absorption that characterizes a score of 9. Often repeats solutions of tasks.
9. Very high absorption in task; willingly repeats solutions of tasks, stays with tasks until they are solved even if they are very difficult; practices tasks until they are thoroughly mastered.

Current Developments in Play Assessment

Practitioners and researchers continue to develop tests of play to use for assessing play development as well as for planning intervention strategies for infants with disabilities. Incorporating play activities that promote social, cognitive, and linguistic development into infant instruction plans is gaining increasing attention among infant interventionists. Play is naturally engaging for the infant; therefore, when intervention is framed in the context of play, the infant is more likely to participate in the intervention.

The Transdisciplinary Play-Based Assessment (TPBA) (Linder 1990) is an example of a play assessment designed for use in infant intervention and early childhood programs. The TPBA is used to assess infant development via observations of play behaviors. Designed for children between six months and six years old, the test uses a team approach to assess play in both modeled and free-play situations. Observational data on free play and elicited play is gathered by a team of teachers, psychologists, physical therapists, and parents. Guidelines are provided for observing play in language and communication, sensorimotor, cognitive, and social-emotional domains. The test directs the observer to look for specific behaviors that document the child's ability in a specific domain. In the social-emotional domain, for example, the observers look at temperament, mastery motivation, and social interactions with a parent. The resulting TPBA assessment data are then used to plan and implement a program that includes activities to promote development in each domain.

Several other assessments currently under development are worth noting. The Play Assessment Checklist for Infants (Bromwich et al. 1981) is an observational instrument used in free-play situations with infants from nine to thirty months old. A specific set of toys is used, and the infant is assessed for cognitive activities with the toys, attention span, social-emotional behaviors during play, and temperament. Another assessment, the Play Observation Scale (Rogers 1986), measures sensorimotor and symbolic play. In the Symbolic Play Scale Checklist developed by Westby (1980), parent-teacher reports and a structured observation session provide data on the cognitive, social, and language aspects of play in children from nine months to five years old.

Overview

It should be evident that there is considerable interest in infants' play. In recent years, efforts have been made to develop useful strategies for analyzing infant and toddler play. The underlying assumption is that play reflects cognitive functioning and offers an avenue for more global assessment of developmental organization.

The play assessments described in this chapter are not standardized, yet assessment of play behaviors holds promise as a measure of infant competence. The utility of these assessments is associated with their ability to identify qualitative and quantitative aspects of play behavior in multiple settings. Further, play assessments can be used to identify individual differences in play progress.

The standardized procedures in traditional infant tests have limited use with infants with handicapping conditions. Free-play assessment techniques, by contrast, are more flexible than traditional measures, thus allowing observation of individual differences in motivation and other cognitive characteristics. Such information can be useful in identifying appropriate cognitive activities and programmatic goals for infants with disabilities.

Summary

Researchers, theoreticians, and practitioners believe that infant play is critical to development and that cognitive competence is both promoted by and reflected in infant play. Because of the importance of play in infancy, scales and procedures have been developed to carefully evaluate how infants play, what their levels of play are, and how well they use cognitive strategies in play situations.

These scales and procedures have been used to identify several developmental play trends in the infant period. Infants first use motion and body actions in play involved with objects in their environment. They then adapt their actions to match the properties of the object. Next, they engage in the functional use of objects. Symbolic play with objects and toys follows; this is more complex play. Finally, infants engage in pretend play that involves symbolic reasoning and representation of objects that might not be present or available.

Researchers have generally agreed on several shared characteristics across types of play. Flexibility is one such characteristic. Play is self-generated and for the infant has no other purpose than enjoyment. Play results in positive affect for the infant.

Free play and modeled play are two methods used to assess infant play. Free-play assessments involve observing infants' play with no prompting or intervention by the observer. Free play is often assessed in naturalistic settings. Modeled play assessments entail demonstrations of play to elicit infant play behaviors. Some play assessments begin with free-play sessions, which are followed by an elicited play sequence.

Mastery motivation assessments measure infant task persistence. Several assessment procedures designed to measure mastery motivation have been developed by Yarrow and his colleagues. These procedures have been used systematically to explore motivational differences between groups of handicapped and nonhandicapped infants and young children.

References

Athey, I. 1984. Contributions of play to development. In *Child's Play: Developmental and Applied*, edited by T. D. Yawkey and A. D. Pellegrini. Hillsdale, NJ: Lawrence Erlbaum Associates.

Bailey, D. B., and M. Wolery. 1984. *Teaching Infants and Preschoolers with Handicaps*. Columbus, OH: Merrill.

Beckwith, L. 1985. Parent-child interaction and social-emotional development. In *Play Interactions: The Role of Toys and Parental Involvement in Children's Development*, edited by C. C. Brown and A. W. Gottfried. Skillman, NJ: Johnson and Johnson.

Belsky, J., L. Garduque, and E. Hrncir. 1984. Assessing performance, competence and executive capacity in infant play: Relations to home environment and security of attachment. *Developmental Psychology* 20:406–417.

Belsky, J., and R. K. Most. 1981. From exploration to play: A cross-sectional study of infant free play behavior. *Developmental Psychology* 17(5):630–639.

Bond, L. A., G. L. Creasey, and C. L. Abrams. 1990. Play assessment. In *Interdisciplinary Assessment of Infants,* edited by E. D. Gibbs and D. M. Teti. Baltimore: Paul H. Brookes.

Bond, L. A., L. D. Kelly, D. M. Teti, and E. D. Gibbs. 1984. Effects of siblings on infant interaction with objects. Paper presented at the annual meeting of the American Psychological Association, Anaheim, CA.

Brockman, L. M., G. A. Morgan, and R. J. Harmon. 1988. Mastery motivation and developmental delay. In *Assessment of Young Developmentally Disabled Children,* edited by T. D. Wachs and R. Sheehan. New York: Plenum Press.

Bromwich, R. M., S. Fust, E. Khokha, and M. H. Walden. 1981. Play Assessment Checklist for Infants. California State University, Northridge.

Cicchetti, D., and A. L. Sroufe. 1976. The relationship between affective and cognitive development in Down's syndrome infants. *Child Development* 47(4): 920–929.

Cicchetti, D., and S. Wagner. 1990. Alternative assessment strategies for the evaluation of infants and toddlers: An organizational perspective. In *Handbook of Early Childhood Intervention,* edited by S. J. Meisels and J. P. Shonkoff. New York: Cambridge University Press.

Clune, C., J. M. Paollella, and J. M. Foley. 1979. Free-play behavior of atypical children: An approach to assessment. *Journal of Autism and Developmental Disorders* 9:61–71.

Fein, G. G., and N. Apfel. 1979. The development of play: Style, structure and situations. *Genetic Psychology Monographs* 99:213–250.

Fenson, L., J. Kagan, R. B. Kearsley, and P. R. Zelazo. 1976. The developmental progression of manipulative play in the first two years. *Child Development* 47:232–235.

Fenson, L., and D. Ramsay. 1980. Decentration and integration of the child's play in the second year. *Child Development* 51:171–178.

Fenson, L., J. Kagan, R. B. Kearsley, and P. R. Zelazo. 1976. The developmental progression of manipulative play in the first two years. *Child Development* 47:232–235.

Fewell, R. R. 1986. Play assessment scale. 5th revision. University of Washington, Seattle.

Fewell, R. R., and R. Kaminski. 1988. Play skills development and instruction for young children with handicaps. In *Early Intervention for Infants and Children with Handicaps: An Empirical Base,* edited by S. L. Odom and M. B. Karnes. Baltimore: Paul H. Brookes.

Fewell, R. R., and J. S. Rich. 1987. Play assessment as a procedure for examining cognitive, communication and social skills in multihandicapped children. *Journal of Psychoeducational Assessment* 2:107–118.

Fromberg, D. P. 1987. Play. In *The Early Childhood Curriculum: A Review of Current Research,* edited by C. Seefeldt. New York: Teachers College Press.

Garvey, C. 1977. *Play*. Cambridge: Harvard University Press.

Gibbs, E. D. 1990. Assessment of mental ability. In *Interdisciplinary Assessment of Infants*, edited by E. D. Gibbs and D. M. Teti. Baltimore: Paul H. Brookes.

Glicker, A. D., G. Couchman, and R. J. Harmon. 1981. *Free Play Social Scale*. Denver: University of Colorado School of Medicine, Infant Development Laboratory.

Greenspan, S., and S. Porges. 1984. Psychopathology in infancy and early childhood: Clinical perspectives on the organization of sensory and affective thematic experience. *Child Development* 55:49–70.

Hall, S. 1990. Observation of sensorimotor development. In *Transdisciplinary Play-Based Assessment*. Baltimore: Paul H. Brookes.

Harmon, R. J., and A. M. Culp. 1981. The effects of premature birth on family functioning and infant development. In *Children and Our Future*, edited by I. Berlin. Albuquerque: University of New Mexico Press.

Howes, C., and P. Stewart. 1987. Child's play with adults, toys, and peers: An examination of family and child-care influences. *Developmental Psychology* 23:423–430.

Hrncir, E. J., G. M. Speller, and M. West. 1985. What are we testing? *Developmental Psychology* 21:226–232.

Jennings, K. D., L. J. Yarrow, and P. P. Martin. 1984. Mastery motivation and cognitive development: A longitudinal study from infancy to 3 ½ years of age. *International Journal of Behavioral Development* 7:441–461.

Johnson, J. E., J. F. Christie, and T. D. Yawkey. 1987. *Play and Early Childhood Development*. Glenview, IL: Scott, Foresman and Company.

Linder, T. W. 1990. *Transdisciplinary Play-Based Assessment*. Baltimore: Paul H. Brookes.

Maslin, C., and G. Morgan. 1984. *Manual for Rating Scales of Child Characteristics*. (Modified IBR). Fort Collins: Department of Human Development and Family Studies, Colorado State University.

McCall, R. B. 1974. Exploratory manipulation and play in the human infant. *Monographs of the Society for Research in Child Development* 39(2), Serial no. 155.

McCune, L. 1986. Symbolic development in normal and atypical infants. In *The Young Child at Play: Reviews of Research*. Vols. 45–61. Edited by G. Fein and M. Riokin. Washington, DC: NAEYC.

McCune, L., B. Kalmanson, M. B. Fleck, B. Glazewski, and J. Sillori. 1990. An interdisciplinary model of infant assessment. In *Handbook of Early Childhood Intervention*, edited by S. J. Meisels and J. P. Shonkoff. New York: Cambridge University Press.

McCune-Nicolich, L. 1983. *A Manual for Analyzing Free Play*. New Brunswick, NJ: Department of Educational Psychology, Rutgers University.

_____. 1981. Toward symbolic functioning: Structure of early pretend games and potential parallels with language. *Child Development* 52:785–797.

McCune-Nicolich, L., and L. Fenson. 1984. Methodological issues in studying early pretend play. In *Child's Play: Developmental and Applied*, edited by T. D. Yawkey and A. D. Pellegrini. Hillsdale, NJ: Lawrence Erlbaum Associates.

Mindes, G. 1982. Social and cognitive aspects of play in young handicapped children. *Topics of Early Childhood Special Education* 2:14–20.

Morgan, G. A., and R. J. Harmon. 1984. Development transformations in mastery motivation: Measurement and validation. In *Continuities and Discontinuities in Development*, edited by R. N. Emde and R. J. Harmon. New York: Plenum Press.

Morgan, G. A., R. J. Harmon, and C. A. Bennett. 1976. A system for coding and scoring infants' spontaneous play with objects. *JSAS Catalog of Selected Documents in Psychology* 6(105), ms. no. 1355.

Musselwhite, C. R. 1986. *Adaptive Play for Special Needs Children*. San Diego: College Hill Press.

Nicolich, L. M. 1977. Beyond sensorimotor intelligence: Assessment of symbolic maturity through analysis of pretend play. *Merrill-Palmer Quarterly* 23:89–99.

Piaget, J. 1962. *Play, Dreams, and Imitation in Childhood*. New York: Norton.

———. 1952. *The Origins of Intelligence*. 2d ed. New York: International Press.

Power, T. G., L. Chapieski, and M. P. McGrath. 1985. Assessment of individual differences in infant exploration and play. *Developmental Psychology* 21:974–981.

Rogers, S. J. 1986. Cognitive characteristics of handicapped children's play: A review. *Journal of Division for Early Childhood* 12:161–168.

Rogers, S. J., and J. K. Sawyer. 1988. *Play in the Lives of Children*. Washington, DC: National Association for the Education of Young Children.

Rosenblatt, D. 1977. Developmental trends in infant play. In *Biology of Play*, edited by B. Tizard and D. Harvey. Philadelphia: J. B. Lippincott.

Rossetti, L. M. 1990. *Infant-Toddler Assessment*. Boston: Little, Brown and Company.

Rubenstein, J., and C. Howes. 1976. The effects of peers on toddler interaction with mothers and toys. *Child Development* 47:597–605.

Rubin, K., and T. Maioni. 1975. Play preference and its relation to egocentrism, popularity, and classification skills in preschoolers. *Merrill-Palmer Quarterly* 21:171–179.

Rubin, K. H. 1980. Fantasy play: Its role in the development of social skills and social cognition. In *New Directions in Child Development: Children's Play*, edited by K. H. Rubin. San Francisco: Jossey-Bass.

Rubin, K. H., G. G. Fein, and B. Vandenberg. 1983. Play. In *Handbook of Child Psychology. Vol. 4: Socialization, Personality, and Social Development*. 4th ed. New York: John Wiley and Sons.

Rubin, K. H., and N. Howe. 1985. Toys and play behaviors: An overview. *Topics in Early Childhood Special Education* 5(3):1–9.

Sachs, J. 1980. The role of adult-child play in language development. In *New Directions for Child Development*, edited by K. H. Rubin. San Francisco: Jossey-Bass.

Saltz, E., and J. Johnson. 1977. Training disadvantaged preschoolers on various fantasy activities: Effects on cognitive functioning and impulse control. *Child Development* 48:367–379.

Sharp, E. 1970. *Thinking Is Child's Play*. New York: E. P. Dutton.

Slade, A. 1987a. A longitudinal study of maternal involvement and symbolic play during the toddler period. *Child Development* 58:367–375.

———. 1987b. Quality of attachment and early symbolic play. *Developmental Psychology* 23:78–85.

Smilansky, S. 1968. *The Effects of Sociodramatic Play on Disadvantaged Preschool Children*. New York: Wiley.

Smith, P. K., and R. Vollstedt. 1985. On defining play: An empirical study of the relationship between play and various play criteria. *Child Development* 56:1042–1050.

Stern, D. 1985. *The Interpersonal World of the Infant*. New York: BasicBooks.

Terrell, B., and R. Schwartz. 1988. Object transformation in the play of language impaired children. *Journal of Speech and Hearing Disorders* 53:459–463.

Turkheimer, M., R. Bakeman, and L. B. Adamson. 1989. Do mothers support and peers inhibit skilled object play in infancy? *Infant Behavior and Development* 12:37–44.

Wehman, P. 1977. *Helping the Mentally Retarded Acquire Play Skills*. Springfield, IL: Charles Thomas.

Westby, C. E. 1980. Assessment of cognitive and language abilities through play. *Language, Speech and Hearing Services in Schools* 11:154–168.

White, R. W. 1959. Motivation reconsidered: The concept of competence. *Psychological Review* 66:297–333.

Wolery, M., and D. B. Bailey. 1989. Assessing play skills. In *Assessing Infants and Preschoolers with Handicaps*, edited by D. B. Bailey and M. Wolery. Columbus, OH: Merrill.

Yarrow, L. J., G. A. Morgan, K. D. Jennings, R. J. Harmon, and J. L. Gaiter. 1982. Infants' persistence at tasks: Relationships to cognitive functioning and early experience. *Infant Behavior and Development* 5:131–141.

Yarrow, L. J., R. P. Klein, S. Lomonaco, and G. A. Morgan. 1975. Cognitive and motivational development in early childhood. In *Exceptional Infant 3: Assessment and Intervention*, edited by G. M. Sterrit and G. E. Kirk. New York: Halstead Press.

Yarrow, L. J., S. McQuiston, R. H. MacTurk, M. McCarthy, R. P. Klein, and P. M. Vietze. 1983. Assessment of mastery motivation during the first year of life: Contemporaneous and cross-age relationships. *Developmental Psychology* 19:159–171.

Zelazo, P., and R. Kearsley. 1980. The emergence of functional play in infants: Evidence for a major cognitive transition. *Journal of Applied Developmental Psychology* 1(2):95–117.

7

Assessing Parent-Infant
Interactions

Shall we dance?

—*Richard Rodgers and Oscar Hammerstein II,*
The King and I

Introduction

Imagine dancing for the first time with someone you don't know, someone who doesn't dance quite the same way you do. At first, both of you are out of sync; you step on each other's toes, move in opposite directions, and don't anticipate the other's moves. Although at first the dance isn't that great, you don't stop; you try again. This time it's better. After an evening of dancing, you both enjoy the experience, and the two of you look and feel good together on the dance floor.

In much the same way, parents and infants learn to "dance" together. The process takes time and practice. They become smoother, begin to read each other's cues, and make appropriate responses. Eventually, they become partners.

For centuries, parents have known that a powerful social relationship begins with the birth of their newborn. Scientists have studied how this relationship begins and how parents and infants contribute to establishing a long-lasting bond. The bond is known as *attachment*. The process of developing parent-infant attachment has been called many different things. Some of these terms are "mutuality," "falling in love," and "the dance."

The attachment process involves reciprocal interactions between parents and infants. For example, a father smiles at his three-month-old baby and the baby smiles back; a mother looks at her five-month-old infant, waves, and says, "Hi," and the baby becomes quiet and looks back intently at her; or a newborn baby girl opens her eyes and gazes at her mother and her mother gazes back. Through such simple beginnings, a complex, synchronous interaction system is built. The system requires both partners to pay attention, signal one another, and continuously adjust their responses to each other's signals. In the normal course of development, interactional systems become increasingly coordinated and involve verbal and gestural communication, facial expressions, turn taking, and mutual responsiveness (Sorce and Emde 1982).

Early parent-infant interactions are the foundation of infants' cognitive, social-emotional, and language development (Sparks et al. 1988). A positive relationship between supportive parent-infant interactions and later development has been well-documented (Beckwith and Cohen 1984; Barnard and Kelly 1990), and researchers have identified elements essential to the interaction process. As a consequence, professionals are now able to use parent-infant assessment scales to target intervention activities designed to correct interaction mismatches.

Recent research supports the need to assess the parent-infant relationship, which is now considered to be critical to the infant's developmental status. Bornstein (1989) found that infants whose mothers were socially responsive performed better on standardized intelligence measures. Through positive early parent-infant interactions, infants learn the social aspect of communicative discourse, such as turn taking (Antoniadis et al. 1984).

Assessment of parent-infant interaction skills can provide information about the strengths, as well as the weaknesses, of the interaction. Mismatches between parent and child may occur when parent or child's affect and behavior are not responsive or reciprocal. Maladaptive patterns are more often found in parents of infants with disabilities or those infants at risk for developmental delay. Maladaptive interactions have been linked with subsequent developmental problems (Greenspan 1983; Clark, Paulson, and Conlin 1993).

In this chapter, we will examine the development of parent-infant interaction skills as well as important elements of the interaction process. Functional and dysfunctional interactive patterns and their effects on development will be described. Finally, interaction measurement approaches and assessment scales will be discussed. To help yourself gain understanding of parent-child interactions, observe infants and parents interacting whenever possible. What we know about parent-infant interactions has come about because we have watched them. Try it yourself. Watch parents and infants together; do it carefully, and see what they do.

Your study of this chapter should increase your knowledge of infants and their social capabilities. You should discover links between parent-infant interactions and infants' skill development. You should be able to

- Outline the course of parent-infant interactions, including their effect on developmental skills
- Describe the effects of dysfunctional parent-infant interactions
- Describe and contrast several parent-infant interaction assessments

Parent-Infant Interaction Patterns

For many years, developmental researchers have studied the relationship between parent-infant interactions and developmental outcomes. Initially, infants were characterized as passive and acted upon by parents. However, this view was challenged by a new model of reciprocity between infant and parent (Bell 1968). According to Richard Bell (1974), the processes underlying attachment are bidirectional.

Attachment is defined as a relationship between two people that lasts over time. The process of attachment involves communication and patterns of interaction between parent and infant that are synchronous and rhythmic (Rossetti 1990). Infants and their caregivers are members of a dyad, with each partner affecting the other's behavior. Their mutual interaction involves coordinated and synchronous communication. Over time and with practice, social interchanges become more regulated, so that interactions match rather than mismatch.

Further interest in parent-child relationships was spurred by theorists who postulated that infants were born with the propensity to promote contact with others (Ainsworth 1973; Bowlby 1982). Research from this perspective found that newborn infants who used behaviors such as crying, gazing, and smiling were observed to promote adults' caregiving efforts.

Systematic studies of interactive patterns between infants and parents have demonstrated strong links between interactive patterns and infant development. Many observations have found that positive maternal-infant interactions are the basis for optimal caregiving (Affleck et al. 1989; Donovan and Leavitt 1989). The importance of building reciprocal interactions is most clearly illustrated when one member of the dyad does not respond to the other's needs and signals. In the case of infants with disabilities or parents who are depressed, interactions may be impaired, resulting in developmental delay or affective disorders (Ainsworth 1982).

Development of Early Interactive Patterns

Seven-month-old Thomas is sitting opposite his father, who leans forward, smiles, and says, "Gonna getcha Tommy." Thomas moves his body forward, his eyes widen, and he smiles. Father moves his hand toward Thomas. Thomas laughs while looking expectantly at his father. They repeat their game.

Elizabeth, a four-month-old infant, is lying in her crib on her back. Her mother leans over her and says, "Hi, Lizzie. Hi, Lizzie." While her mother is speaking to her, Elizabeth is quiet and looks intently at her. As soon as mother stops speaking, Elizabeth smiles, kicks, and waves her arms.

Right from the start, newborn infants are social. They begin life with a behavioral repertoire that shapes their caregivers' attitudes and social exchanges with them. Babies signal to their caregivers through vocalizations, looks, and touch. Simply gazing at their caregivers captures their undivided attention. They move in rhythm to the sound of their parent's voice. Parents usually interpret these expressions as communication, and they in turn respond by looking, talking, and attending to their infant's needs. Early reflexive smiling elicits caregivers' attention, and newborn reflexes such as sucking and rooting promote nursing activities and close parental contact (Condon and Sander 1974).

During the first few months of life, the parent-infant communication process becomes refined through transactions that involve rhythmicity and mutual adaptations (Brazelton, Koslowski, and Main 1974). Consider how early turn taking, an important component of early interaction exchanges between mother and infant, is learned through the newborn suck-and-jiggle response. When nursing infants slow their sucking, mothers jiggle them and the infants resume sucking (Kaye 1976). Since jiggling actually inhibits the resumption of sucking, it appears that the infant is learning to respond to mother's action. In fact, after a few times, infants will wait to be jiggled before they resume sucking. What is necessary to establish early parent-infant reciprocal interactions? First, the infant's signaling system must be intact. This means that the infant must signal clearly to caregivers, using signals such as cooing, babbling, differentiated crying, and facial expressions (Bernal 1972). Second, the infant must be attentive and responsive to the environment (Robson and Moss 1970).

The caregiver's part in the dialogue requires sensitivity to infant needs, cues, and behavioral states as well as skill at responding appropriately to the infant. The accuracy of caregivers' perceptions about the meaning of infants' signals influences the quality of interactions. The caregiver's ability to read and interpret infant cues has been termed *affect attunement* (Stern 1984).

Each partner in the dyad contributes unique elements to the development of a synchronous parent-infant relationship. This is an adaptive process involving coordination, matching, and repair (Tronick and Cohn 1989). An infant girl, for example, expresses delight by widening her eyes and cooing when her father shakes a small stuffed toy in front of her. He continues to move the toy while smiling at her, and she in turn increases her vocalizations and movements. Her father continues his actions, but she begins to fuss. As the father continues to attempt to engage his infant, she turns away. What was a matched behavior sequence initially is now a mismatch. Communication repair is needed and will occur when the father and infant adjust their behaviors to regain reciprocal communication. They may do this by the father stopping interaction until his baby looks at him, indicating she is ready to resume interactions. The father then slowly initiates play again.

This process has been labeled the "mutually adaptive dance" (Barnard et al. 1989) According to these authors, four components are essential for a smooth dance. First, each partner must have the abilities and skills needed to read and respond effectively to the other. Second, the partners' responses must be contingent on the other's behavior. Third, the interactive content must be enriched through the availability of toys, range of activities, and parent-infant time together. Fourth, the interactive patterns must adapt as the infant develops.

Interaction between parent and infant is a dyadic process and requires the caregiver to be emotionally available to the infant (Emde, Osofsky, and Butterfield 1993). Others have termed the concepts of "mirroring" (Stern 1985), "connectedness" (Clark 1985), and "shared meaning" (Emde, Osofsky, and Butterfield 1993) as important to the parent-infant attachment process. When the caregivers are sensitive and responsive to the infant's cues, they support the infant's developing sense of competence and promote independent functioning. Sroufe (1979) termed this process "scaffolding," which not only helps the child successfully complete a task but expands the child's skills and knowledge.

Impact of Parent-Infant Interactions on Development

The idea that there is a strong relationship between parent-infant interaction and infant competence has been overwhelmingly supported in the research literature (Lewis and Goldberg 1969; Clarke-Stewart 1973; Olson, Bates, and Bayles 1984; Beckwith and Cohen 1984). Positive contingent interactions affect infants' development of social skills (Tronick and Gianino 1986a), language, attachment, and cognitive abilities (Bee et al. 1982).

Furthermore, maternal characteristics such as dimensions of emotional involvement, warmth, and attention to infant's cues have been positively related to accelerations in infant development, whereas mothers whose interactions with their babies were chaotic had infants with disorganized behaviors (Stern et al. 1973). Infants of parents who are depressed have been found to have developmental delay in language and cognitive skills as well as a low affect (Cogill et al. 1986; Lyons-Rut et al. 1986). In addition, maternal contingent responsiveness is linked to infant exploration and to more advanced communication (Yarrow et al. 1971).

Through repeated positive interactions with parents, infants become securely attached, a condition that has many advantages for an infant's development. Securely attached infants view their parents as a security base from which they can explore their environment. Securely attached infants have been found to be more socially competent toddlers (Waters, Wippman, and Sroufe 1979). In comparison to children classified as insecurely attached infants, children who are securely attached are more cooperative, more competent problem solvers, and more likely to have internal controls.

The strong link shown between parent-infant interactions and developmental competence underscores the need to assist parents when interactions are troubled or fail. Toward this end, professionals are teaching parents how to enhance parent-infant interactions in neonatal intensive care nurseries (Field 1987; Wyly and Allen 1990; Wyly, Allen, and Wilson 1995) and in early intervention programs (Rosenberg and Robinson 1985). Further, during recent years, assessment instruments have been developed to guide and evaluate intervention approaches.

Maladaptive Interaction Patterns

Positive interactive relationships between parents and infants can provide a rich foundation for later relationships as well as enhancing the development of the infant (Simeonsson et al. 1986). Normally, the interactions are bidirectional, with each agent regulating a shared reciprocity process through transactions that involve continuous negotiations (Bell 1968). However, the development of normal interactive exchanges is jeopardized when one member of the interactional pair does not read accurately or respond appropriately to the cues of the other. As a result, affective or interactive disturbances may occur (Field 1987).

Because of the overwhelming evidence that a positive relationship exists between high-quality caregiver mutuality and infant competence, researchers have examined factors that can affect interaction patterns. Edward Tronick and Andrew Gianino (1986a) employed a "still-face" paradigm in which mothers of infants were asked to be unresponsive to their infant for several minutes as they faced their alert infant. The infants initially tried to engage their mothers in an interaction and after several minutes became distressed. In another experiment, mothers were instructed to read a newspaper as their infant played and attempted to interact with them. Fifteen-month-old infants played and explored less under conditions where their mothers were preoccupied (Sorce and Emde 1982).

Studies of interaction patterns of parents and infants at risk have for the most part looked at the infant's role in shaping interactions (Rosenberg and Robinson 1988). More recently, investigators have examined affective parental disturbances and their effect on parent-child relationships (Clark, Paulson, and Conlin 1993).

The presence of infant disabling conditions poses a risk for adaptive parent-infant interactions. Parents must cope with infants who are less responsive, are fragile, have a lower activity level, and make fewer social initiations compared with normally developing infants (Barnard and Kelly 1990; Ramey, Bell, and Gowen 1980). Infants with visual impairments smile less than normal infants and maintain contact through the use of auditory and tactile cues (Kastein, Spaulding, and Scharf 1980; Fraiberg 1975). Depressed activity levels have been noted in infants with perinatal complications such as prematurity or respiratory distress syndrome (Field 1987). Less eye contact has been noted in interactions between Down syndrome infants and their mothers (Jones 1980a).

Consider several examples of interactive problems:

Six-month-old Michael has severe cerebral palsy. His condition restricts coordinated head and body movement. His father sits close to him, leans forward, smiles, and says, "Hi, Michael." Then he picks up a brightly colored pop-up toy and says, "Michael look at this!" Michael attempts to move toward his father. His eyes widen while he looks at his father's face. Michael sustains the gaze for several seconds until he can no longer support holding his head erect. Michael's head drops toward his chest, and his father stops his interaction with him.

A mother with a history of psychiatric problems tries to soothe her crying four-month-old baby. The baby continues to flail her arms and cry as her mother bounces her, while vigorously hitting her back in a stereotyped rhythm. During this interaction, the mother does not speak. She glances briefly at the baby, who stops crying momentarily. Then she again begins to vigorously bounce her baby, and the crying resumes.

Rachel is a three-week premature infant, who is now described as a "growing preemie." This means she is out of the critical stage and beginning to make medical gains, but she is still quite fragile and must remain in an incubator most of the time. Her parents have traveled sixty miles from their home to the neonatal intensive care nursery where Rachel is hospitalized. Upon their arrival in the nursery, they talk to her through the incubator portholes. Rachel does not open her eyes.

Jason, an eight-month-old baby with Down syndrome, is playing with his father. His father initiates a game of peekaboo by covering his eyes, then saying "peekaboo" as he removes his hands. Jason looks at his father but does not grin or smile. His father tries again, first covering his own eyes and then Jason's. Jason continues to look at his father, but his emotional expression does not indicate surprise or joy. His father stops playing the game.

In a study of mother-child dyads, the overall responsiveness of infants with mental retardation was lower than their normal counterparts. Infants with mental retardation made significantly fewer social initiations toward their mothers. Comparison studies of parent-infant interactions of Down syndrome infants provide evidence of a number of significant behavioral differences between these children and normal infants. There is less interactive turn taking, less gaze behavior, and fewer directed vocalizations (Hanson 1981; Richard 1986). These findings suggest that the social interactional process may be disrupted because of lower levels of active engagement in high-mutuality exchanges between such infants and their caregivers. Consequently, to elicit appropriate responses from their infant, parents must be more sensitive and work harder and better to elicit and sustain interactions (Kelly 1982). This increased demand on parents can create stress as well as feelings of inadequacy. Parents may also experience less pleasure and more frustration in their interactions.

Differences in maternal directiveness and control of interactions through verbal commands have been found in studies that compare the interactions between mothers and infants who are disabled or who are nondisabled but matched in mental age (Hanzlick and Stevenson 1986; Jones 1980b). Qualitative differences in mother-infant turn taking was observed in interactions involving infants with Down syndrome. When compared to a group of normal infants, disabled infants engaged in more vocal "clashes," situations where mothers and infants vocalized at the same time (Berger and Cunningham 1983). Analysis of interactions between mothers and infants with cognitive delays shows that these mother-infant dyads make fewer interactive responses than normal mother-infant dyads (Eheart 1982). One explanation for this is that the mothers of infants with delays are just as responsive as the mothers of normal infants, but they respond less often because their delayed infants give them fewer cues than normally developing infants would.

Empirical investigations of parent–preterm infant dyads have shown that in face-to-face and feeding interactions, mothers of preterm infants are more active in stimulating their unresponsive infants (Field 1977; Brown and Bakeman 1979). Yet, mothers of sick preterm babies are less likely to talk to, touch, or cuddle them (DiVitto and Goldberg 1979). These early interactions have long-term effects, as illustrated by the results of a study of game playing between parents and groups of four-month-old infants. Compared to parents and normal infants, there was less game playing, for example, peekaboo and patty-cake, between parents and preterm infants (Field 1979). Documentation of game-playing interactions between parents and their eight-month-old sick preterms and parents and their healthy full-term infants revealed that the parents of the sick preterms were more active in their interactions, even though the sick preterms fretted and played less (Goldberg, Brachfield, and DiVitto 1980).

In summary, the research suggests that fragile, unresponsive, and sick preterm infants affect the early interactional dyad. Parents work harder to elicit responses from these infants, who do not respond readily to subtle cues (Farren and Briggs 1986). During such attempts to stimulate their infants, parents often overstimulate the infants, which causes the infants to look away or fuss in an attempt to disengage. The parents' extra efforts to arouse and stimulate their high-risk infants persist through the first year of life (Field 1983a).

Interactions are also altered when the parent is unresponsive. Field et al. (1990) filmed depressed and nondepressed mothers with their three-month-old infants. Not only was there less matched play between depressed mothers and infants, but more of the interaction time was spent in anger or protest or in disengagement. Less-synchronous interactions have been observed with parents who are mentally ill or have been abused as children (Rutter 1990). Such interactions have negative outcomes for infants, who respond with agitated and depressed behaviors.

Consider each of the three examples that follow. Each illustrates a situation in which the caregiver needs assistance in reading the infant's interactional signals. The caregivers also need to modify their interactions to better match those of their infant.

A single mother, age twenty-six, and her seven-month-old male infant have been referred by the child and family services agency to an early intervention program. Until recently, the infant showed no signs of developmental problems, although a visiting home nurse noted at three months that the infant did not smile much or show interest in others. The mother lives alone and has little in the way of social support from her family. For the past ten months, she has experienced bouts of severe depression. In a recent developmental screening test, the baby showed a mild developmental delay.

A grandfather thoroughly enjoys playing with his eight-month-old granddaughter, Kyle. She likes rough-and-tumble play, peekaboo, and "gotcha." Her grandfather expresses concern that although Kyle giggles and laughs during the games, she sometimes appears distracted and looks away after several minutes of turn taking.

Jesse, a thirteen-month-old infant with Down syndrome, has just been admitted to an infant intervention program. A developmental assessment shows that he has a four-month cognitive delay and a three-month gross motor delay. Jesse's mother reports she tries to play games with him but doesn't feel very successful because she has to work so hard to gain his interest and he gives little indication of enjoying play with her.

The context of early social interactions allows parents and infants to begin a reciprocal relationship. In this process, parents gain confidence in "reading" their baby and making contingent responses to their overtures. Infants, too, acquire confidence in knowing they have an effect on their environment. Poor or dysfunctional interaction patterns may contribute to affective and developmental disorders for the infant and to inappropriate caregiver interaction skills.

Methodology for Assessing Parent-Infant Interactions

Methods for observing parent-infant interactions were first developed and used by academic researchers concerned with the nature of early social interactions and their contribution to child development. This early focus changed somewhat in the 1960s as intervention efforts with infants at risk for disabilities began to expand and became necessary to increase our understanding of interactions involving infants with disabilities. The considerable body of evidence that shows that the interactions between parents and their disabled infants are different from those between parents and nondisabled infants shifted intervention efforts from an infant focus to a broader family focus. Moreover, it became more likely that assessments of parent-infant interactions in families with high-risk infants would be used to formulate intervention plans (Bryant and Graham 1993).

Since 1985, a number of empirically based scales have been developed to assess parent-infant functioning and to guide interventions with parents and disabled infants. Whereas some scales were designed primarily for research or clinical purposes, others were developed as part of specific infant intervention programs (Bromwich 1981).

Methodological Issues

The choice of an assessment procedure depends first on the purpose of assessing the interaction and on the specific behaviors to measured. Once it is clear why you are doing an assessment and what it is you want to study, you can choose among a number of parent-infant interaction assessments that vary in several dimensions. These variables include the setting of the observation, number of observations, types of behaviors observed, materials used, structure of the observation, and measurement format.

Generally, an evaluation of the parent-infant interaction pattern is part of a more comprehensive assessment that includes a structured assessment of the infant's developmental status. In addition, information is gathered from parents on the child's developmental history, medical conditions, and family history.

The setting used for observing interactions can be the infant's home environment, a clinic, or a laboratory observation room. Some assessment protocols specify exactly where observations must take place, whereas others are more flexible. Viewing interactions in the home is an advantage in that the participants' behavior may be more realistic. But practical considerations such as scheduling, expense, and time required to make home visits may eliminate this as a choice. Laboratory studies offer more control across observations. In addition, often the interactions you want to study can be elicited more easily in a laboratory setting than in a home. However, the behaviors may not be as natural as in the home setting.

An important consideration in assessing parent-infant interaction is the structure of the observation. How observations are structured depends on the assessment goals. Parents and infants can be observed during bathing or feeding times (Barnard 1979) or while playing. Some procedures require parents to teach their infants to do something (Mahoney et al. 1986). As an alternative, parents and infants might be observed for a specific time period just doing what they would normally do in each other's presence.

The length of the observation is usually determined by the activities being observed. Some scales specify a minimum observation time, whereas others have several five- to ten-minute observations within one session. Total observation time in most assessments usually does not exceed twenty to thirty minutes.

Observational formats include direct observation and videotapes. Observers must be trained to high scoring reliability. Trained observers are usually allowed to move or shift attention during the observation, but their presence may inhibit some parent-infant behaviors. The use of videotapes for observation depends on the availability of videotape facilities. A decided advantage of using videotapes is that they can be viewed and rewatched at later times. If the presence of a video camera is distracting to either partner in the dyad, the behaviors may not accurately portray typical parent-infant interactions. In some cases, videos can serve both as an assessment and as a teaching tool. Videotapes can be used for demonstrations, feedback, and practice. Intervention staff can use a video to teach effective interactions to parents.

The behaviors assessed by the various scales are typically behaviors that the research literature on parent-infant interactions has identified as essential to high-quality early relationships. For example, reading and responding to infant clues, regulating stimulation, and signaling with clarity are included in most scales. The organization of these behaviors in increasingly complex levels of interactional competence is used in several assessments (Bromwich 1983; Greenspan and Lieberman 1980).

Assessment Approaches

Parent-infant interactive behaviors are measured in several different ways. Binary checklists wherein the rater indicates the presence or absence of the specific behavior are used in some scales. Behavioral rating scales involving judgments about the quality of the observed behaviors are frequently used as a data source. Finally, time-triggered coding procedures are used to measure the frequency of specified behaviors as they occur within specific timed intervals.

Parent-infant assessments measure two levels of behaviors. *Molar* categories are global behavioral dimensions such as responsiveness, warmth, or directiveness. Such behaviors establish the overall tone of the interactions. *Molecular* categories are more specific parent or infant behaviors that constitute the overall interactions. Behaviors such as gestures, smiles, eye contact, and turning away are examples of molecular categories. Ratings that use molar scores provide a general summary of the observed interaction. Molar assessments, for example, can provide information on the level of negative or positive affect, on interaction style, and on the dyad's sensitivity. Molecular ratings can identify more narrowly defined behaviors that can be used in structuring interventions, for example, use of prompts in play or vocal imitation. Although these categories are convenient observation devices, trained observers conducting interactional assessments must be aware that behaviors do not always fit neatly into the defined molecular or molar categories (Comfort 1988).

Measures of Parent-Infant Interactions

A number of assessment scales have been developed to assess the overall quality of parent-infant interactions. These measures have been used principally for research or in clinical settings. Assessing the quality of parent-infant interaction provides a more comprehensive evaluation of infants when used in conjunction with assessments of a child's developmental functioning. When interventionists are selecting a parent-infant interaction assessment for infants who are disabled or delayed, an important criterion is that the assessment reliably measure behaviors in dyads (Rosenberg and Robinson 1985). In addition, the scale should pinpoint useful interaction strategies that can easily be incorporated into the intervention system to plan for families and their disabled infants.

This section describes eight scales for assessing parent-infant interaction. The scales represent different approaches to observing parents and infants.

Family-Administered Neonatal Activities (FANA)

The FANA is used as a hospital-based family support instrument to empower and support parents following the birth of their baby. Its purpose is to provide a vehicle whereby parents can interpret their perceptions of their newborns. It is used as an intervention tool when families have experienced a difficult birth or are concerned about their ability to care for infants at home (Cardone and Gilkerson 1990).

The FANA is conducted on day two postpartum and includes (1) a chart review, (2) a parent perception interview, (3) administration of the Brazelton Neonatal Behavioral Assessment Scale, and (4) an integrated summary by a trained facilitator. The administration of the FANA takes approximately forty minutes. Parents are encouraged to share their perceptions of their infant's behaviors and to integrate these with observations during the assessment.

Parent Behavior Progression (PBP)

The PBP (Form I and II) (Bromwich 1981) was constructed by the University of California at Los Angeles Infant Studies Project to evaluate interactions between parents and their high-risk infants. The results are to be used as guides for intervention efforts. The test has been used to sensitize interventionists to the unique properties of a parent-infant dyad and to promote increased parental enjoyment of their infants.

Form I is used with infants between birth and nine months, and Form II spans the period from nine to thirty-six months. The scale serves as a diagnostic and intervention tool that focuses the examiner on positive behaviors in the parent-infant repertoire. The scale focuses on the parent rather than the infant. The assessment is used to plan intervention strategies to assist parents in acquiring new behavior patterns. The scales are composed of a checklist of parent questions and structured observations of parents' interactions with their infants. The PBP identifies six hierarchical levels of parent involvement, ordered according to increasing parental competencies (see Table 7.1).

The PBP level sequence is proposed to follow the normal course of parent-infant involvement, in which parents first enjoy their babies through learning to recognize their cues and then provide experiences for growth and development. Rose Bromwich (1983) points out that parent interventions do not have to follow the PBP level sequence strictly. Parents can be encouraged to engage in play activities with infants at Level IV or V, which would result in mutually satisfying interactions and feelings of competence, for example, at Levels II and III.

The Maternal Behavior Rating Scale (MBRS)

The MBRS (Mahoney, Finger, and Powell 1985) is a molar rating scale that assesses the quality of maternal interactive behaviors with one-, two-, and three-year-old infants who are mentally retarded. First, a ten-minute mother-infant play session is videotaped. The videotape interactions between the mother and child are then rated using the five-point Likert scale on eighteen maternal behavior items and four infant behaviors. Test observers should be trained to achieve 90 percent interrater reliability. The free-play testing situations should be as similar as possible. The maternal items in the scale were drawn from other maternal behavior scales reported in the literature. A factor analysis of the eighteen items yielded three independent factors: child-oriented or maternal pleasure, quantity of stimulation, and maternal controller directiveness. The eighteen MBRS items are listed in Table 7.2.

A seven-item short form of the MBRS (Mahoney, Powell, and Finger 1986) was developed as a more time-efficient means of assessing mother-child interactions. The authors propose that the shortened form may be useful for evaluating the effects of intervention programs specifically designed to modify mother-infant play interactions.

Parent/Caregiver Involvement Scale (PCIS)

The PCIS (Farren et al. 1987) rates caregivers' involvement during interactive free play with an infant or toddler during a twenty-minute live or videotaped observation. The scale focuses on the caregiver's rather than the

TABLE 7.1   Levels of the Parent Behavior Progression

Level	Parent Behavior
I	Enjoyment of the infant
II	Parent is a sensitive observer of the infant; reads infant cues and responds to them
III	Parent engages in quality and quantity interaction; interactions are mutually satisfying and provide an opportunity for the development of attachment
IV	Parent demonstrates an awareness of developmentally appropriate materials and activities
V	Parent initiates new play activities based on principles internalized from own experience or modeled demonstration
VI	Parent independently generates new developmentally appropriate activities that are interesting to the infant

SOURCE: R. Bromwich, *Working with Parents and Infants: An Interactional Approach* (Baltimore: University Park Press, 1981).

TABLE 7.2   Maternal Behavior Rating Scale

Maternal Behavior Items

Expressiveness
Enjoyment
Warmth
Sensitivity to child interest
Sensitivity to child state
Responsivity
Achievement orientation
Appropriate stimulation
Inventiveness
Physical stimulation
Social stimulation
Playfulness
Degree of comfort
Effectiveness
Approval
Permissiveness
Patience
Directiveness

SOURCE: G. Mahoney, A. Powell, and I. Finger, "The Maternal Behavior Rating Scale," *Topics in Early Childhood Special Education* 6 (1986): 44–56.

infant's contribution to interactions. Eleven behaviors, for instance, vocalization, physical responsiveness, positive and negative emotions, control, and teaching behavior, are rated on a one-to-five Likert scale.

Behaviors are evaluated using three criteria: (1) the quality or effectiveness of the caregiver's behavior, acceptance, and warmth; (2) the amount of care, which refers to the level and quantity of the caregiver's behavior; and (3) the appropriateness, that is, the match between the infant and caregiver behaviors. An overall interaction rating is also included in the assessment.

The PCIS scale has been used with populations that include environmentally high-risk infants and developmentally delayed infants.

The assessment profile of the caregiver's interactive behaviors with the child has been useful clinically in designing individualized family plans. It has been pointed out that one drawback of the PCIS is its focus on caregiver behavior, which precludes information on the development of reciprocal exchanges between parent and child (Barnard and Kelly 1990).

Nursing Child Assessment Teaching and Feeding Scales (NCAST)

The NCAST (Barnard 1979) is a binary checklist designed to assess reciprocity and contingency in parent-child interactions in two situations, feeding and teaching a task. The first situation, feeding, is viewed as a familiar activity that provides the most opportunities for interaction between parent and infant. In the second situation, caregivers are asked to teach two tasks to their infant, one task at age level and another that is about six weeks' beyond. Following three to five minutes of observing the teaching or feeding, the trained observer checks the behaviors observed (feeding includes 76 yes/no items; teaching includes 73 yes/no items). The items are organized into six subcategories, including four caregiver categories, which are sensitivity to cues, fostering socioemotional growth, fostering cognitive growth, and response to infant distress, and two child/infant categories, which are responsiveness and clarity of cues. NCAST results are expressed as subscale, caregiver, infant, and total scores.

The teaching scale has been found to be more strongly correlated with the infants' cognitive development than the feeding scale (Farren, Clark, and Ray 1990). Helen Bee et al. (1982) found that at thirty-six months, the teaching scale was moderately correlated with developmental status.

Greenspan-Lieberman Observation System for Assessment of Caregiver-Infant Interaction During Semistructured Play (GLOS)

The GLOS (Greenspan and Lieberman 1980) is a clinical observation tool used to assess adaptive and maladaptive parent-infant interactions in a laboratory setting. This scale was developed for use with multirisk families. The assessment is based on the Stanley Greenspan (1981) model of infant emotional development, which assumes that newborn infants begin to regulate and adapt to their environment. As their adaptation processes become more organized, they demonstrate the capacity to establish an attachment to caregivers. Further, although there are age-related adaptive behaviors, there are individual differences in the process, since infants use their unique coping skills to become invested in caregivers.

The GLOS scales measure fifty-three caregiver behaviors and forty-three infant behaviors. The caregiver behaviors include contingent responses to the infant, pleasurable or aversive tactile experiences with the infant, and level of stimulation with the infant. Infant behaviors, by contrast, focus on matters such as disengagement, seeking physical contact with the caregiver, and responses to caregiver behaviors. Trained observers code behaviors occurring in a ten-minute videotaped caregiver-infant play sequence filmed in a laboratory setting. The complexity of the GLOS has promoted the development of a shorter version that employs a five-page rating system for eighty parent and infant behaviors.

The GLOS has been used principally as a research tool to describe the parenting interactions of adolescent and other groups of high-risk parents (Hofheimer, O'Grady, and Packer 1988). The authors propose that the scale can provide useful clinical information for planning and implementing interventions for caregivers and infants with maladaptive interactions. Because of its length and complexity, the GLOS has not been widely used for clinical purposes. The final version of the test has not yet been published.

Mother-Infant Play Interaction Scale (MIPIS)

The MIPIS (Walker and Thompson 1982) assesses the interactive strategies used by mothers and infants in an unstructured play situation. Play is considered to be a rich medium for interactive behaviors and subsequent attachment. The scale measures mutuality and responsiveness of mothers and infants between four to six weeks after birth. Qualities of play interactions are rated in a five-minute live or videotaped session. The sixteen-item scale contains three subscales: maternal, infant, and dyadic. The maternal subscale includes maternal holding style, vocalization style, expression of affect, and visual interaction. The infant subscale consists of the predominant infant affect level, wakeful response, and visual interaction. Measures in the dyadic subscale include dyadic quality of interaction, interaction affect synchrony, and termination of interaction. Some examples from the MIPIS scale are as follows:

- Maternal holding style
- Maternal expression of affect—quality of contingency to infant
- Maternal caregiving style
- Predominant infant wakeful response level

- Predominant infant mood/affect
- Maternal visual interaction
- Infant visual interaction
- Style of play—animate versus inanimate—interaction
- Maternal vocalization style—general (tone and content)
- Maternal vocalization style—quantity of contingency (to holding style)
- Maternal attempts at smile elicitation
- Kinesthetic quality of interaction
- Overall dyadic quality of interaction
- Synchrony of affect
- Termination of interaction

The MIPIS has been used as a research tool, and the authors provide instructions for clinical use of this instrument. Normative data on this scale are limited to normal mother-infant dyads and may not accurately reflect high-risk infant-mother interactive behaviors.

Observation of Communicative Interaction (OCI)

The OCI is a scale devised to guide observations of mother-infant interaction (Klein and Briggs 1986). The scale is used to assess the strengths and weaknesses and quality and style of the interaction. Ten interaction categories are included on the scale:

- Mother provides appropriate tactile and kinesthetic communication
- Mother shows pleasure when interacting with infant
- Mother responds to infant's distress
- Mother positions self and infant to maximize eye-to-eye contact
- Mother smiles contingently at infant
- Mother varies pitch and uses exaggerated intonation
- Mother encourages conversation
- Mother responds contingently to infant's behavior
- Mother modifies interaction in response to infant's stress cues
- Mother uses communication to teach language and conceptual skills

The OCI is intended to be used in a clinical setting as an informal guide to the observer. There are no data on the instrument's reliability and validity.

Conclusion

Given the evidence regarding the contributions of early parent-infant interactions to developmental outcomes, evaluating interactions between at-risk parents and infants can provide valuable information for planning appropriate interventions. Until recently, there were few available interaction scales. Those described here have been designed for practitioners to systematically observe parent-infant dyads. Although the development of the scales is an important first step, rigorous standardization of the scales, accompanied by empirical evaluation of their reliability and validity, is still needed.

Using Intervention to Improve Parent-Infant Interactions

Optimal parent-infant social interactions rely on rhythmicity, contingent responding, predictability, and the readability of each partner in the dyad (Brazelton, Koslowski, and Main 1974; Goldberg 1977). When infants or caregivers are impaired, their communication can be chaotic and confusing. As a result, often neither the infant nor the caregiver responds appropriately to the initiations of the other, and often both make trial-and-error responses to chaotic signals. Recently, effective procedures have been developed to improve parent-infant interactions in such dyads. These are promising beginnings in family-infant interventions (Marfo 1988).

Translating parent-infant interaction assessments into intervention goals involves several steps. First, a systematic observational assessment of the interaction must be carried out. The assessment should be strengthened with information about the family. Ideally, this information would include the availability of family support systems, current concerns about the infant and interactive process, medical status of the child and caregivers, resources, and needs. In addition, assessment of the infant's developmental status should be included. Second, the strengths and weaknesses and overall style of the observed interaction must be identified. Third, information should be shared with parents to plan reasonable interventions that fit the family context. Finally, in collaboration with the caregivers, reasonable goals should be set to foster competence and mutually satisfying interactions.

A parent-infant observation measure can be useful for planning and adopting a workable intervention plan. Care should be taken, however, to facilitate the goal-setting process by coupling these data with other information about the family and its value system. Professionals must also recognize that infants with disabling conditions do not always have maladaptive interactions. They may have qualitatively different interactions that parents often match.

At their best, parent-infant interaction assessments provide a window on the total family system. To set meaningful intervention goals and provide a foundation for successful interventions, assessments should be used to identify the strengths as well as the weaknesses of current interactions. It is inappropriate to design interventions based solely on low-scoring items or items missed in the observation. Instead, interventionists can use the assessment data to better understand the interaction strategies that do and can work for the parent-infant dyad both within the family and in other situations. Interpretation of assessment outcomes should attend to the individual differences that occur in a dynamic relationship. Individual differences should not always be interpreted as deficits. Successful treatment plans incorporate techniques tailored to the family's individual style and needs.

Intervention programs that in the past used only child-focused goals now emphasize family strengths that include the infant. Investigators found that programs emphasizing infant development that included strategies to enhance parent-infant interaction resulted in improved parent interactional skills (Rosenberg and Robinson 1985). Intervention approaches with the goal of modifying the quality of parent-infant interactions have used either direct training techniques or interventions that focus on modifying the needs and resources of the family system. The nondirective strategies have addressed family factors such as the parents' attitudes toward their infant, family stress, and the availability of support (Crnic, Greenberg, and Slough 1986). Although there is general agreement in the field that there is an association between family functioning and parent-infant interactions, the relative effectiveness of nondirective and direct interventions has not been effectively evaluated.

Direct approaches use modeling, formal classes, or direct instruction techniques to teach parents not sure how these differ. Some programs use videotapes of parent-infant interactions as an instructional base (Filler 1976). In others, professionals and parents engage in dyadic teaching that involves demonstration and feedback to parents (Clark and Siefer 1983; Rosenberg and Robinson 1985). Field (1983b), however, has used interaction coaching techniques to modify the behaviors of mothers of high-risk infants. In face-to-face interactions, mothers were asked to imitate their infant's behavior. Mothers became more attentive to the arousal cues of their infants, and infants became more attentive and decreased their gaze aversion. Videotaped interactions of parent-infant interactions have been used to provide structured feedback to the parent (McCollum 1984). Rose Bromwich (1981) developed an interactive program model for improving the nature and quality of interaction between high-risk infants and their parents. The Parent Behavior Progression is used to assess parent-infant interaction and serves as the base for intervention plans. Goals from a sample intervention plan are presented in Table 7.3 (Bromwich 1983).

Creating opportunities for families with at-risk infants to improve their interactions can enhance parent competencies and infant outcomes. Intervention programs whose goals address the improvement of interaction can empower parents and reduce parental stress. Further, intervention staff who systematically measure interactions and plan interaction goals will enhance their understanding of parents' perceptions and values in their ongoing relationship with their infant.

TABLE 7.3   Sample Goals from Parent Behavior Progression Intervention Program

Goals	Rationale and Considerations	Program Plan	Evaluation Plan
Increase social behavior of infant with parents; increase parents' valuing of infant's social behavior and consequently their responses to it.	Infant's vocalizations are pleasurable to the infant; minimal eye contact observed between infant and mother; no social games observed or reported with infant. Mother enjoys talking to interventionists.	Respond to and reward infant's vocalizations. Point out that infant is like mother—likes to "talk," too. Discuss with mother the importance of eye contact. In response to mother's questions, provide list of, and bring, suitable records and books. Model social games, nursery rhyme games.	Look for increase in infant's social and affective behavior with parent by second summary time, 4 months hence.
Develop third caregiver's skills in play interaction with infant.	Third caregiver is teenager who spends several hours a day caring for infant.	Model presenting toys to infant and interacting with infant to increase infant's interest and attention span.	Look for infant's increased pleasure in play and a longer attention span.

SOURCE: R. Bromwich, *Parent Behavior Progression: Manual and 1983 Supplement* (Northridge, CA: Center for Research Development and Services, Department of Educational Psychology, California State University, 1983).

Summary

Parent-infant interactions are the foundation for effective relationships later in development. A harmonious interactive relationship features responsiveness to social cues, ability to modulate arousal, turn taking, and affective displays. Research strongly suggests that early social interactions characterized by warmth and high mutuality promote the development of communication and language abilities, cognitive skills, and social-emotional stability.

Studies of parent-infant interactions when one member of the pair is disabled or affectively unresponsive show that interactions are likely to be characterized by less mutuality than is typical in normal dyads. High-risk infants are more likely to give confusing communication signals and to be less responsive to parents. Parents may also be the source of interactive disturbances. Their interactional skills may be lacking in synchrony and balance. For example, findings show that depressed or cognitively impaired parents are more likely to be affectively unresponsive to their infants' social initiations.

A number of assessments have been developed to measure parent-infant interactions. Most scales employ direct behavioral observations of molar or molecular categories of interactive behaviors. Molar categories are broad categories of behavior such as sensitivity and responsiveness within the dyad. More discrete units of behavior such as eye contact, gaze, or smile are termed molecular units. The eight parent-infant scales described in this chapter are the Family-Administered Neonatal Activities, Parent Behavior Progression, Maternal Behavior Rating Scale, Parent/Caregiver Involvement Scale, Nursing Child Assessment Teaching and Feeding Scales, Greenspan-Lieberman Observation System for Assessment of Caregiver-Infant Interaction During Semistructured Play, Mother-Infant Play Interaction Scale, and Observation of Communicative Interaction.

Procedures for assessing parents and infants with disabilities have been incorporated into infant intervention programs. Interventions that focus on improving parent-infant interactions have gained increasing emphasis in intervention programs.

References

Affleck, G., H. Tennen, J. Rowe, B. Roscher, and L. Walker. 1989. Effects of formal support on mother's adaptation to the hospital-to-home transition of high-risk infants: The benefits and costs of helping. *Child Development* 60:488–495.

Ainsworth, M. 1982. Early caregiving and later attachment problems. In *Birth-Interaction and Attachment*. Skillman, NJ: Johnson and Johnson.

Ainsworth, M.D.S. 1973. The development of infant-mother attachment. *In Review of Child Development Research*. Vol. 3. Edited by B. M. Caldwell and H. W. Ricciuti. Chicago: University of Chicago Press.

Antoniadis, A., S. Didow, S. Lockhart, and P. Moroge. 1984. Screening for early cognitive and communicative behaviors. *Communique* 9:14–20.

Barnard, K. E. 1979. *Instructor's Learning Resource Manual*. Seattle: NCAST Publications, University of Washington.

Barnard, K. E., and J. E. Kelly. 1990. Assessment of parent-child interactions. In *Handbook of Early Childhood Intervention*, edited by S. J. Meisels and J. P. Shonkoff. New York: Cambridge University Press.

Barnard, K. E., M. A. Hammond, C. L. Booth, H. L. Bee, S. K. Mitchell, and S. J. Spieker. 1989. Measurement and meaning of parent-child interaction. In *Applied Developmental Psychology*. Vol. 3. Edited by F. Morrison, C. Lord, and D. Keating. New York: Academic Press.

Beckwith, L., and S. E. Cohen. 1984. Home environment and cognitive competence in preterm children during the first 5 years. In *Home Environment and Early Cognitive Development*, edited by A. W. Gottfried. New York: Academic Press.

Bee, H. L., K. E. Barnard, S. J. Eyres, C. A. Gray, M. A. Hammond, A. L. Spietz, C. Snyder, and B. Clark. 1982. Prediction of IQ and language skill from perinatal status, child performance, family characteristics, and mother-infant interaction. *Child Development* 53:1134–1156.

Bell, R. 1968. A reinterpretation of the differentiation of effects in studies of socialization. *Psychological Review* 75:81–95.

Bell, R. Q. 1974. Contributions of human infants to caregiving and social interaction. In *The Effect of the Infant on Its Caregiver*, edited by M. Lewis and L. R. Rosenblum. New York: John Wiley and Sons.

Berger, J., and C. C. Cunningham. 1983. Development of early vocal behaviors and interactions in Down's syndrome and non-handicapped infant-mother pairs. *Developmental Psychology* 19:322–331.

Bernal, J. 1972. Crying during the first ten days of life and the maternal responses. *Developmental Medicine and Child Neurology* 14:362–372.

Bornstein, M. H. 1989. Stability in early mental development: From attention and information processing in infancy to language and cognition in childhood. In *Stability and Continuity in Mental Development*, edited by M. H. Bornstein and N. A. Kaasnegar. Hillsdale, NJ: Lawrence Erlbaum Associates.

Bowlby, J. 1982. *Attachment*. 2d ed. New York: BasicBooks.

Brazelton, T. B., B. Koslowski, and M. Main. 1974. The origins of reciprocity: The early mother-infant interaction. In *The Effect of the Infant on Its Caregiver*, edited by M. Lewis and L. R. Rosenblum. New York: John Wiley and Sons.

Bromwich, R. 1983. *Parent Behavior Progression: Manual and 1983 Supplement*. Northridge, CA: Center for Research Development and Services, Department of Educational Psychology, California State University.

_____. 1981. *Working with Parents and Infants: An Interactional Approach*. Baltimore: University Park Press.

Brown, J. V., and R. Bakeman. 1979. Relationships of human mothers with their infants during the first year of life. In *Maternal Influences and Early Behavior*, edited by R. W. Bell and W. P. Smotherman. New York: Spectrum.

Bryant, D. M., and M. A. Graham. 1993. *Implementing Early Intervention: From Research to Effective Practice*, edited by D. M. Bryant and M. A. Graham. New York: Guilford Press.

Cardone, I. A., and L. Gilkerson. 1990. Family Administered Neonatal Activities: An exploratory method for the integration of parental perceptions and newborn behavior. *Infant Mental Health Journal* 11:127–141.

Clark, G. N., and R. Siefer. 1983. Facilitating mother-infant communication: A treatment model of high-risk and developmentally delayed infants. *Infant Mental Health Journal* 4:67–82.

Clark, R. 1985. *The Parent-Child Early Relational Assessment.* Madison, WI: University of Wisconsin Medical School.

Clark, R., A. Paulson, and S. Conlin. 1993. Assessment of developmental status and parent-infant relationships: The therapeutic process of evaluation. In *Handbook of Infant Mental Health,* edited by C. H. Zeanah. New York: Guilford Press.

Clarke-Stewart, K. A. 1973. Interactions between mothers and their young children: Characteristics and consequences. *Monographs of the Society for Research in Child Development* 38(6–7 serial no. 153):1–109.

Cogill, S., H. Caplan, H. Alexandra, K. Robson, and R. Kumar. 1986. Impact of maternal postnatal depression on cognitive development of young children. *British Medical Journal* 292:1165–1167.

Comfort, M. 1988. Assessing parent-child interaction. In *Family Assessment in Early Intervention,* edited by D. B. Bailey and R. J. Simeonsson. Columbus, OH: Merrill.

Condon, W., and Sander, L. 1974. Synchrony demonstrated between movements of the neonate and adult speak. *Child Development* 45:456–462.

Crnic, K., M. T. Greenberg, and N. M. Slough. 1986. Early stress and social support influences on mothers' and high-risk infants' functioning in late infancy. *Infant Mental Health Journal* 7:34–58.

DiVitto, B., and S. Goldberg. 1979. The effects of newborn medical status on early parent-infant interaction. In *Infants Born at Risk: Behavior and Development,* edited by T. M. Field, A. M. Sostek, S. Goldberg, and H. H. Shuman. New York: Spectrum.

Donovan, W., and L. Leavitt. 1989. Maternal self-efficacy and infant attachment: Integrating physiology, perceptions, and behavior. *Child Development* 60:460–470.

Eheart, B. 1982. Mother-child interactions with nonretarded and mentally retarded preschoolers. *American Journal of Mental Deficiency* 87:20–25.

Emde, R. N., J. O. Osofsky, and P. M. Butterfield. 1993. *The IFEEL Pictures: A New Instrument for Interpreting Emotions.* Madison, CT: International Universities Press.

Farren, D., and M. Briggs. 1986. *Observation of Communicative Interaction: A Model Program to Facilitate Positive Communication Interactions Between Caregivers and Their High-Risk Infants.* DHHS Publication no. MCJ 06351–01–0. Washington, DC: Government Printing Office.

Farren, D. C., C. Kasari, P. Yoder, L. Harber, G. S. Huntington, and M. Comfort-Smith. 1987. Rating mother-child interactions in handicapped and at-risk infants. In *Stimulation and Intervention in Infant Development,* edited by T. Tamir. London: Freund Publishing House.

Farren, D. C., K. S. Clark, and A. R. Ray. 1990. Measures of parent-child interaction. In *Interdisciplinary Assessment of Infants,* edited by E. D. Gibbs and D. M Teti. Baltimore: Paul H. Brookes.

Field, T. 1987. Affective and interactive disturbances in infants. In *Handbook of Infant Development,* edited by J. D. Osofsky. 2d ed. New York: John Wiley and Sons.

_____. 1983a. High-risk infants "have less fun" during early interactions. *Topics in Early Childhood Special Education* 3:77–87.

_____. 1983b. Early interactions and interaction coaching of high-risk infants and parents. In *Development and Policy Concerning Children with Special Needs: The Minnesota Symposia on Child Psychology,* edited by M. Perlmutter. Hillsdale, NJ: Lawrence Erlbaum Associates.

Field, T., B. Healy, S. Goldstein, and M. Guthertz. 1990. Behavior-state matching and synchrony in mother-infant interactions of nondepressed versus depressed dyads. *Developmental Psychology* 20:7–14.

Field, T. M. 1979. Interaction patterns of high-risk and normal infants. In *Infants Born at Risk: Behavior and Development,* edited by T. M. Field, A. M. Sostek, S. Goldberg, and H. H. Shuman. New York: Spectrum.

_____. 1977. Effects of early separation, interactive deficits and experimental manipulations on infant-mother face-to-face interaction. *Child Development* 48:763–771.

Filler, J. 1976. Modifying maternal teaching style: Effects of task arrangement on the match-to-sample performance of retarded preschool-age children. *American Journal of Mental Deficiency* 87:20–25.

Fraiberg, S. 1975. The development of human attachments in infants blind from birth. *Merrill-Palmer Quarterly* 21:315–334.

Goldberg, S. 1977. Social competence in infancy: A model of parent-infant interaction. *Merrill-Palmer Quarterly* 23:163–177.

Goldberg, S., S. Brachfield, and B. DiVitto. 1980. Feeding, fussing and play: Parent-infant interaction in the first year as a function of prematurity and perinatal medical problems. In *High-Risk Infants and Children: Adult and Peer Interactions,* edited by T. Field. New York: Academic Press.

Greenspan, S. 1983. Parenting in infancy and early childhood: A developmental structuralist approach to delineating adaptive and maladaptive pattern. In *Minimizing High-Risk Parenting,* edited by J. Sasserath and R. Hoekelman. Skillman, NJ: Johnson and Johnson.

_____. 1981. *Psychopathology and Adaptation in Infancy and Early Childhood: Principles of Clinical Diagnosis and Preventive Intervention.* New York: Viking Press.

Greenspan, S., and A. Lieberman. 1980. Infants, mothers and their interactions: A quantitative clinical approach to developmental assessment. In *The Course of Life: Psychoanalytic Contributions Toward Understanding Personality Development. Vol. 1: Infancy and Early Childhood* (pub. no. ADM 80–786). Washington, DC: U.S. Government Printing Office.

Hanson, M. 1981. Down's syndrome children: Characteristics and intervention research. In *The Uncommon Child: Genesis of Behavior.* Vol. 2. Edited by M. Lewis and L. Rosenblum. New York: Plenum Press.

Hanzlick, J., and M. Stevenson. 1986. Interaction of mothers with their infants who are mentally retarded, retarded with cerebral palsy, or nonretarded. *American Journal of Mental Deficiency* 90:513–520.

Hofheimer, J. A., K. E. O'Grady, and A. B. Packer. 1988. Infants born to adolescents: Predicting development at four years from early interaction and social risk. Paper presented at the International Conference on Infant Studies, Los Angeles, March–April.

Jones, O. 1980a. Mother-child communication in very young Down's syndrome and normal children. In *High-Risk Infants and Children: Adult and Peer Interactions*, edited by T. Field, S. Goldberg, D. Stern, and A. Sostek. New York: Academic Press.

_____. 1980b. Prelinguistic communication skills in Down's syndrome and normal infants. In *High-Risk Infants and Children: Adult and Peer Interactions*, edited by T. Field. New York: Academic Press.

Kastein, S., I. Spaulding, and B. Scharf. 1980. *Raising the Young Blind Child: A Guide for Parents and Educators*. New York: Human Sciences Press.

Kaye, K. 1976. Infants' effects on their mothers' teaching strategies. In *The Social Context of Learning and Development*, edited by J. Glidwell. New York: Gardner Press.

Kelly, J. F. 1982. Effects of intervention on caregiver-infant interaction when the infant is handicapped. *Journal of the Division for Early Childhood* 5:53–63.

Klein, D., and M. Briggs. 1986. *Observation of Communicative Interaction*. A Model Program to Facilitate Positive Communication Interactions Between Caregivers and Their High-Risk Infants. DHHS Publication no. MCJ 06351–01–0. Washington, DC: Government Printing Office.

Lewis, M., and S. Goldberg. 1969. Perceptual-cognitive development in infancy: A generalized expectancy model as a function of the mother-infant interaction. *Merrill-Palmer Quarterly* 15:81–100.

Lyons-Rut, K., D. Zoll, D. Connell, and H. Grunebaum. 1986. The depressed mother and her one-year-old infant: Environment interaction, attachments, and infant development. In *Maternal Depression and Infant Disturbance: New Directions for Child Development*, edited by E. Tronick and T. Field. San Francisco: Jossey-Bass.

Mahoney, G., A. Powell, and I. Finger. 1986. The Maternal Behavior Rating Scale. *Topics in Early Childhood Special Education* 6:44–56.

Mahoney, G., A. Powell, C. Finnegan, S. Fors, and S. Wood. 1986. The transactional intervention program, theory, procedures and evaluation. In *The Family Support Network Series: Individualizing Family Services* (Monograph 4), edited by D. Gentry and J. Olson. Moscow, ID: Warren Center on Human Development, University of Idaho.

Mahoney, G., I. Finger, and A. Powell. 1985. Relationship of maternal behavioral style to the development of organically impaired mentally retarded infants. *American Journal of Mental Deficiency* 90:296–302.

Marfo, K., ed. 1988. *Parent-Child Interaction and Developmental Disabilities: Theory, Research and Intervention*. New York: Praeger.

McCollum, J. 1984. Social interaction between parents and babies: Validation of an intervention procedure. *Child: Care, Health and Development* 10:301–315.

Olson, S. L., J. E. Bates, and K. Bayles. 1984. Mother-infant interactions and the development of individual difference in children's cognitive competence. *Developmental Psychology* 20:166–179.

Ramey, C. T., P. B. Bell, and J. W. Gowen. 1980. Parents as educators during infancy: Implications from research for handicapped infants. In *New Directions for Exceptional Children*, edited by J. J. Gallagher. San Francisco: Jossey-Bass.

Richard, N. B. 1986. Interaction between mothers and infants with Down syndrome: Infant characteristics. *Topics in Early Childhood Special Education* 6:54–71.

Robson, K. S., and H. A. Moss. 1970. Patterns and determinants of maternal attachment. *Journal of Pediatrics* 11:976–985.

Rosenberg, S., and C. Robinson. 1985. Enhancement of mothers' interactional skills in an infant education program. *Education and Training of the Mentally Retarded* 20:163–169.

Rosenberg, S. A., and C. C. Robinson. 1988. Interactions of parents with their young handicapped children. In *Early Intervention for Infants and Children with Handicaps*, edited by S. L. Odom and M. B. Karnes. Baltimore: Paul H. Brookes.

Rossetti, L. M. 1990. *Infant-Toddler Assessment*. Boston: Little-Brown and Company.

Rutter, M. 1990. Commentary: Some focus and process considerations regarding effects of parental depression on children. *Developmental Psychology* 26:60–67.

Simeonsson, R. J., D. B. Bailey, G. S. Huntington, and M. Comfort. 1986. Testing the concept of goodness of fit in early intervention. *Infant Mental Health Journal* 7:81–94.

Sorce, J. F., and R. N. Emde. 1982. The meaning of infant emotional expression: Regularities in caregiving responses in normal and Down's syndrome infants. *Journal of Child Psychology and Psychiatry* 23:145–158.

Sparks, S., M. Clark, D. Oas, and R. Erickson. 1988. Clinical services to infants at risk for communication disorders. Paper presented at the annual convention of the American Speech-Language-Hearing Association, Boston, April.

Sroufe, L. A. 1979. Socioemotional development. In *Handbook of Infant Development*, edited by J. D. Osofsky. New York: Wiley.

Stern, D. 1985. *The Interpersonal World of the Infant*. New York: BasicBooks.

Stern, D. N. 1984. Mother and infant at play: The dyadic interaction involving facial, vocal and gaze behaviors. In *The Effect of the Infant on Its Caregiver*, edited by M. Lewis and L. R. Rosenblum. New York: John Wiley and Sons.

Stern, G. G., B. M. Caldwell, L. Hersher, E. L. Lipton, and J. B. Richmond. 1973. Early social contacts and social relations: Effects of quality of early relationships. In *The Competent Infant*, edited by L. J. Stone, T. Smith, and L. B. Murphy.

Tronick, E., and A. Gianino. 1986a. The transmission of maternal disturbance to the infant. In *Maternal Depression and Infant Disturbance*, edited by E. J. Tronick and T. Field. San Francisco: Jossey-Bass.

Tronick, E. Z., and A. Gianino. 1986b. Interactive mismatch and repair: Challenges to the coping infant. *Zero to Three* 6 (3):1–6.

Tronick, E. Z., and J. F. Cohn. 1989. Infant-mother face-to-face interaction: Age and gender differences in coordination and occurrence of miscoordination. *Child Development* 60:85–92.

Walker, L. O., and E.T. Thompson. 1982. In *Analysis of Current Assessment Strategies on the Health Care of Young Children and Childbearing Families*, edited by S. Smith-Humenick. Norwalk, CT: Appleton-Century Crofts.

Waters, E., J. Wippman, and L. A. Sroufe. 1979. Attachment, positive affect and competence in the peer group: Two studies in construct validation. *Child Development* 50:821–829.

Wyly, M. V., and J. Allen. 1990. *Stress and Coping in the Neonatal Intensive Care Nursery*. Tucson, AZ: Therapy Skill Builders.

Wyly, M. V., J. Allen, and J. R. Wilson. 1995. *Premature Infants and Their Families: Developmental Interventions*. San Diego: Singular Publishing.

Yarrow, L., J. Rubenstein, F. Pedersen, and J. Janowski. 1971. Dimensions of early stimulation and their different effects on development. *Merrill-Palmer Quarterly* 18:205–218.

8

Measuring Infant
Emotion and Temperament

Sweet baby in thy face
Soft desires I can trace
Secret joys and secret smiles
Little pretty infant wiles.

—*William Blake, "A Cradle Song"*

Introduction

I have a friend who has a two-year-old daughter and a three-month-old infant. She is constantly saying they're as different as night and day. She says that even as a newborn, her two-year-old was rarely quiet, whereas her new baby has a low activity level, and both girls have very different mood swings. Her younger child cries infrequently and doesn't seem bothered by much, whereas her two-year-old has always had intense moods and does not adapt well to new situations. Moreover, the two-year-old walked at eight months, said her first word at ten months, always seems to be moving ahead, and is somewhat precocious. By contrast, the baby seems to be on a more normal developmental course.

Like this mother, parents recognize differences in their children and often give thumbnail descriptions of their infants' personality traits. They might describe their newborn baby as quiet but alert or as fussy and very active. Although parents and pediatricians have long known that infants have distinct and unique personalities, to a large extent the scientific basis for human identity has been developed since 1976. The word *temperament* is used to describe the behavior style that contributes to infants' individual differences. Infants' temperaments determine the way they react to their environment and the people around them. Early on, individual differences in behavior style can be seen in infants' prevailing moods, as well as in the intensity of their responses and their coping efforts.

There is a large and growing body of research that supports the idea that some aspects of temperament are evident in the early life of infants. Some temperament characteristics appear to be adaptive and relatively stable, though their continuity through the life span is not fully understood. The

169

interplay of environmental and biological influences on temperament is an important question for infant researchers. There is consensus that temperament has a constitutional basis, but scientists disagree about the definitions and dimensions of temperament (Bates 1987).

Measures of temperament have been designed to improve our understanding of infants. Temperament assessments have been used by pediatricians to identify the elements of a difficult temperament style. Alexander Thomas and Stella Chess (1984) noted that infants with a difficult temperament style were more likely to have behavior problems in early and middle childhood. Parents' response to their infants' behavior style has been found to be a powerful predictor of later behavior problems (Parker and Zuckerman 1990). The continuity of temperament, parents' perceptions of their infants' temperament, and the "goodness of fit" between parents' and infants' temperaments are also analyzed using assessments of temperament.

In recent years, important advances have been made in studying emotions in infants and in the affective aspects of communication between infants and caregivers. The first two years are critical to the development of infants' emotional systems. What the infant experiences, the caregivers' effectiveness in reading infant emotional signals, and the caregivers' own emotional regulation have an impact on the infant's affect system. Investigators are interested not only in how emotions develop but also in the link between emotions the infant experiences and later developmental outcomes (Tronick 1989).

As infant emotions develop, they provide a framework for caregivers' responses to the infants. As emotions become more complex, the interactions between caregivers and infants also become more complex as both partners integrate and effectively monitor their emotional signals (Emde 1993). Assessment of infant emotion is believed important to understanding infant difficulties and parent-infant relationships. Assessment of infant emotions has primarily focused on interpretation of infants' facial expressions (Saarni 1975).

In this chapter, we will examine the concept of temperament and emotion and consider how these concepts are commonly defined. Types and examples of temperament and emotion assessments will be discussed, along with problems associated with these measures. In addition, the concepts of easy and difficult temperaments will be presented.

Your study of this chapter should focus on the constructs of temperament and emotion and their use as a tool in describing infant personality. When you have finished studying this chapter, in addition to having increased your knowledge of the variety of issues in temperament and emotion research, you should be able to

- Define temperament and emotion
- Describe aspects of temperament, including dimensions and stability

- Describe infant emotion patterns
- Describe several temperament and emotion instruments
- Outline the uses of temperament and emotion assessments

Infant Temperament

Carlos was active from birth. He moved his body, turned his head, and kicked his arms and legs. At two months old, he squirmed, moved, and would often arch his body when he was held. He rarely slept longer than two hours at a time. His parents found it difficult to soothe him once he began to fuss or cry. At ten months old, he was described as a busy infant. He would play briefly with one toy, then throw it down and pick up another. He crawled and explored almost constantly. By two, Carlos was always in motion, moving from activity to activity. At four, he entered a preschool center, where his teacher described him as distractible. In first grade, he was reported to disrupt his classmates with his behavior. He did not sit quietly for longer than five minutes and did not stay with activities for longer than a few minutes.

Myra's parents often remarked that even when she was only a few hours old, she would open her eyes and look intently at them. They described her as a good baby. They said it wasn't long before she began to sleep for longer periods. She cried infrequently and was easily comforted. In fact, she quieted herself by tucking her legs in under her body and putting her fist in her mouth. By three months old, she had a moderate level of activity and periods of quiet time. At nine months, when given objects, she would examine them first by turning them over and then play with them for short periods of time. At eighteen months, she joined a play group and, with the exception of infrequent temper tantrums, was a quiet child who presented few problem behaviors. In kindergarten, Myra was initially hesitant but adapted to the schedule. Her teacher noted that she was cooperative and played well with other children.

These examples illustrate the concept of temperament. Temperament is the individual style of behavior evident from birth. This concept was first introduced via the New York Longitudinal Study (NYLS) (Thomas and Chess 1977; Thomas and Chess 1980), in which individual clusters of traits were identified. As in these two cases, temperament characteristics such as activity, sociability, emotionality, soothability, and adaptability are salient and stable very early in life. Infant temperament has consequences for social interactions and the ability to adapt to new situations. Temperament characteristics give infants their unique social identity.

Temperament, then, can be thought of as those characteristics that are the foundation of personality. Usually, personality is described in terms of temperament characteristics. If, for example, you were asked to describe the personality of some of your friends you might describe your friend Jim as optimistic, even-tempered, and intense. Another friend, Beth, might be characterized as impassive, not very adaptable, and sober. Your descriptions of these two people are based on your experiences with them. You assume that they are much the same way with others.

New York Longitudinal Study

The first major investigation of infant temperament in the New York Longitudinal Study began in 1956 (Thomas, Chess, and Birch 1968; Thomas and Chess 1977). The investigators asked two questions: Are there individual temperament characteristics in early infancy? And if there are, are these characteristics consistent throughout childhood?

A group of 141 children was studied over a twenty-year period. Parent interviews about their children's behavior style were the primary data source; later, behavioral observations were added. Because the original sample was primarily upper middle class, samples of working-class and at-risk infants were subsequently added to the study population (Thomas and Chess 1980).

Nine dimensions of temperament were identified during the NYLS (see Table 8.1 for descriptions of temperament characteristics during infancy). The dimensions include activity level, adaptability, approach to or from new stimuli, sensory threshold, distractibility, persistence/attention span, rhythmicity of biological function, and predominant quality of mood. A three-point scale, which ranged from "shows very little" to "shows a large amount," was used to rate infants on each of the nine characteristics.

A factor analysis of these ratings indicated that most children fell into three temperament categories: easy, difficult, and slow-to-warm-up. Approximately 40 percent of infants were identified as easy, 15 percent as difficult, and 5–10 percent as slow-to-warm-up. Infants classified as easy have (1) moderate, pleasant mood expression, (2) regular biological functions, and (3) are adaptable and react positively to new situations. In contrast, difficult babies have (1) intense and often negative moods, (2) irregular sleep and eating patterns, and (3) do not adapt readily to new stimuli. The slow-to-warm-up group is (1) slow in reacting or adapting positively to new stimuli and (2) displays a somewhat negative mood. About 35 percent of the children in the study did not fit into any of the three types. Instead, they displayed mixed-temperament styles.

According to this model, the infants' temperament category will guide interactions with caregivers and experience in the environment. Infants with different temperament features elicit different behaviors from their caregivers. It has been suggested that fit between parents' temperaments and their infant's temperament is important to the quality of the parent-child relationship (Plomin 1990).

TABLE 8.1 Nine Expressions of Temperament Characteristics at Different Ages in Infancy

Temperamental Characteristics	Rating	2 Months	6 Months	1 Year	2 Years
Activity level	high	moves during diaper change	bounces; crawls after people	eats rapidly, walks quickly	climbs furniture; explores actively
	low	little movement during sleep	plays alone quietly	goes to sleep easily, eats slowly	likes quiet play; listens to music
Rhythmicity	regular	regular feeding and sleep patterns	consistent food intake; goes to sleep and awakes same time each day	naps after lunch; regular bowel movements	always snacks in the afternoon and before bedtime
	irregular	awakes at different times each day	food intake varies, as does sleep pattern	wakes at different times; no pattern in bowel movements	nap times change daily; problems in toilet training
Distractibility	not distractible	will stop crying if comforted and rocked	stops crying if mother talks or sings; quiets if given a toy during diapering	is comforted by toy or game during diapering or face washing	tantrums cease when given a substitute toy
	distractible	will not stop crying during diapering	cries until fed	is not comforted by toy or game	tantrum if not given desired toy
Approach or withdrawal	positive	smiles	smiles and expresses enjoyment; pleasure with new foods	approaches strangers easily	slept well first time at grandparents' house

(continues)

TABLE 8.1 (*continued*)

Temperamental Characteristics	Rating	2 Months	6 Months	1 Year	2 Years
	negative	cries at appearance of strangers; rejects first cereal	wary of strangers	stiffens when picked up	avoids new children
Adaptability	adaptable	enjoys bathing	did dislike new faces, now accepts them	was afraid of toy animals, now likes to play with them	obeys quickly
	not adaptable	startled by sudden noises; resists diapering	fusses and is uncooperative during dressing	keeps rejecting new foods when offered	cries each time hair is cut

SOURCE: Adapted from A. Thomas and S. Chess, *The Dynamics of Psychological Development* (New York: Brunner/Mazel, 1980).

Thomas and Chess viewed the template of temperament as innate and also found that temperament is strongly influenced by experience. They believed that the way an infant's temperament matched the environment could alter how the infant's temperament was expressed. They saw the match as a goodness-of-fit situation. For example, if an infant with a difficult temperament has tolerant parents who are patient, allow their child time to adapt to new situations, and tolerate negative moods, the infant may learn to adapt and incorporate effective coping strategies. If, however, the same infant has parents who are restrictive and punish the infant for being reluctant to cooperate in a new routine, the infant may learn to react negatively to new people and situations. Thus, according to Thomas and Chess, how an infant's temperament and environment fit will influence how the infant's temperament will be expressed.

Temperament Definition

How we study and measure temperament depends on our definition of temperament. Researchers today would not agree on a single definition of temperament (Goldsmith et al. 1987). Most formulations of temperament focus on individual expression of behaviors (the "how") rather than on the content of the behaviors (the "why") (Buss and Plomin 1975). Thomas and Chess (1977), for example, defined temperament broadly as an individual behavior style of reacting to the environment. Temperament has also been proposed to be an individual response to environmental changes and self-regulation that is stable and biologically based (Rothbart and Derryberry 1981). Other investigators have viewed temperament as individual differences in the probability of expressing and experiencing emotions and arousal (Goldsmith and Campos 1982).

Despite different approaches to defining temperament, there are some common areas of agreement. Researchers generally agree that temperament has a genetic basis, includes dimensions that can be identified in early infancy, is relatively stable, and can be modified by environmental influence. Nevertheless, there is still not a universally accepted definition.

Dimensions of Temperament

Different investigators approach temperament from different perspectives. Theorists agree neither on a universal definition of temperament nor on the traits or dimensions that make up temperament. This is an important point, since the assessments developed by researchers to measure temperament reflect their particular definition of the dimensions of temperament.

Thomas and Chess (1977) identified nine dimensions of temperament in their NYLS, whereas Arnold Buss and Robert Plomin (1975) listed four dimensions: emotionality, activity, sociability, and impulsivity. Rothbart and Derryberry (1981) were even more parsimonious. Their conceptualization of temperament consisted of two factors: reactivity and self-regulation. Re-activity includes response systems such as the autonomic nervous system and brain activation processes. These interface with the infant's self-regulatory system, which monitors the infant's ability to regulate reactivity. John E. Bates (1980) took yet another approach with the Infant Characteristics Questionnaire. This scale, which is used to identify difficult infant temperament, focuses on four dimensions of infant temperament: fussy-difficult, unadaptable, dull, and unpredictable (Bates 1986).

Despite the lack of consensus on the dimensions of temperament, there is some overlap across descriptions. Theorists do agree that activity level and reactivity to the environment are temperament characteristics and that these characteristics affect infants' social interactions and personality expression.

In fact, considerable study has been devoted to infants characterized by "difficult" temperaments (Wolkind and DeSalis 1982; Bates 1980). Difficult infants may affect parents' perceptions of their infant's abilities, which may in turn alter or negatively affect the interactive processes between parents and these infants (Broussard and Hartner 1970).

Origins of Temperament

What are the determinants of temperament? Researchers have recently raised questions regarding the sources of temperament. Like cognitive theorists, they ask whether temperament is inborn or acquired through experience (Derryberry and Rothbart 1984).

Several theorists (Buss and Plomin 1975; Rothbart and Derryberry 1981) maintain that temperament is essentially biologically determined and that its expression is only minimally affected by the environment. Temperament, in their view, is not permanently altered by interfacing with the environment. Instead, temperament is thought to be relatively enduring. Thomas and Chess (1977), however, argue that although there is a sizable genetic component in temperament, prenatal and postnatal influences can alter infant temperament.

Despite different interpretations regarding the relative influences of environment and heredity on temperament, a substantial body of evidence suggests that temperament dimensions are present at birth (Goldsmith et al. 1980). Characteristics such as activity, emotionality, and sociability appear to have strong biological roots (Goldsmith 1983). Irritability, sensitivity, and soothability were found to be stable in infants during the first four months of life (Birns, Barten, and Bridger 1969). Activity level and attentiveness have also been identified early in infancy (Bates and Bayles 1984; McDevitt and Carey 1981). These dimensions remain fairly stable throughout life and have consequences for infants' interactions with others and for their own personality development.

Difficult Temperament

The first formal identification of difficult temperament in infants occurred in the New York Longitudinal Study (Thomas, Chess, and Birch 1968). Here, infants were considered to be temperamentally difficult if they were characterized by a constellation of behaviors that included negative affect, irregular biological functioning, slow adaptability to environmental changes, intense reactions, and withdrawal. Thomas and Chess (1984) described difficult temperament as constitutionally based and believed that it might result in an increased risk for later behavior problems.

Several findings have suggested that there are links between temperament attributes in infancy and behavioral adjustment (Rutter 1970; Thomas, Chess, and Birch 1968). Correlations have been shown between difficult temperament from one year old onward and later behavior problems, when considered in relation to the child's sex and parenting problems (Cameron 1978). Mothers' ratings of their six-month-old infants as difficult were found to be predictive of maternal perceptions of aggression and acting out at three, four, and five years in age (Bates, Petit, and Bayles 1985). The predictive power of maternal ratings was supported by Elsie Broussard's work (Broussard and Hartner 1970, 1971). A group of 104 infants was followed from infancy to age ten. Mothers who rated their infants as "average" or "worse than average" were more likely to have children with behavior problems at ages four and ten.

Although these findings indicate that it is possible to conduct early assessment of the temperamentally difficult infant, the concept of "difficultness" and its predictability for future expression of behavioral disorders has met with controversy by prominent researchers in the field. A number of investigators have found that a mother's depression is linked to infant difficultness and later behavior problems (Woldkind and DeSalis 1982; Lee 1983). Bates (1987) has suggested that difficult infants behave in ways that predispose parents to perceive them negatively.

It appears that labeling an infant as difficult may indicate more about the parents' perceptions of their infant than of the infant's temperament (Vaughn et al. 1987). For example, Brian Vaughn and his colleagues found that prenatally assessed maternal characteristics, particularly anxiety, were more likely to be linked to maternal diagnosis of temperament difficulty for their young infants. Bates (1986) found that first-time mothers are more likely to rate their infants as difficult. These data make two interpretations possible: Either first-born infants are temperamentally more difficult or mothers may be unfamiliar with new infants and interpret their behaviors negatively. The infant temperament dimensions of manageability and regularity were found to be more important for multiparous mothers than first-time mothers (Hagebull and Bohlin 1990).

In summary, there is a substantial body of evidence that shows a set of early appearing temperament characteristics that are relatively enduring. Some evidence suggests that infant "difficultness" places the infant at risk for later adjustment problems. However, there is evidence, too, that the parents' perceptions of difficultness is stable and that parental perceptions may be what is being rated rather than the infant's difficultness. M. K. Rothbart (1982) pointed out that caution should be used in labeling an infant or young child as difficult. Her concern is that the label will lead to adults' behaving toward the child in ways that would foster negative interactions and result in behavioral disturbances.

Assessment of Early Temperament

A number of instruments have been designed to measure temperament in infants and young children. Some temperament measures have been developed to identify infants with difficult temperaments, and other scales are used to assess the relationship between early temperament and social and cognitive development. Assessing temperament is considered important in measuring the goodness of fit between infant and caregiver. Infants at risk for developmental disabilities and their caregivers are vulnerable to mismatches in parent-infant interactions; therefore, a temperament assessment is considered to be an essential part of a comprehensive developmental assessment (Parker and Zuckerman 1990). Because of the complexity of the temperament construct, assessments of temperament are believed to reflect a behavior pattern that is being shaped by infants' reactions to social interactions and home environments.

Measurement Methods

In general, most temperament instruments reflect Thomas and Chess's theoretical view of temperament and consequently focus on the nine temperament dimensions identified in the NYLS. Other temperament measures, however, are guided by different investigators' theories of temperament. Whatever the theoretical view, three approaches have been used. They are as follows: parent reports, which include both parent questionnaires and interviews; infant observations; and controlled laboratory procedures (Rothbart and Goldsmith 1985).

Parent Reports.   By far the most frequently used temperament measures are parent questionnaires. Thomas and Chess used maternal reports as the major data source in the NYLS because they felt that mothers' frequent interactions with their babies would result in mothers being most knowledgeable about their infant's behavior. Moreover, because questionnaires are economical and time efficient, generally taking no more than twenty minutes to complete, they are used often in clinical practice. Thus, many temperament assessments are based on the parent's perceptions of the infant. For example, parents are often asked to respond to questions about the regularity of their infant's feeding and sleep patterns, soothability, impulsivity, and emotionality. Typically, there are about ten to twenty items per instrument, with each item rated on a five-, six-, or seven-point scale. Descriptions of items are usually presented within a particular context, eliciting opinions on such matters as, for example, whether the baby is fussy when being dressed or whether the infant turns away when new foods are offered.

Parent interviews are also used to rate and describe infants' behavior style. Usually parents are the raters, although teachers or other caregivers may be included in the interview. The interview protocol usually includes questions that address temperament dimensions as well as the expression of temperament characteristics. Standardized interviews allow in-depth and expanded questions about infants' behavior. However, standardized interviews are costly and time-consuming.

Because of the possible subjectivity of parent responses, questions have been raised about using parent questionnaires to assess infant temperament (Vaughn, Deinard, and Egeland 1980). A number of investigators have concluded that questionnaires assess parents' temperament and attitudes about their infant more accurately than they assess an infant's behavior style (Sameroff, Seifer, and Elias 1982). Studies of mothers' ratings of their infants' temperaments consistently show that maternal characteristics, such as anxiety and socioeconomic status, have more effect on mothers' ratings than infant variables do (Sameroff, Seifer, and Zax 1982). Bates and his colleagues found that maternal life circumstances and psychological functioning predicted infants' temperament scores better than the infants' behavior did (Bates, Freeland, and Lounsbury 1979). In one study, preterm infants were generally rated as more difficult than full-term infants at three and six months (Gennaro, Tulman, and Fawcett 1990).

Studies comparing parent and outside observer reports of infant temperament have been undertaken to address the inadequacy of parental reports. However, parent and outside observer ratings of infant temperament have been characterized by considerable variability (Vaughn et al. 1981). When different people, for example, parent versus teacher or father versus mother, evaluate an infant's temperament, the ratings are not as similar as when one person rates the infant's temperament in different settings (Greenberg and Field 1982; Field and Greenberg 1982). There is even more variability when two different raters rate a baby's temperament in different infant environments.

A related concern with parent reports grows out of the nature of parents' experience with infants. Whereas a mother of six children may easily recognize subtle differences in temperament among her children, a first-time parent with limited infant experience may not accurately rate temperament dimensions or may conclude that a baby who fusses now and then is a very difficult baby. Questions of parent bias in questionnaire reports have led researchers to suggest that in order to insure a more accurate assessment of infant temperament, observations of infant behaviors should be included as part of the data base (McDevitt and Carey 1978). Bates (1983) has suggested, however, that clinicians should regard parent perceptions as an integral part of the social reality. Understanding the parent perceptions leads to an understanding of the meaning of difficult temperament.

Home Observations.   Infant temperament may be assessed by observing infants' behavior in the home setting. In a typical home observation, a trained observer visits the home for a one- to three-hour period. During that time, the observer codes the infant's behaviors over a number of routine activities such as playing, feeding, toileting, and dressing. The observer uses a rating scale and usually includes observation notes. Temperament decisions are made after several observations.

Although the home observation eliminates possible biases, several methodological problems remain. Home observations allow a look at the natural responses of the infant but may tap only a limited sample of the infant's behaviors during the observation period. While the observation is taking place, parents may work actively to control their infant's negativity or their own level of reactions. The presence of the observer in the home may affect both parents' and infants' behaviors. Finally, it is often difficult to record the array of infant responses needed to make an informed evaluation.

Laboratory Measures.   In laboratory situations, infants and their parents are observed in a controlled setting. Often, a play format is used to elicit specific behaviors. Observers watch and record behaviors, or the situation is videotaped for analysis.

There are several research advantages associated with laboratory observations. The controlled laboratory format is often used in temperament research studies because it provides greater objectivity than home observations or parent reports. Greater precision in measuring infant temperament can be obtained in a laboratory observation. Further, multiple measures are possible, particularly when videotapes are used. There are, however, some disadvantages to laboratory observation. Compared to the home setting, the laboratory may inhibit the normal behaviors of the infant. Some investigators have pointed out a serious disadvantage of laboratory measures—that parents of difficult infants may be unwilling to come to a laboratory for testing (Rothbart and Goldsmith 1985). Finally, laboratory assessment, by virtue of its control, may limit infants' range of responses.

Psychometric Considerations

The psychometric adequacy of available temperament measures varies considerably. In a review of twenty-six available instruments for infants, preschoolers, and school-age children, it was found these instruments to have high interrater reliability but only moderate internal consistency and test-retest reliability (Hubert et al. 1982).

Reliability data are available for most temperament instruments. In comparison, validity data are not as readily available. In a review of temperament instruments, it was found that there are no empirical findings on convergent, concurrent, and predictive data available for over one-half of the twenty-six instruments (Hubert et al. 1982). In the validity studies of these measures, there are such methodological problems as small sample sizes, conclusions based on low but significant correlation, and the use of retrospective reports. In general, validity data yield inconsistent findings.

Temperament Measures

There are a number of measures of temperament designed for infants, preschoolers, and school age children. For the most part, the instruments have been designed for research rather than clinical purposes. A notable exception is the Infant Temperament Questionnaire, used by clinics to determine temperament style for infants under one year old. In the sections that follow, several infant temperament assessments will be described.

Neonatal Perception Inventories.   The Neonatal Perception Inventories (NPI) was designed to measure maternal perceptions of their newborns (Broussard and Hartner 1971). It was intended as a screening measure for infants at risk for psychosocial disorders. In this assessment, parents first rate the "average" infant on six behavioral characteristics and then rate their own infants on the same characteristics. The six behavioral areas are crying, bowel movements, predictability, sleeping, spitting up, and feeding.

The test is first administered several days after birth, and then a somewhat different form is given at one month in age. A Likert five-point scale is used to rank the various areas of function. Scores are summed over the items pertaining to the "average" infant and the parents' "own" baby. The "average" baby total is then subtracted from the "own" baby total. A negative score or a score of zero is the criterion for high risk. That is, if parents rate the average baby higher than their own baby, their child is considered to be a high-risk infant. A score of equal to or higher than +1 indicates low risk, since parents are rating their infant as better than the average baby. Table 8.2 shows an example of an NPI rating category.

TABLE 8.2   Example of a Neonatal Perception Inventories Rating Category

How much crying do you think the average baby does?				
a great deal	a good bit	moderate amount	very little	none
5	4	3	2	1

How much crying do you think your baby will do?				
a great deal	a good bit	moderate amount	very little	none
5	4	3	2	1

SOURCE: E. R. Broussard and M.S.S. Hartner, "Further Considerations Regarding Maternal Perception of the Firstborn," in *Exceptional Infant: Studies in Abnormality*, vol. 2, ed. J. Hellmuth (New York: Brunner/Mazel, 1971).

Infant Temperament Questionnaire.   In 1970, William Carey developed a parent report measure, the Infant Temperament Questionnaire (ITQ), to assess infant temperament. The ITQ is a seventy-item test derived from the temperament dimensions identified by Thomas and Chess. It measures the temperament categories of activity, rhythmicity, approach or withdrawal, adaptability, intensity, mood, persistence, distractibility, and threshold. Parents are asked to provide information on their baby's responses to new foods, reactions to bathing, responses to dressing, and sleep and eating patterns. Since the ITQ was developed as a screening tool for detecting difficult temperament, parents are asked to provide their impressions of their baby's "difficultness."

The revised ITQ (Carey and McDevitt 1978) was designed for infants between four and eight months old. The questionnaire consists of ninety-five items organized in nine subscales (see Table 8.3). Based on rating scores, infants are placed in one of five categories: (1) difficult, (2) slow-to-warm-up, (3) intermediate-high (difficult), (4) intermediate-low (easy), and (5) easy. In addition to rating their infants on the nine temperament dimensions, parents are asked to provide global ratings of their infant's temperament.

Perception of Baby Temperament Scales.   The Perception of Baby Temperament Scales (PBT) consists of fifty-four items, six items for each of the nine dimensions identified by Thomas and Chess. For example, the rhythmicity scale has the range of items described in the next section. On each scale, three of the six items are at one end of a behavioral continuum, and the other three are at the opposite end. Parents rate their infant on all nine categories.

TABLE 8.3 Sample Items by Category from the Revised Infant Temperament Questionnaire

The mother rates each of the following items as follows:					
Almost *Never*					*Almost* *Always*
1	2	3	4	5	6

Category	Description
1. Activity	The infant moves about much (kicks, grabs, squirms) during diapering and dressing. The infant plays actively with parents—much movement of arms, legs, body.
2. Rhythmicity	The infants wants and takes milk feedings at about the same times (within one hour) from day to day. The infant's bowel movements come at different times from day to day (over one hour's difference).
3. Approach	The infant accepts right away any change in place or position of feeding or person giving it. For the first few minutes in a new place or situation (new store or home), the infant is fretful.
4. Adaptability	The infant objects to being bathed in a different place or by a different person, even after two or three tries. The infant accepts regular procedures (hair brushing, face washing, etc.) any time without protest.
5. Intensity	The infant reacts strongly to foods, whether positively (smacks lips, laughs, squeals) or negatively (cries). The infant reacts mildly to meeting familiar people (quiet smiles or no response).
6. Mood	The infant is pleasant (smile, laughs) when first arriving in unfamiliar places (friend's house, store). The infant cries when left to play alone.
7. Persistence	The infant amuses self for half an hour or more in crib or playpen (looking at mobile, playing with toy). The infant watches other children playing for under a minute and then looks elsewhere.
8. Distractibility	The infant stops play and watches when someone walks by. The infant continues to cry in spite of several minutes of soothing.
9. Threshold	The infant reacts even to a gentle touch (startle, wriggle, laugh, cry). The infant reacts to a disliked food even if it is mixed with a preferred one.

SOURCE: W. B. Carey and S. C. McDevitt, 1978. "Revision of the Infant Temperament Questionnaire," *Pediatrics* 61: 735–739.

Scale II: Rhythmicity

1. She generally goes to sleep at about the same time each day for naps and nighttime sleep. She does not vary more than a half hour from one day to the next.
2. She generally takes about the same amount of food (milk) each day. It is not hard to anticipate how much she will eat.
3. She likes to be fed at about the same time each day. Hungry times do not vary more than a half hour from day to day.
4. She is unpredictable in when she likes to be fed. Hungry times vary by more than an hour from one day to the next.
5. She is unpredictable in the time when she will awaken from a nap or nighttime sleep. Awakening time may vary one to two hours from one day to the next.
6. The time when bowel movements occur shows no particular pattern from one day to the next.

A study of the psychometric properties of the PBT (Huitt and Ashton 1982) revealed that the nine temperament categories lacked internal consistency. Twenty-eight mothers and fathers completed the PBT over six-week intervals, rating their babies beginning at age nineteen weeks and ending at forty-nine weeks. The results showed that mothers and fathers agree on certain aspects of infant temperament when they appear in the context of specific situations such as feeding or napping.

Infant Behavior Questionnaire.   The Infant Behavior Questionnaire (IBQ) (Rothbart 1978, 1981) was designed as a parent report instrument on infant temperament. It consists of ninety-four questions about the occurrence of specific infant behaviors during the week prior to completing the form. A sample question from the IBQ is as follows: "During the past week, when being undressed, how often did your baby cry, smile, or laugh?" Possible answers to this question range from "never" to "always" (Rothbart 1978, 1981).

IBQ subscales assess activity level (gross motor and locomotor activity), fear (distress and extended latency to approach intense or novel stimuli), soothability (reduction in fussiness when soothing techniques are used), distress at limitations (crying or fussiness while waiting for food or when prevented access to a toy), smiling and laughter, and duration of orienting (vocalizing, playing with or looking at object for extended time period). A longitudinal analysis (Rothbart 1981) of the IBQ subscales revealed stability of the activity and the smiling and laughter dimensions from three through twelve months in age. Less stability over this period was shown for the dimensions of orienting and soothability. The fear and distress dimensions did not show stability from three to twelve months in age.

In one study, the results of a multivariate approach in temperament assessments were reported (Rothbart and Goldsmith 1985). Home observations (Rothbart and Derryberry 1981) were used to cross-validate the Infant Behavior Questionnaire. Low correlations were demonstrated between home observations and parent reports. Laboratory observations of infants' behaviors and reactivity have provided some initial evidence of significant convergence between laboratory observations and parent reports.

Infant Emotion

Emotional development is a concept that encompasses complexly interrelated processes that mature and adapt to experience. As such, emotions in infancy are organized and engaged in dynamic changes. Emotions are essential to maintaining attention and thought and are central to the development of self. Emotions are viewed as inseparable from other mental functions such as cognition and motivation (Emde 1993). Thus, emotions play a critical role in caregiver-infant interactions and infants' self-directed regulatory behaviors. It has been proposed that emotions develop from a basic core of emotions, that they modify the infant's cognitive experience, and in turn, that both cognition and emotions become more sophisticated (Fischer, Shaver, and Carnochan 1990). This self-organizing process continues throughout infancy.

Emotional expressions such as facial and vocal expressions are now thought to reflect infants' inner experiences. Looking at infants' faces has become an accepted procedure for assessing infant emotions. Clinicians are therefore trained to interpret the emotional signals given in facial changes and actions.

In the section that follows, we will review development of infant emotion. In addition, a recent assessment of infant emotion will be highlighted.

Background

Scientific interest in infant emotions is not new. In 1872, Charles Darwin first described his own infant's emotional expression. He identified basic organized patterns of emotion that emerged during infancy. Ninety years later, Silvan Tomkins (1962) incorporated Darwin's basic categories of emotion (e.g., joy, disgust, interest, anger, surprise, fear, sadness) into his theory of emotional development. In the 1940s, a number of investigators described the emotional deprivation observed in infants reared in institutions (Hunt 1941; Spitz 1945). Carrolle Izard (1971, 1975) identified the emergence of emotions during infant development and provided evidence of facial patterns of emotion.

During recent years, empirical research has focused on emotional development during infancy (Greenspan 1990). The ways that infants communicate their emotions via facial expressions and nonverbal cues has generated considerable interest. Infant expressions of emotion are now viewed as emotional communication that can be measured and used as an assessment of infants' emotional state (Tronick 1989; Emde, Osofsky, and Butterfield 1993).

Emotional Development

Infants, at birth, are capable of expressing pleasure and displeasure (Stern 1985). During this period, infants can organize sleep-wake cycles and rhythms and move synchronously to words spoken by their caregiver. The young infant is increasingly able to regulate arousal states (Tronick 1989), which is crucial for affective communication with caregivers.

As infants develop, emotional expressions such as cries become more complex. At around four months old, cries are accompanied by kicking or pushing. Such directed actions signal the emergence of a new emotion—anger. Anger is expressed between four to six months, often in response to a frustrating situation such as encountering a barrier. At two to three months, a social smile is evident; that is, infants smile at their caregivers. Generally at around four to five months old, infants begin to become wary around strangers.

Between five and eight months, infants show an increasing array of complex emotional patterns. Anger is more clearly expressed. Disgust may be seen in response to distasteful stimuli or events. At around five months, infants show the beginnings of interest and excitement in events in their environment. At around seven months, babies laugh when playing games with their caregivers. Stranger wariness becomes more clearly manifest between seven and eight months.

During the period between nine and twelve months, infants display more intense forms of anger, surprise, joy, fear, security, and affection. Their emotions are intricately linked to their ability to cognitively assess environmental events. They show an increasing ability to cope with heightened levels of positive and negative emotions, a process known as *emotional regulation* (Kopp 1987). Infants of nine months are able to interpret the emotional state of their caregiver and will modify their own emotional behaviors to match those of the caregiver (Termine and Izard 1988).

Over the second year of life, infants develop more organized and integrated behavioral and emotional patterns. Their own self-awareness increases dramatically. They have greater awareness of others' emotional states. With the advent of language, infants of fifteen to eighteen months are able to verbally express emotions and may use some form of emotional signaling to their caregivers when at a distance. Between eighteen and twenty-four months, infants begin to incorporate emotion into their pretend play.

Assessing Infant Emotion

The need for assessing infant emotion is driven by the knowledge that developmental problems are often linked to relationship disorders between infants and their caregivers. Clinicians who carry out early intervention point out the need for assessments of infant emotions and emotional signaling in order to implement effective interventions. It is hoped that such assessment tools will identify problems with infants' regulatory behaviors and affective signaling or difficulties in early caregiving.

The assessment instruments that have been developed are for the most part used for research purposes and are not applicable for clinical interventions. Most instruments measure emotional availability of infant or caregiver and emotional communication between infant and caregiver. The assessments have generally used parent interviews or observational methods. Several existing instruments employ parent questionnaires. The IFEEL Pictures (IFP), described later, is a picture-based assessment for assessing emotional availability.

Parent Interviews

The interview method has been used primarily in research to obtain information about parents' perceptions, hopes, concerns, and satisfaction with their infant. Because of the time and cost involved in conducting an open-ended interview, semistructured interviews have been designed to elicit categories of information from parents. One such instrument is the Parent Attachment Interview (Bretherton et al. 1989).

Observational Methods

Observational methods are used to assess the emotional communication and availability between infant and caregiver. Often, the observer uses a rating scale of caregiver-infant interactions. The Maternal Sensitivity Scales have been used to rate the caregiver's level of responsiveness to the infant's signals during interactions in the home (Ainsworth et al. 1978). In 1987, the instrument was revised and is now titled the Emotional Availability Scales (Biringen, Robinson, and Emde 1987).

The Ainsworth Strange Situation procedure has been widely used in the laboratory to measure emotional signaling and the degree of security between infant and caregiver (Ainsworth et al. 1978). Although this method does not directly assess infant emotions, it assesses emotional security within the context of a series of maternal separations and reunions with the infant. It is designed for assessing infants from eleven to twenty-four months in age.

Picture-Based Instruments

One approach to investigating the expression and recognition of infant emotions is judging infant emotions from photographs. The rationale for using judgments of infants' facial expressions is that preverbal infants communicate affect via facial expressions (Best and Queen 1989). These expressions are emotional signals to caregivers who recognize the signals and respond to them. In cases of disturbed caregiver-infant interactions or parents who are at risk for infant abuse or neglect, the caregivers might have difficulty reading their infant's signals.

Expressions of the major categories of emotion, for instance, joy, fear, and sadness, have been documented to show regularities across cultures (Ekman and Friesen 1978). Studies of the accuracy of judgments of adult facial expressions of emotions demonstrated that adult judges consistently identified seven categories of emotion (Izard 1972; Ekman, Friesen, and Ellsworth 1982). Robert Emde and his colleagues further documented that untrained adult judges agreed on the emotional content of pictures of infant facial expressions (Emde et al. 1985). This work led to the development of the IFEEL Pictures (Emde, Osofsky, and Butterfield 1993), an instrument for interpreting infant emotions.

The IFEEL Pictures is a standard set of thirty photographs of infants representing nine emotion categories: (1) enjoyment-joy, (2) interest-excitement, (3) distress-anguish, (4) passive-bored, (5) surprise-startle, (6) anger-rage, (7) fear-terror, (8) disgust-contempt, and (9) shame-humiliation. Respondents are asked to judge the feelings expressed in the pictures. The instrument has been used primarily as a research tool to assess the ways that parents interpret infant emotions, particularly parents at risk for problematic interactions, for example, depressed caregivers, adolescent parents, and parents of premature infants (Zahn-Waxler and Wagner 1993).

Summary

The concept of temperament has been defined as an individual way of reacting to the environment. Individual differences in behavior style have been found to be consistent and somewhat stable. Some researchers have posited that temperament is primarily genetic and is little modified by experience. Others argue that temperament characteristics can be adapted to the demands of the environment.

Classic work (Thomas, Chess, and Birch 1968) identified the dimensions of temperament as well as the temperament categories of easy, difficult, and slow-to-warm-up. The nine dimensions of temperament described are activity level, rhythmicity, distractibility, approach or withdrawal, adaptability, attention span, intensity of reaction, threshold of responsiveness, and mood quality. Theorists differ both on the definition of temperament and on the dimensions that constitute it.

Assessment of temperament is generally done during infancy, a time when stable traits predictive of later behavior are identified. Three methods are used to measure infant temperament: parent reports, infant observations at home, and observations in controlled laboratory situations. Parent perception measures are used most frequently. However, the bias that is inherent in parent reports has called into question whether such instruments are valid measures of infant temperament. Rather, it has been suggested that instead, these are measures of parents' attitudes about their infants.

Infant emotion is considered central to parent-infant relationships. Infant emotions are organized and become more complex as the infant develops. Infants' facial expressions convey emotion and are essential components in emotional signaling.

Measures of infant emotion have primarily focused on assessing emotional availability and emotional regulation within caregiver-infant interactions. A new instrument, the IFEEL Pictures, assesses caregivers' judgment of infant emotion via infant facial expression.

References

Ainsworth, M.D.S., M. Blehan, E. Waters, and S. Wall. 1978. *Patterns of Attachment: A Psychological Study of the Strange Situation.* Hillsdale, NJ: Lawrence Erlbaum Associates.

Bates, J. 1987. Temperament in infancy. In *Handbook of Infant Development,* edited by J. D. Osofsky. 2d ed. New York: John Wiley.

Bates, J. E. 1986. The measurement of temperament. In *The Study of Temperament: Change, Continuities, and Challenges,* edited by R. Plomin and J. Dunn. Hillsdale, NJ: Lawrence Erlbaum Associates.

_____. 1983. Issues in the assessment of difficult temperament: A reply to Thomas, Chess, and Korn. *Merrill-Palmer Quarterly* 29:89–97.

_____. 1980. The concept of difficult temperament. *Merrill-Palmer Quarterly* 26:300–319.

Bates, J. E., and K. Bayles. 1984. Objective and subjective components in mothers' perceptions of their children from age 6 months to 3 years. *Merrill-Palmer Quarterly* 30:111–130.

Bates, J. E., C. A. Freeland, and M. L. Lounsbury. 1979. Measurement of infant difficultness. *Child Development* 50:794–803.

Bates, J. E., G. S. Petit, and K. Bayles. 1985. Infancy and preschool antecedents of behavior problems at 5 years. Paper presented at the biennial meeting of the Society for Research in Child Development, Toronto, Canada, April.

Best, C. T., and H. F. Queen. 1989. Baby, it's in your smile: Right hemiface bias in infant emotional expressions. *Developmental Psychology* 25:264–276.

Biringen, Z., J. Robinson, and R. N. Emde. 1987. *Emotional Availability Scales.* Denver: University of Colorado Health Science Center.

Birns, B., S. Barten, and W. Bridger. 1969. Individual differences in temperamental characteristics of infants. *Transactions of the New York Academy of Sciences* 31:1071–1082.

Bretherton, I., Z. Biringen, D. Ridgeway, C. Maslin, and M. Sherman. 1989. Attachment: The parental perspective. *Infant Mental Health Journal* 10:203–221.

Broussard, E. R., and M.S.S. Hartner. 1971. Further considerations regarding maternal perception of the firstborn. In *Exceptional Infant: Studies in Abnormality.* Vol. 2. Edited by J. Hellmuth. New York: Brunner/Mazel.

_____. 1970. Maternal perception of the neonate as related to development. *Child Psychiatry and Human Development* 1:16–25.

Buss, A. H., and R. Plomin. 1975. *A Temperament Theory of Personality Development.* New York: Wiley Interscience.

Cameron, J. R. 1978. Parental treatment, children's temperament, and the risk of childhood behavioral problems: 2. Initial temperament, parental attitudes, and the incidence and form of behavioral problems. *American Journal of Orthopsychiatry* 48:140–147.

Carey, W. B. 1970. A simplified method for measuring infant temperament. *Journal of Pediatrics* 77:188–194.

Carey, W. B., and S. C. McDevitt. 1978. Revision of the Infant Temperament Questionnaire. *Pediatrics* 61:735–739.

Darwin, C. [1872] 1965. *The Expression of Emotions in Man and Animals.* Chicago: University of Chicago Press.

Derryberry, D., and M. K. Rothbart. 1984. Emotion, attention, and temperament. In *Emotion, Cognition, and Behavior*, edited by C. E. Izard, J. Kagan, and R. Zajonc. New York: Cambridge University Press.

Ekman, P., W. Friesen, and P. Ellsworth. 1982. *Emotion in the Human Face.* New York: Pergamon Press.

Ekman, P., and W. U. Friesen. 1978. *Facial Action Coding System.* Palo Alto, CA: Palo Alto Consulting Psychologists Press.

Emde, R., C. Izard, R. Huebner, J. F. Sorce, and M. D. Kinnert. 1985. Adult judgments of infant emotions: Replication studies within and across laboratories. *Infant Behavior and Development* 8:79–88.

Emde, R. N. 1993. A framework for viewing emotions. In *The IFEEL Pictures: A New Instrument for Interpreting Emotions*, edited by R. N. Emde, J. D. Osofsky, and P. M. Butterfield. Madison, CT: International Universities Press.

Emde, R. N., J. D. Osofsky, and P. M. Butterfield, eds. 1993. *A New Instrument for Interpreting Emotions.* Madison, CT: International Universities Press.

Field, T., and R. Greenberg. 1982. Temperamental ratings by parents and teachers of infants, toddlers, and preschool children. *Child Development* 51:160–163.

Fischer, K. W., P. Shaver, and P. Carnochan. 1990. How emotion develops and how they organize development. *Cognition & Emotion* 4:81–127.

Gennaro, S., L. Tulman, and J. Fawcett. 1990. Temperament in preterm and full-term infants at three and six months of age. *Merrill-Palmer Quarterly* 36:201–215.

Goldsmith, H. H. 1983. Genetic influences on personality from infancy to adulthood. *Child Development* 54:331–355.

Goldsmith, H. H., A. H. Buss, R. Plomin, M. K. Rothbart, H. Thomas, S. Chess, R. A. Hinde, and R. B. McCall. 1987. Roundtable: What is temperament? Four approaches. *Child Development* 58:505–529.

Goldsmith, H. H., and J. J. Campos. 1982. Toward a theory of infant temperament. In *The Development of Attachment and Affiliative Systems*, edited by R. N. Emde and R. J. Harmon. New York: Plenum Press.

Goldsmith, H. H., J. J. Campos, N. Benson, C. Henderson, and P. East. 1980. Genetics of infant temperament: Parent report and laboratory observations. Paper presented at the International Conference on Infant Studies, New Haven, April.

Greenberg, R., and T. Field. 1982. Temperament ratings of handicapped infants during classroom mother and teacher interactions. *Journal of Pediatric Psychology* 7:387–405.

Greenspan, S. I. 1990. Comprehensive clinical approaches to infants and their families: Psychodynamic and developmental perspectives. In *Handbook of Early Childhood Intervention*, edited by S. J. Meisels and J. P. Shonkoff. New York: Cambridge University Press.

Hagebull, B., and G. Bohlin. 1990. Early infant temperament and maternal expectations related to maternal adaptation. *International Journal of Behavioral Development* 13:199–214.

Hubert, N. C., T. D. Wachs, P. Peters-Martin, and M. J. Gandour. 1982. The study of early temperament: Measurement and conceptual issues. *Child Development* 53:571–600.

Huitt, W. G., and P. T. Ashton. 1982. Parents' perceptions of infant temperament: A psychometric study. *Merrill-Palmer Quarterly* 28:95–109.

Hunt, J. M. 1941. Infants in an orphanage. *Journal of Abnormal Social Psychology* 36:338.

Izard, C. 1975. On the ontogenesis of emotions and emotion-cognition relationships in infancy. In *The Development of Affect*, edited by M. Lewis and L. A. Rosenblum. New York: Plenum Press.

_____. 1972. *Patterns of Emotion: A New Analysis of Anxiety and Depression.* New York: Academic Press.

_____. 1971. *The Face of Emotion.* New York: Meredith and Appleton-Century Crofts.

Kopp, C. B. 1987. Regulation of distressed negative emotions: A developmental view. *Developmental Psychology* 25:343–354.

Lee, C. 1983. Adult characteristics and their relationship to teaching/disciplinary strategies with compliant and noncompliant children. Ph.D. diss., Indiana University.

McDevitt, S. C., and W. B. Carey. 1981. Stability of ratings vs. perceptions of temperament from early infancy to 1–3 years of age. *American Journal of Orthopsychiatry* 51:342–345.

_____. 1978. The measurement of temperament in 3–7-year-old children. *Journal of Child Psychology and Psychiatry* 19:245–253.

Parker, S. J., and B. S. Zuckerman. 1990. Therapeutic aspects of the assessment process. In *Handbook of Early Childhood Intervention*, edited by S. J. Meisels and J. P. Shonkoff. New York: Cambridge University Press.

Plomin, R. 1990. *Nature and Nurture: An Introduction to Human Behavioral Genetics.* Pacific Grove, CA: Brooks/Cole.

Rothbart, M. K. 1982. The concept of difficult temperament: A critical analysis of Thomas, Chess, and Korn. *Merrill-Palmer Quarterly* 28:35–40.

_____. 1981. Measurement of temperament in infancy. *Child Development* 52:569–578.

_____. 1978. The infant behavior questionnaire. Department of Psychology, University of Oregon, Eugene.

Rothbart, M. K., and D. Derryberry. 1981. Development of individual differences in temperament. In *Advances in Developmental Psychology.* Vol. 1. Edited by M. E. Lamb and A. L. Brown. Hillsdale, NJ: Lawrence Erlbaum Associates.

Rothbart, M. K., and H. H. Goldsmith. 1985. Three approaches to the study of infant temperament. *Developmental Review* 5:237–260.

Rutter, M. 1970. Psychological development: Predictions from infancy. *Journal of Child Psychiatry* 11:49–62.

Saarni, C. 1975. Cognitive and communication features of emotional experience, or do you show what you feel. In *The Development of Affect*, edited by M. Lewis and L. A. Rosenblum. New York: Plenum Press.

Sameroff, A. J., R. Seifer, and M. Zax. 1982. Early development of children at risk for emotional disorders. *Monograph of the Society for Research in Child Development* 47(7).

Sameroff, A. J., R. Seifer, and P. K. Elias. 1982. Sociocultural variability in infant temperament ratings. *Child Development* 53:164–173.

Spitz, R. 1945. Hospitalism. *Psychoanalytic Study of the Child* 1:53.

Stern, D. N. 1985. *The Interpersonal World of the Infant.* New York: Basil Books.

Termine, N. T., and C. E. Izard. 1988. Infants' responses to their mothers' expression of joy and sadness. *Developmental Psychology* 24:223–229.

Thomas, A., and S. Chess. 1984. Genesis and evolution of behavioral disorders: From infancy to early adult life. *American Journal of Psychiatry* 141:1–9.

_____. 1980. *The Dynamics of Psychological Development.* New York: Brunner/Mazel.

_____. 1977. *Temperament and Development.* New York: Brunner/Mazel.

Thomas, A., S. Chess, and C. H. Birch. 1968. *Temperament and Behavior Disorders in Children.* New York: New York University Press.

Tomkins, S. S. 1962. *Affect, Imagery, Consciousness.* Vol. 1. New York: Springer.

Tronick, E. 1989. Emotions and emotional communication in infants. *American Psychologist* 44:112–119.

Vaughn, B., E. Deinard, and B. Egeland. 1980. Measuring temperament in pediatric practice. *Pediatrics* 96:510–514.

Vaughn, B., E. Tarelson, L. Crichton, and B. Egeland. 1981. The assessment of infant temperament: A critique of the Carey Infant Temperament Questionnaire. *Infant Behavior and Development* 4:1–17.

Vaughn, B. E., L. S. Joffe, C. F. Bradley, R. Seifer, and P. Barglow. 1987. Maternal characteristics measured prenatally are predictive of ratings of temperamental "Difficulty" on the Carey Infant Temperament Questionnaire. *Developmental Psychology* 23:152–161.

Wolkind, S. N., and W. DeSalis. 1982. Infant temperament, maternal mental state and child behavior problems. In *Temperamental Differences in Infants and Young Children*, edited by R. Porter and G. M. Collins. Ciba Foundation Symposium 89. London: Pittman Books.

Zahn-Waxler, C., and E. Wagner. 1993. Caregivers' interpretation of infant emotions: A comparison of depressed and well mothers. In *The IFEEL Pictures: A New Instrument for Interpreting Emotions*, edited by R. N. Emde, J. D. Osofsky, and P. M. Butterfield. Madison, CT: International Universities Press.

9

Assessment of Developmental Status: Issues and New Directions

A baby is the most complicated object made by unskilled labor.

—Unknown

Introduction

Infant assessment is a progressive and rapidly changing field. Since 1960, assessment practices have changed greatly, and hundreds of measures, including observational guides, norm-referenced instruments, criteria-referenced measures, caregiver interview strategies, and behavioral analysis measures, have been developed. Researchers and clinicians now agree that multiple assessment methods, rather than one assessment approach, are the "best practice" (Ensher and Clark 1994). Assessment practices are moving toward a more integrated approach that employs interdisciplinary strategies. This is considered necessary in order to comprehensively assess the complexity of young children.

As a result of developmental research, infants have been shown to be capable, complicated, socially interactive beings. Although their development is guided by biological determinates, it is also influenced by the infant's social and cultural matrix. New assessment processes have been designed to capture the complexities of infant development.

Developmental assessment is a process designed to measure infants' competence and areas of concern. A systematic and comprehensive assessment process, to be meaningful, should include information on the cultural context of an infant's caregiving environment. The process of developmental assessment not only includes an evaluation of the infant's status but also evaluates caregivers' relationships with the infant. Parents are considered an integral part of the assessment process (Clark, Paulson, and Conlin 1993). To meet the goal of a comprehensive assessment of infants, multiple assessment strategies are used to allow for a holistic sampling of infant behavior within the family context.

Infant assessment has been influenced by a variety of factors. The intelligence-testing movement of the early twentieth century influenced the development of infants' cognitive tests. In the 1920s and 1930s, standardized developmental tests evolved naturally from the growing body of information about the unfolding of infants' skills (Bayley 1933). Longitudinal studies of mental development found a lack of stability between early test performance and later IQ (Rose and Feldman 1995). The lack of stability was thought to be the result of qualitative changes in mental development from infancy to childhood. At that time, the developmental changes measured by standardized tests were primarily sensorimotor and were thought to be qualitatively different from the symbolic and abstract reasoning measured by child and adult intelligence tests. Recent studies indicate that measures of information processing—for example, habituation and recognition memory in infancy—are more predictive of later cognitive outcomes that characterize intelligence than standardized developmental tests are (McCall and Carriger 1993).

Today, in the 1990s, assessing infant intelligence is emphasized less than previously, and greater attention is being devoted to measuring the processes that drive infant development. The interrelationship of developmental domains is also being assessed, as is the quality of the caregiving environments. Infant assessment now includes specific tests of infant language (Bzoch and League 1971), coping strategies (Williamson and Zeitlin 1990), attachment (Ainsworth 1982), neuromotor capabilities (Chandler, Andrews, and Swanson 1980), and attentional processing (Brooks-Gunn and Lewis 1981).

Infant research has broadened its scope to include an emphasis on atypical infant development. This new area of research resulted from an increase in the survival rate of infants at risk for developmental dysfunction (Kopp 1987) and from the concomitant growth in the number of infant intervention programs that provide educational and therapy services for infants with handicaps and for their families. In response to the need to identify and measure the developmental progress of disabled infants, alternative assessment strategies are being developed that allow flexibility in measuring individual infants' abilities (McCune et al. 1990). These assessments are being used to plan and evaluate instructional programs for infants with handicaps.

In this chapter, we will look at some new directions in infant assessment. The rationale for multiple measures and for the interdisciplinary assessment of at-risk infants will be presented. Finally, the integration of infant-focused and family-focused assessment in planning intervention strategies will be discussed.

Applications of Infant Assessment: Providing Comprehensive Assessment

In early intervention programs and clinics, where infants are monitored or treated over time, comprehensive developmental assessments are replacing the one-time specific assessment approach that uses a standardized test. Although some assessments do have limited goals such as measuring habituation to a repeated stimulus or auditory pitch discrimination, most assessments are done to obtain information for the purpose of diagnosing a problem or planning an intervention program. These assessments are comprehensive and integrated. Thus, a comprehensive assessment includes assessment of developmental status and competencies as well as investigation of the infant's caregiving and learning environments.

Several concerns have been raised about using one specific assessment approach for screening or evaluation. Assessments and screenings are often conducted in a strange setting by an unfamiliar clinician over a brief time period. Assessments may require infants to react quickly in unfamiliar situations. Researchers are concerned that although such assessments provide information on the normative level of development, they do not provide information on the quality of responses. Further, conventional standardized assessments may be inappropriate for high-risk and developmentally disabled infants (Barnett, Macmann, and Carey 1992). Greenspan and his colleagues (1994) have argued that current assessment approaches often provide fragmented views of infants rather than an integrated understanding of infants and their relationships within their family, community, and culture. Moreover, there is a tendency to assess only those functions for which there are tests. Aspects of development that are difficult to measure, for instance, parent-infant communication, are often overlooked by assessors.

Clinicians now propose that a meaningful assessment should include a standardized assessment, informal measures, and structured observations. Assessments of infants with developmental or emotional delays should not only measure the core functional areas of development—language, motor, sensory, and cognitive functioning and emotional and social capacities—but they should also assess family and cultural patterns that impact on the infant (Berkeley and Ludlow 1992). To meet the challenge of assessing infants who have handicaps or who are medically fragile, assessment instruments should be flexible in administration and be capable of measuring the dynamic developmental processes that occur during infancy (Neisworth and Bagnato 1992).

Conducting a comprehensive assessment for at-risk infants involves choosing appropriate assessment instruments and strategies. The choice will vary depending on the infant, the needs of the family, and the available intervention services. Gail Ensher and David Clark (1994) suggest that the choice of assessment strategies should address some of the following concerns:

• Are strategies sensitive to cultural diversity?
• Can the instruments be used in diverse settings?

- Are the measures valid and reliable over time?
- Do the measures allow for information input from caregivers and professionals who work with the infant?
- Do the selected measures provide an adequate sampling of behavior over time?
- Do the strategies provide an understanding of the infant's functioning as well as the infant's behaviors?

In 1994, the Zero to Three Work Group on Developmental Assessment reviewed the limitations of current assessment approaches when used to assess infants and young children at developmental risk (Greenspan and Meisels 1994). The group proposed basic principles of assessment intended to guide practitioners in assessing an infant's optimal level of functioning and in assessing the caregiver, family, community, and cultural patterns that influence development. According to the group's guidelines, an assessment should first involve a discussion with parents, which involves listening to their views, outlining the assessment goals, and obtaining a developmental history. Next, the infant and caregiver should be observed in unstructured play, followed by specific assessments of individual functions of the infant as needed. The data gathered should be integrated and discussed with the infant's primary caregivers. The Zero to Three group proposed that the assessment should be guided by the following basic principles:

- Assessment requires multiple sources of information and strategies.
- Assessment requires knowledge of typical development in order to assess typical and at-risk infants.
- The particular assessment should focus on the infant's level and pattern of organizing experience and on the integration of emotional and cognitive abilities.
- The assessment should identify the infant's current strengths and competencies as well as the competencies the infant needs to develop to attain developmental milestones.
- During assessment, infants should not be separated from caregivers or assessed by an unfamiliar examiner.
- Structured tests should not be the primary source of assessment information.
- Assessments should not be considered adequate unless they provide an integrated understanding of the infant's development.
- Assessment is an ongoing collaboration between professionals and parents.
- Assessment is viewed as the first step in a potential intervention process.

The comprehensive assessment approach is driven by efforts to aid professionals and to help caregivers better understand their infant's competencies. Different measures provide the pieces of information for a total, integrated view of the infant. Comprehensive assessments of infants can guide the planning of intervention approaches.

Issues and New Directions in Infant Assessment

Linking Research and Application

Infant assessment has significantly changed since the 1970s. Research on infant competence has provided the base for clinical assessment and interventions for infants at risk for disabilities. But linking basic research to assessment practice is not always practical.

Assessments developed by researchers are often inappropriate for use in clinical settings. Research-oriented assessments may be too lengthy or require equipment that is too expensive or too cumbersome in a clinical context. Some research methodology has been developed for observing infant play, but observation strategies developed to observe parent-infant interactions in laboratories need to be adapted for applied work with infants and their families.

Still, basic research has opened doors and focused on new ways to observe infants and infant behaviors. Researchers have also conceptualized the relationship of the family system to infant development. The derivation of clinically useful assessments from basic infant research will continue as a major contribution to infant assessment.

Interdisciplinary Assessment

The interdisciplinary team approach to the assessment of infants with handicaps is an outgrowth of current knowledge about the multidimensional nature of infant development. The field of clinical infancy is a composite of education, medicine, developmental and clinical psychology, occupational therapy, physical therapy, nursing, social work, and speech and language pathology. This blend is increasingly reflected in current practice, where teams of professionals collaborate to assess family and child and to determine needed interventions (Rossetti 1990).

A team approach to assessment can take several forms. An integrated team might work together with one examiner administering a core battery of tests, while other team members observe and consult. In many situations, a physician or hospital clinic team conducts the initial screening battery, then refers the infant to an infant program, where a team of professionals uses comprehensive assessments to delineate the extent and salient characteristics of the delay or disability. The format of the assessment procedure will vary depending on the infant and family. For example, formal structured assessments may be combined with less-structured observations.

Practitioners agree that multiple measures, rather than a single assessment, should be used to assess both quantitative and qualitative aspects of infant development (McCune et al. 1990). The selection of particular scales and procedures depends on the purpose of the assessment. Although a standardized norm-referenced developmental assessment is generally used as part of the test pool, the choice of other instruments depends on whether the purpose of the assessment is screening for developmental problems, diagnosis, planning educational intervention, or conducting research.

Bridging Assessment and Intervention

The passage of federal legislation Public Law 99-457 in 1986 had an enormous impact on infants with disabilities. Under this law, the federal government assists states in planning, developing, and implementing an interagency system of early intervention for infants and their families. The implementation of Public Law 99-457 Part H of IDEA has challenged professionals to identify and serve infants at developmental risk and their families (Bailey and Wolery 1992).

The commitment to providing services to infants and toddlers with developmental delays has dramatically increased since 1986. Guided by the prevailing view that "infants can't wait," comprehensive intervention for this population begins at birth. Consequently, detecting developmental problems must be systematic and ongoing. Personnel trained in infant assessment need to examine newborn infants before hospital discharge, and follow-up clinics and referral networks designed to detect infants with developmental delays must be in place and operating effectively.

Assessment procedures, then, are used to refer infants and young children to early intervention programs. Once in the program, infants must be monitored to determine their developmental level, progress, and functional skills. Based on assessment information, decisions need to be made regarding appropriate family-infant intervention strategies. The role of assessment is central to early intervention. Because of the importance of infant assessment to intervention, the assessment process is being carefully scrutinized and evaluated as never before (Wachs and Sheehan 1988; Bailey and Wolery 1989).

Alternative Assessment Methods

Work aimed at developing improved assessments for infants has led to a number of alternative methods and procedures. One impetus for developing new assessment strategies is that traditional infant tests do not provide much useful information about the functional capacities of infants with handicaps. Because infants who are disabled develop at different rates and may show dissimilar developmental patterns, clinicians have needed to look beyond traditional measures and toward ways of assessing qualitative aspects of development.

One requirement of Public Law 99-457 is that the families of at-risk infants are to be assessed. The assessment is to focus on the family's strengths and needs that relate to enhancing the optimal development of their at-risk infant. This mandate has challenged professionals in the field to review the process and content of family assessment. The assessment must be culturally sensitive and assess the needs of families without being intrusive. A number of family assessment instruments have been developed to obtain information about family needs and the infant's development within the family context (Bailey and Simeonsson 1988).

As a result of the increased knowledge about infants' competence and development, assessments have been developed that can measure different developmental domains and the ways these domains interact. Infant assessment now includes observation of infants' play, motor skills, language, social interactions, information processing, and temperament. The need to extend the scope of infant assessment can be seen in a variety of assessment strategies. Several of these assessment areas are highlighted in this section.

Language Assessment

Assessing communication and language in infants is considered a requisite in a comprehensive evaluation of infants with disabilities. Early language assessment generally addressed (1) the pragmatic aspect of language, that is, the rules governing use of language; and (2) the structural aspect of language, that is, syntax and phonological and syntactic language rules. In the 1990s, language assessment looks not only at how these two aspects of language are developing but also at infants' ability to communicate. Communicative competence is assessed by evaluating preverbal and verbal communication. Preverbal language assessment measures infants' signs, gestures, looking, and sound production. Verbal language development assessments measure infants' verbalizations, such as one-word utterances, grammatical structure of sentences, and word combinations.

Several coding systems have been developed to measure preverbal infants' communication (Bates, Camaioni, and Volterra 1975; Dore 1974; Halliday 1975). These systems measure communicative intention. For example, whereas an infant of four months might reach for an interesting object while making babbling sounds, an infant of eight or nine months may point or use gestures to convey a request or acknowledge the presence of a person. The Communication Intention Inventory (Coggins and Carpenter 1981) assesses intention categories such as attention seeking, requests for action, requests for objects, protest, acknowledging, and answering. These are measured by frequency of gestural and verbal actions. Phillips Dale (1980) devised an assessment system to classify communicative intentions expressed as one-word utterances.

It has been suggested that early gestural communication is the source of children's verbally expressed communication and that one-word utterances represent "primitive speech acts" (Dore 1975). The nine categories used to describe these utterances are as follows:

- Repeating
- Answering
- Labeling
- Request for action
- Request for answer
- Calling
- Protesting
- Practicing
- Greeting

The Assessing Prelinguistic and Early Linguistic Behaviors in Young Children test battery monitors gesture development in infants and young children (Olswang et al. 1987). Gesture behaviors are observed in six categories: (1) social regulation and social games; (2) greetings, signs of affection, and bedtime; (3) eating and drinking; (4) dressing, grooming, and washing; (5) adult activities; and (6) toys and games. For example, in the category of greetings, signs of affection, and bedtime, the examiner notes the appearance of such behaviors as these: waves hi or bye; puts doll to bed; hugs dolls, animals, or people.

There are a variety of procedures designed to measure language comprehension in verbal infants. One standardized instrument is the Receptive-Expressive Emergent Language Scale (REEL) (Bzoch and League 1971). The REEL is a 132-item test that measures both receptive and expressive language in infants from birth to thirty-six months. Used primarily as a screening instrument, the REEL relies on a parent interview to collect data about an infant's understanding and use of language. Direct observation of the infant is also used to obtain data.

Another standardized language scale is the Sequenced Inventory of Communication Development-Revised (SICD-R) (Hedrick, Prather, and Tobin 1984). The SICD-R evaluates the receptive and language abilities of infants and children from four months to four years old. Through parent report and direct observation of infants, sound discrimination, comprehension, and verbal expressions are measured.

A recent trend in evaluating communication and language of infants with disabilities is to use standardized language assessments in combination with nonstandardized tests and observations of verbal and nonverbal skills (Roberts and Crais 1989). One investigator has suggested that standardized testing be combined with observation measures to obtain a more accurate picture of how infants use language to communicate (Miller 1981).

The Communication and Symbolic Behavior Scales (CSBS) is an instrument designed to detect communication problems in infants and toddlers

(Weatherby and Prizant 1989). The scales assess communication, affective, social, and symbolic abilities of infants between nine and twenty-four months in age. The test is designed to detect infants at risk for communication disorders and to plan appropriate interventions.

Criterion-referenced tests are often used by infant interventionists to assess an infant's language performance. The Preschool Language Scale-Revised (Zimmerman, Steiner, and Pond 1979) is an example of a criterion-referenced language screening instrument for infants one to six years old. Developmental aspects of articulation, grammatical form and structure, and auditory comprehension are measured.

Since 1986, new strategies for assessing language development and comprehension have emerged. Language assessment has broadened to include parent-infant interaction and communication, gestural communication, and symbolic communication. As clinicians have become aware of the importance of language and communication to development, language assessment has been included in comprehensive assessments of at-risk infants.

Coping Assessment

Examining how effectively infants cope with the demands of their environments is a relatively new assessment approach. All infants must cope with the stressors of everyday living. The coping efforts made by infants depend on the resources available to them as well as on their ability to adapt these resources to meet situational demands. Coping requires infants to judge the meaning of an event, decide on a course of action, and then make a coping effort (Williamson and Zeitlin 1990). Assessments ask this question: What is the infant's coping competence? Because coping involves cognition, self-regulation, and the integration of responses, an assessment of coping contributes to a greater understanding of infant capacities and how they are used.

Coping is being examined at the earliest age—in the responses of premature infants. Premature infants in neonatal intensive care units are often overwhelmed by the stress of the noisy, busy intensive care environment, and their precarious medical condition necessitates frequent handling and medical procedures. Consequently, health professionals in NICUs are being trained to observe fragile premature infants for behavioral and physiological signs of stress and coping. Based on their observation, health professionals can then provide appropriate developmental interventions (Wyly and Allen 1990; Wyly, Allen, and Wilson 1995). In 1982, Als published the Assessment of Preterm Infant Behavior (APIB), a scale that addresses preterm infants' early ability to cope.

Before, during, and following environmental maneuvers, the APIB is used to assess five subsystems identified in Als's synactive theory: physiologic, motoric, state system, attentional-interactional, and self-regulation

(Als and Duffy 1989). The examiner determines how well the infant adapts to these maneuvers and what the tolerance level of the infant is for the stimuli. Signs of coping stability and instability are assessed in each of the four areas.

In 1988, Shirley Zeitlin, Gordon Williamson, and Margery Szczepanski designed the Early Coping Inventory to assess the coping of infants and young children. The inventory is made up of forty-eight items, each a behavioral characteristic identified as important to child coping. The items are grouped into three behavioral categories that assess specific actions that are used to manage the challenges of functional living. These categories are sensorimotor organization, reactive behavior, and self-initiated behavior.

Sensorimotor organization items include behaviors such as movements to reach, look at, or obtain objects, organization of information from several different sensory modalities, and adaptation to touch or physical handling. Representative items from the reactive behavior category assess movements and actions made by the infant in response to changes in the environment and to the social overtures of others. Self-initiated behavior items address infants' own actions to solve problems or achieve a goal.

Coping effectiveness is rated using a five-point scale in which a score of 1 indicates ineffective behavior and a 5 means that the behavior is effective across a variety of situations. The behaviors of infants are observed and rated in many different circumstances. In addition to the numerical ranking, a qualitative rating determines whether the behavior is (1) appropriate for the infant's developmental level, (2) appropriate to the particular situation, and (3) used successfully by the infant. The rating and scoring of the inventory takes approximately thirty minutes. Three types of information are obtained. An adaptive behavior index yields information about the infant's overall coping competence. The infant's level of effectiveness in each of the three categories is provided in a coping profile. Finally, the infant's individual coping strengths and weaknesses are listed.

The coping inventory has been used to compare the effectiveness of coping patterns in disabled and nondisabled children under three years old (Williamson, Zeitlin, and Szczepanski 1989). Young children with disabilities were less effective than nondisabled children in their coping efforts, specifically in the self-initiated behavior category. Infants and young children with disabilities may have more difficulty in managing their stressors because their disabling condition may limit their developmental resources and, in turn, their available coping strategies (Zeitlin, Williamson, and Rosenblatt 1987).

Motor Assessment

Crawling, reaching, and walking allow infants to explore their world. Motor activity brings new experiences within reach. Infants can test the texture, shape, and movement of objects. They can learn to adapt to their ever-changing environment.

Infants with motor dysfunction, however, are at risk for normal development (Rosenbloom 1975). The evidence suggests that physical impairments directly affect certain developmental processes and have a detrimental effect on interactions with the environment. For example, infants who have difficulty sitting or holding their heads up will be restricted in looking at objects and at tracking people. Their ability to move toward objects or others will be limited. If accommodations are not made to provide them with opportunities to look and explore, they are likely to be delayed in reaching normal developmental milestones.

Concern about delays in the development of infants with disabilities has led to an increase in early intervention services for such infants, and as services have increased, greater effort has been directed at assessing their motor development. Particular attention has been paid to the utility of motor assessments. Some investigators have proposed that to be useful, motor instruments must assess the variability in motor skills of individual children as well as the neuromotor dimensions essential to manipulation and mobility (Gallagher and Cech 1989). Motor assessments should include enough items to determine developmental level in addition to providing measures of muscle tone, muscle strength, postural reactions, and structural mobility and integrity.

A number of motor instruments for the assessment of infants and young children are available. Recently, several assessments have been developed that evaluate patterns of movement rather than motor milestones (Case-Smith 1996). Some examples of these assessments are highlighted here.

The Bayley Scales of Infant Development contains motor scales used to assess both the fine and gross motor skills of infants from two weeks to thirty months in age (Bayley 1969). The motor scale is designed to assess body control, large muscle coordination, and fine motor coordination of hands and fingers. The infant's motor developmental age level is computed on a psychomotor development index (PDI). Because the scales include only a limited number of items, it should be used as a screening test rather than as a comprehensive motor evaluation.

The Movement Assessment of Infants (MAI) (Chandler, Andrews, and Swanson 1980) is a neurodevelopmental scale developed to measure infants' motor abilities through the first year of life. It tests four movement components: tone, primitive reflexes, automatic reactions, and volitional movement. Because each item is criterion referenced, the assessment can be linked with intervention goals. To determine the level of maturity of the response, each item is scored on a scale of one to four, except for one level that is scored on a one to five scale. A set of risk scores is provided for infants aged four or eight months.

The Peabody Developmental Motor Scales (PDMS) was designed to assess the gross motor and fine motor skills (Folio and Fewell 1983) of children from birth to 6.9 years of age and to plan intervention strategies for physically impaired infants and children. The PDMS gross motor section includes ten items at each age level and is divided into five skill areas: reflexes, balance, nonlocomotion, locomotion, and receipt and propulsion. The fine motor section, which contains eight items at each level, is divided into four skill areas: hand use, grasping, eye-hand coordination, and manual dexterity. Items are scored as 0, 1, or 2, with a score of 2 indicating success, a score of 1 meaning partial success, and 0 standing for no success. A developmental quotient and age-equivalent scores are obtained for each scale. Each scale takes approximately thirty minutes to administer. Validity and reliability data have been documented for the PDMS. It is a relatively easy assessment to administer.

Several motor assessments based on the dynamic systems theory have recently been developed. This theory posits that although certain motor goals are shared by infants, infants use a wide variety of movements to attain their motor goals (Thelen 1995). Assessments of this sort are the Alberta Infant Motor Scale (AIMS) (Piper and Darrah 1994), the Toddler and Infant Motor Evaluation (TIME) (Miller and Roid 1994), and the Test of Infant Motor Performance (TIMP) (Campbell et al. 1994). These assessments measure infants' functional movements in the infant's natural environment. In each test, the examiner is allowed to modify the environment to elicit the infant's best performance. In addition, qualitative aspects of movement and postural control are measured rather than single motor acts or milestones.

Family Assessment

The contribution of the family system to the well-being of infants is now recognized by both developmentalists and interventionists (Bailey and Simeonsson 1988). For infants and young children with disabilities, family functioning is considered crucial to the child's development. The importance of the family's effect on long- and short-term infant outcomes is affirmed by the passage of Public Law 99-457, which mandates individualized family service plans for families of disabled infants and toddlers. Families are central in planning interventions for their disabled child, and individual family needs are considered in the process. Thus, family assessment scales and procedures are currently being developed to assist practitioners in determining the areas of family needs and potential inputs.

Donald Bailey and Rune Simeonsson (1988) have suggested five areas of family assessment: (1) parent-child interactions, (2) family stress and needs, (3) critical events, (4) family roles and supports, and (5) family environments. Although some assessments have been developed, the number of instruments available is still quite limited.

Family assessment strategies are used to measure the family home environment (Caldwell 1972), levels of parent-infant attachment (Ainsworth 1982), family resources (Leet and Dunst 1985), family coping (Hymovich 1984), and family functioning (Skinner, Steinhauer, and Santa-Barbara 1983). Observations of mother-infant interactions are used to determine levels of maternal involvement with the infant (Mahoney, Finger, and Powell 1986). The Family Needs Survey has been developed to measure family needs for assistance in six areas (Bailey and Simeonsson 1988). The assessment considers needs for (1) information, (2) support, (3) explaining to others, (4) community services, (5) financial aid, and (6) family functioning. Family members are asked to identify whether they need help, do not need help, or are not sure if they need help in each area. An eighteen-item self-report assessment of social support was developed to measure family social support (Dunst, Jenkins, and Trivette 1984). It measures the degree to which family members with at-risk infants perceive support as being available to them.

Conclusion

Infancy is one of the most challenging and exciting periods in the human life span. During the 1980s, infancy, as a period in the life cycle, came into its own in terms of recognition from professionals and the public. Television shows, popular books, and articles were devoted to the subject of infancy—even *Time* magazine produced a special infancy issue. Colleges and universities introduced infant curricula designed to train professionals to work with infants and their families. Infant intervention programs expanded rapidly throughout the United States.

Infant assessment, like no other area in the field of infancy, reflects the burgeoning attention paid to the infant period. The rapid development of assessments of infant behaviors and experiences should be evident in the chapters of this text. There is no question that the next twenty years will bring considerable sophistication to the field. The melding of research, applied areas, and interdisciplinary efforts hold great promise for innovative approaches to infant assessment.

Summary

The process of infant assessment has evolved from the use of traditional norm-referenced assessments to using a comprehensive assessment model. This change in assessment focus is the result of knowledge about the dynamic and complex nature of infant development and an understanding of the importance of the family to the infant's development. The passage of Public Law 99-457 in 1986 heralded a decade of change in the theory and practice of infant assessment.

Comprehensive assessment involves multiple assessments that include a variety of disciplines and that measure family needs and functioning in promoting infant development. Recent research has identified motor and language functioning as central components of development. A number of new assessment tools have been designed to measure motor and language functioning. These domains are included in comprehensive assessments.

References

Ainsworth, M.D.S. 1982. Attachment: Retrospect and prospect. In *The Place of Attachment in Human Behavior*, edited by C. M. Parke and J. Stevenson-Hinde. New York: BasicBooks.

Als, H. 1982. Toward a synactive theory of development: Promise for the assessment and support of infant individuality. *Infant Mental Health Journal* 3:229–243.

Als, H., and F. Duffy. 1989. Neurobehavioral assessment in the newborn period: Opportunity for early detection on later learning disabilities and for early intervention. *Birth Defects* 25:127–152.

Bailey, D. B., and M. Wolery. 1992. *Teaching Infants and Preschoolers with Disabilities*. 2d ed. New York: Merrill.

———. 1989. *Assessing Infants and Preschoolers with Handicaps*. Columbus, OH: Merrill.

Bailey, D. B., and R. J. Simeonsson. 1988. *Family Assessment in Early Intervention*. Columbus, OH: Merrill.

Barnett, D. W., G. M. Macmann, and K. T. Carey. 1992. Early intervention and the assessment of developmental skills: Challenges and directions. *Topics in Early Childhood Special Education* 12:21–43.

Bates, E., L. Camaioni, and V. Volterra. 1975. The acquisition of performatives prior to speech. *Merrill-Palmer Quarterly* 21:205–206.

Bayley, N. 1969. *Bayley Scales of Infant Development: A Manual*. New York: Psychological Corporation.

———. 1933. Mental growth during the first three years. *Genetic Psychology Monograph* 14:1–92.

Berkeley, T. R., and B. L. Ludlow. 1992. Developmental domains: The mother of all interventions; or the subterranean early development blues. *Topics in Early Childhood Special Education* 11:13–21.

Brooks-Gunn, J., and M. Lewis. 1981. Assessing young handicapped children: Issues and solutions. *Journal of the Division for Early Childhood* 2:84–95.

Bzoch, K. R., and R. League. 1971. *The Bzoch-League Receptive-Expressive Emergent Language Scale: For the Measurement of Language Skills in Infancy*. Baltimore: University Park Press.

Caldwell, B. 1972. *HOME Inventory*. Little Rock: University of Arkansas.

Campbell, S. K., T.H.A. Kolobe, E. Osten, G. L. Girolami, and M. Lenki. 1994. *Test of Infant Motor Performance*. Chicago: Department of Physical Therapy, University of Illinois.

Case-Smith, J. 1996. Analysis of current motor development theory and recently published infant motor assessments. *Infants and Young Children* 9:29–41.

Chandler, L., M. Andrews, and M. Swanson. 1980. *The Movement Assessment of Infants: A Manual*. Rolling Bay, WA: Infant Movement Research.

Clark, R., A. Paulson, and S. Conlin. 1993. Assessment of developmental status and parent-infant relationships: The therapeutic process of evaluation. In *Handbook of Infant Mental Health*, edited by C. H. Zeanoh. New York: Guilford Press.

Coggins, T. E., and R. I. Carpenter. 1981. The communicative intention inventory: A system for coding children's early intentional communication. *Applied Psycholinguistics* 2:235–252.

Dale, P. S. 1980. Is early pragmatic development measurable? *Journal of Child Language* 2:21–40.

Dore, J. 1975. Holophrases, speech arts and language universals. *Journal of Child Language* 2:21–40.

_____. 1974. A pragmatic description of early language development. *Journal of Psycholinguistic Research* 4:343–350.

Dunst, C. J., V. Jenkins, and C. M. Trivette. 1984. The family support scale: Reliability and validity. *Journal of Individual, Family and Community Wellness* 4:45–52.

Ensher, G. L., and D. A. Clark. 1994. *Newborns at Risk: Medical Care and Psychoeducational Intervention*. Gaithersburg, MD: Aspen.

Folio, M. R., and R. R. Fewell. 1983. *Peabody Developmental Motor Scales and Activity Cards: A Manual*. Allen, TX: DLM Teaching Resources.

Gallagher, R. J., and D. Cech. 1989. Motor assessment. In *Assessment of Young Developmentally Disabled Children*, edited by T. D. Wachs and R. Sheehan. New York: Plenum Press.

Greenspan, S., and S. Meisels, with Zero to Three Work Group. 1994. Toward a new vision for developmental assessment. *Zero To Three* 14:1–8.

Halliday, M.A.K. 1975. *Learning How to Mean: Explorations in the Development of Language*. London: Edward Arnold.

Hedrick, D., E. Prather, and A. Tobin. 1984. *Sequenced Inventory of Communication Development*. Seattle: University of Washington Press.

Hymovich, D. P. 1984. Development of the Chronicity Impact and Coping Instrument: Parent Questionnaire (CICI:PQ). *Nursing Research* 33:218–222.

Kopp, C. B. 1987. Developmental risk: Historical reflections. In *Handbook of Infant Development*, edited by J. Osofsky. 2d ed. New York: Wiley.

Leet, H. E., and C. J. Dunst. 1985. *Family Resource Scale: Reliability and Validity*. Morgantown, NC: Family, Infant, and Preschool Program.

Mahoney, G., I. Finger, and A. Powell. 1986. The maternal behavior rating scale. *Topics in Early Childhood Special Education* 6:44–56.

McCall, R. B., and M. S. Carriger. 1993. A meta-analysis of infant habituation and recognition memory performance as predictors of later IQ. *Child Development* 64:57–79.

McCune, L., B. Kalmanson, M. Fleck, B. Glazewski, and J. Sillari. 1990. An interdisciplinary model of infant assessment. In *Handbook of Early Childhood Intervention*, edited by S. J. Meisels and J. P. Shonkoff. New York: Cartridge Press.

Miller, J. 1981. *Assessing Language Production in Children: Experimental Procedures*. Baltimore, MD: University Park Press.

Miller, L. J., and R. G. Roid. 1994. *The TIME: Toddler and Infant Motor Evaluation: A Standardized Assessment*. Tucson, AZ: Therapy Skill Builders.

Neisworth, J. T., and S. J. Bagnato. 1992. The case against intelligence testing in early intervention. *Topics in Early Childhood Special Education* 12 (1):1–20.

Olswang, L., C. Stoel-Gammons, T. Coggins, and R. Carpenter. 1987. *Assessing Linguistic Behaviors*. Seattle: University of Washington Press.

Piper, M. C., and J. Darrah. 1994. *Motor Assessment of the Developing Infant*. Philadelphia: W. B. Saunders.

Roberts, J. E., and E. R. Crais. 1989. Assessing communication skills. In *Assessing Infants and Preschoolers with Handicaps*, edited by D. B. Bailey and M. Wolery. Columbus, OH: Merrill.

Rose, S. A., and J. F. Feldman. 1995. Prediction of IQ and specific cognitive abilities at 11 years from infancy measures. *Developmental Psychology* 31:685–696.

Rosenbloom, L. 1975. The consequence of impaired movement: A hypothesis and review. In *Movement and Child Development*, edited by K. S. Holt. Philadelphia: J. B. Lippincott.

Rossetti, L. M. 1990. *Infant-Toddler Assessment: An Interdisciplinary Approach*. Boston: College-Hill.

Skinner, H. A., P. D. Steinhauer, and J. Santa-Barbara. 1983. The family assessment measure. *Canadian Journal of Community Mental Health* 2:91–105.

Thelen, E. 1995. Motor development: A new synthesis. *American Psychologist* 50:79–95

Wachs, T. D., and R. Sheehan. 1988. *Assessment of Young Developmentally Disabled Children*. New York: Plenum.

Weatherby, A., and B. Prizant. 1989. *Communication and Symbolic Behavior Scales*. San Antonio, TX: Special Press.

Williamson, G. C., and S. Zeitlin. 1990. Assessment of coping and temperament contributions to adaptive functioning. In *Interdisciplinary Assessment of Infants*, edited by E. D. Gibbs and O. M. Teti. Baltimore: Paul H. Brookes.

Williamson, G. C., S. Zeitlin, and M. Szczepanski. 1989. Coping behavior: Implications for disabled infants and toddlers. *Infant Mental Health Journal* 10:3–13.

Wyly, M. V., and J. Allen. 1990. *Stress and Coping in the Neonatal Intensive Care Unit*. Tucson, AZ: Therapy Skill Builders.

Wyly, M. V., J. Allen, and J. Wilson. 1995. *Premature Infants and Their Families: Developmental Interventions*. San Diego: Singular Press.

Zeitlin, S., G. C. Williamson, and M. Szczepanski. 1988. *Early Coping Inventory*. Bensenville, IL: Scholastic Testing Services.

Zeitlin, S., G. C. Williamson, and W. P. Rosenblatt. 1987. The coping with stress model: A counseling approach for families with a handicapped child. *Journal of Counseling and Development* 65:443–446.

Zimmerman, I. L., V. G. Steiner, and R. E. Pond. 1979. *Preschool Language Scale*. Columbus, OH: Merrill.

About the Book
and Author

Infancy is one of the most fascinating periods in the human life cycle. In two short years, infants become thinking, speaking, social beings. As this book explains, over the past three decades researchers and clinicians have developed an array of assessment methods for measuring infant development and diagnosing infants with developmental delays.

The field of infant assessment has broadened from a major focus on cognitive development to an emphasis on parent-infant interaction, play assessment, and newer strategies that involve naturalistic observations. Because of the need to look at the whole infant, assessment often involves multiple disciplines. The interdisciplinary approach measures the infant domains of motor skills, cognitive abilities, and language acquisition and evaluates the infant's psychosocial environment.

The chapters in this volume provide a solid overview of the current trends in infant assessment measures and procedures. The book can be used in undergraduate and graduate infant development courses and for advanced courses in infant assessment.

M. Virginia Wyly is professor of psychology at the State University College at Buffalo. Currently project director of the NICU Training Project, she is also the coauthor of *Stress and Coping in the NICU* and author of the text *Developmental Interventions for Premature Infants and Their Families.*

Index